BLACK LEGACY PRESS™
WWW.BLACKLEGACYPRESS.ORG

SLAVE NARRATIVES

VOLUME II
ARKANSAS NARRATIVES
PART 2

By
United States.
Work Projects Administration

Copyright © 2024 by BLACKLEGACYPRESS.ORG

All rights reserved. No part of this publication may be reproduced or transmitted in any form or by any means electronic or mechanical, including information storage and retrieval systems without permission in writing from the publisher, except for student research using the appropriate citations.

ISBN: 978-1-63652-206-7

SLAVE NARRATIVES

A Folk History of Slavery in the United States.
From Interviews with Former Slaves

**UNITED STATES.
WORK PROJECTS ADMINISTRATION**

TYPEWRITTEN RECORDS PREPARED BY
THE FEDERAL WRITERS' PROJECT
1936-1938
ASSEMBLED BY
THE LIBRARY OF CONGRESS PROJECT
WORK PROJECTS ADMINISTRATION
FOR THE DISTRICT OF COLUMBIA
SPONSORED BY THE LIBRARY OF
CONGRESS

WASHINGTON 1941

VOLUME II
ARKANSAS NARRATIVES
PART 2

Prepared by
The Federal Writers' Project of
The Works Progress Administration
For the State of Arkansas

CONTENTS

Frank Cannon 1
Zenie Cauley 3
Liney Chambers 7
Willie Buck Charleston 11
Lewis Chase 13
Katherine Clay 17
Maria Sutton Clemments 19
Maria Sutton Clemments 27
Maria Sutton Clemments 33
Fannie Clemons 35
Joe Clinton 37
Betty Coleman 45
Lucy Cotton 47
T.W. Cotton 49
Ellen Cragin 53
Sallie Crane 63
Isaac Crawford 71
Mary Crosby 73
Mrs. Mildred Thompson 75
Richard Crump 77
Zenia Culp 83
Albert Cummins 87
Betty Curlett 89
Betty Curlett 97

J.H. Curry	101
Lyttleton Dandridge	107
Ella Daniels	111
Mary Allen Darrow	117
Alice Davis	121
Charlie Davis	123
D. Davis	125
James Davis	135
Jim Davis	139
Jim Davis	141
Jeff Davis	145
Jeff Davis	147
Jordan Davis	153
Mary Jane Drucilla Davis	157
Minerva Davis	161
Rosetta Davis	165
Jennie Davis	167
Winnie Davis	171
Leroy Day	173
Hammett Dell	175
James Dickey	185
Benjamin Diggs	187
Katie Dillon	189
Alice Dixon	193
Luke D. Dixon	199
Martha Ann Dixon	203
Railroad Dockery	207

Callie Donalson	211
Charles Green Dortch	215
Fannie Dorum	227
Silas Dothrum	233
Sarah Douglas	239
Sarah Douglas	241
Tom Douglas	243
Sarah and Tom Douglas	247
Tom & Sarah Douglas	253
Sebert Douglas	257
Henry Doyl	259
Willie Doyld	263
Wade Dudley	267
Isabella Duke	269
Wash Dukes	273
Lizzie Dunn	277
Nellie Dunne	279
William L. Dunwoody	281
Lucius Edwards	291
John Elliott	293
Millie Evans	299
Millie Evans	307
Mose Evans	311
Rachel Fairley	317
Pauline Fakes	323
Mattie Fannen	325
Robert Farmer	331

Mrs. Lou Fergusson	339
Jennie Ferrell	345
Frank Fikes	347
J.E. Filer	351
Orleans Finger	353
Molly Finley	359
Fanny Finney	363
Gate-eye Fisher	367
Ellen Fitzgerald	371
Henry Fitzhugh	375
Mary Flagg	381
Doc Flowers	385
Frances Fluker	391
Ida May Fluker	395
Wash Ford	399
Wash Ford	401
Judia Fortenberry	403
Emma Foster	407
Emma Foster	409
Ira Foster	411
Ira Foster	413
Leonard Franklin	415
Eliza Frazier	419
Mary Frazier	423
Tyler Frazier	425
Mittie Freeman	429
Mattie Fritz	437

Interviewer: Miss Irene Robertson
Person interviewed: Frank Cannon
R.F.D., two miles, Palestine, Arkansas
Age: 77

FRANK CANNON

"I was born three miles west of Starkville, Mississippi on a pretty tolerable large farm. My folks was bought from a speculator drove come by. They come from Sanders in South Ca'lina. Master Charlie Cannon bought a whole drove of us, both my grandparents on both sides. He had five farms, big size farms. Saturday was ration day.

"Our master built us a church in our quarters and sont his preacher to preach to us. He was a white preacher. Said he wanted his slaves to be Christians.

"I never went to school in my life. I was taught by the fireside to be obedient and not steal.

"We et outer trays hewed out of logs. Three of us would eat together. We had wooden spoons the boys made whittling about in cold rainy weather. We all had gourds to drink outer. When we had milk we'd get on our knees and turn up the tray, same way wid pot-liquor. They give the grown up the meat and us pot-liquor.

"Pa was a blacksmith. He got a little work from other plantations. The third year of the surrender he bought us a cow. The master was dead. He never went to war.

He went in the black jack thickets. His sons wasn't old enough to go to war. Pa seemed to like ole master. The overseer was white looking like the master but I don't know if he was white man or nigger. Ole master wouldn't let him whoop much as he pleased. Master held him off on whooping.

"When the master come to the quarters us children line up and sit and look at him. When he'd go on off we'd hike out and play. He didn't care if we look at him.

"My pa was light about my color. Ma was dark. I heard them say she was part Creek (Indian).

"Folks was modester before the children than they are now. The children was sent to play or git a bucket cool water from the spring. Everything we said wasn't smart like what children say now. We was seen and not heard. Not seen too much or somebody be stepping 'side to pick up a brush to nettle our legs. Then we'd run and holler both.

"Now and then a book come about and it was hid. Better not be caught looking at books.

"Times wasn't bad 'ceptin' them speculator droves and way they got worked too hard and frailed. Some folks was treated very good, some killed.

"Folks getting mean now. They living in hopes and lazing about. They work some."

Interviewer: Bernice Bowden
Person Interviewed: Zenie Cauley
1000 Louisiana
Pine Bluff, Ark.
Age: 78
[-- 7 1938]

ZENIE CAULEY

"I member when they freed the people.

"I was born in Bedie Kellog's yard and I know she said, 'Zenie, I hate to give you up, I'd like to keep you.' But my mother said, 'No, ma'am, I can't give Zenie up.'

"We still stayed there on the place and I was settled and growed up when I left there.

"I'm old. I feels my age too. I may not look old but I feels it.

"Yes ma'am, I member when they carried us to church under bresh arbors. Old folks had rags on their hair. Yes'm, I been here.

"My father was a Missionary Baptist preacher and he was a preacher. Didn't know 'A' from 'B' but he was a preacher. Everbody knowed Jake Alsbrooks. He preached all over that country of North Carolina. They'd be as many white folks as colored. They'd give him money and he never called for a collection in his life. Why one Sunday they give him sixty-five dollars to help buy a horse.

"Fore I left the old county, I member the boss man, Henry Grady, come by and tell my mother, 'I'm gwine to town now, have my dinner ready when I come back—kill a chicken.' She was one of the cooks. Used to have us chillun pick dewberries and blackberries and bring em to the house.

"Yes, I done left there thirty-six years—will be this August.

"When we was small, my daddy would make horse collars, cotton baskets and mattresses at night and work in the field in the daytime and preach on Sunday. He fell down in Bedie Kellog's lot throwin' up shucks in the barn. He was standin' on the wagon and I guess he lost his balance. They sent and got the best doctor in the country and he said he broke his nabel string. They preached his funeral ever year for five years. Seemed like they just couldn't give him up.

"White folks told my mother if she wouldn't marry again and mess up Uncle Jake's chillun, they'd help her, but she married that man and he beat us so I don't know how I can remember anything. He wouldn't let us go to school. Had to work and just live like pigs.

"Oh, I used to be a tiger bout work, but I fell on the ice in 'twenty-nine and I ain't never got over it. I said I just had a death shock.

"I never went to school but three months in my life. Didn't go long enough to learn anything.

"I was bout a mile from where I was born when I professed religion. My daddy had taught us the right way. I tell you, in them days you couldn't join the church unless you had been changed.

"I come here when they was emigratin' the folks here to Arkansas."

United States. Work Projects Administration

Interviewer: Miss Irene Robertson
Person interviewed: Liney Chambers, Brinkley, Arkansas
Age:

[TR: Some word pronunciation was marked in this interview. Letters surrounded by [] represent long vowels.]

LINEY CHAMBERS

"I was born in Tennessee close to Memphis. I remember seein' the Yankees. I was most too little to be very scared of them. They had their guns but they didn't bother us. I was born a slave. My mother cooked for Jane and Silas Wory. My mother's name was Caroline. My father's name was John. An old bachelor named Jim Bledsoe owned him. When the war was over I don't remember what happened. My mother moved away. She and my father didn't live together. I had one brother, Proctor. I expect he is dead. He lived in California last I heard of him.

"They just expected freedom all I ever heard. I know they didn't expect the white folks to give them no land cause the man what owned the land bought it hisself foe he bought the hands whut he put on it. They thought they was ruined bad enouf when the hands left them. They kept the land and that is about all there was left. Whut the Yankees didn't take they wasted and set fire to it. They set fire to the rail fences so the stock would get out all they didn't kill and take off. Both sides was mean. But it seemed like cause they was fightin' down here on the Souths ground it was the wurst here. Now that's just the way I sees it. They done one more thing too. They put any colored man in the front where he would get killed first and they stayed sorter behind in the back lines. When they come along they try to get the colored men to go with them and that's the way they got treated. I didn't know where anybody was made to stay on after the war. They was lucky if they had a place to stay at. There wasn't anything to do with if they stayed. Times was awful unsettled for a long time. People whut went to the cities died. I don't know they caught diseases and changing the ways of eatin' and livin' I guess whut done it. They died mighty fast for awhile. I knowed some of them and I heard 'em talking.

"That period after the war was a hard time. It sho was harder than the depression. It lasted a long time. Folks got a lots now besides what they put up with then. Seemed like they thought if they be free they never have no work to do and jess have plenty to eat and wear. They found it different and when it was cold they had no wood like they been used to. I don't believe in the colored race being slaves cause of the color but the war didn't make times much better for a long time. Some of them had a worse time. So many soon got sick and died. They died of Consumption and fevers and nearly froze. Some near 'bout starved. The colored folks just scattered 'bout huntin' work after the war.

"I heard of the Ku Klux but I never seen one.

"I never voted. I don't believe in it.

"I never heard of any uprisings. I don't know nobody in that rebellion (Nat Turner).

"I used to sing to my children and in the field.

"I lived on the farm till I come to my daughters to live. I like it better then in town. We homesteaded a place at Grunfield (Zint) and my sister bought it. We barely made a living and never had money to lay up.

"I don't know what they'll (young generation) do. Things going so fast. I'm glad I lived when I did. I think it's been the best time for p[o]r folks. Some now got too much and some not got nothin'. That what I believe make times seem so hard."

United States. Work Projects Administration

Interviewer: Miss Irene Robertson
Person interviewed: Willie Buck Charleston, Jr., Biscoe, Arkansas
Age: 74

WILLIE BUCK CHARLESTON

"I was born up here on the Biscoe place before Mr. Biscoe was heard of in this country. I'm for the world like my daddy. He was light as I is. I'm jus' his size and make. There was three of us boys. Dan was the oldest; he was my own brother, and Ed was my half-brother. My daddy was a fellar of few words and long betwix' 'em. He was in the Old War (Civil War). He was shot in his right ankle and never would let it be took out. Mother had been a cook. She and my grandmother was sold in South Carolina and brought out here. Mother's name was Sallie Harry. Judging by them being Harrys that might been who owned them before they was sold. She was about as light as me. Mother died when I was a litter bit er of a fellar. Then me and Dan lived from house to house. Grandma Harry and my Aunt Mat and Jesse Dove raised us. My daddy married right er way ag'in.

"I recollect mighty little about the war. We lived back in the woods and swamps. I was afraid of the soldiers. I seen them pass by. I was so little I can barely recollect seeing them and hiding from them.

"When we lived over about Forrest City I seen the Ku Klux whoop Joe Saw and Bill Reed. It was at night. They was tied to trees and whooped with a leather snake whoop. I couldn't say how it come up but they sure poured it on them. There was a crowd come up during the acting. I was scared to death then. After then I had mighty little use for dressed-up folks what go around at night (Ku Klux). I can tell you no sich thing ever took place as I heard of at Biscoe. We had our own two officers and white officers and we get along all the time tollerably well together."

Interviewer: Miss Irene Robertson
Person interviewed: Lewis Chase; Des Arc, Arkansas
Age: 90?

[TR: Some word pronunciation was marked in this interview. Letters surrounded by [] represent long vowels.]

LEWIS CHASE

"I answer all your questions I knows lady.

"When de Civil War goin on I heard lots folks talking. I don't know what all they did say. It was a war mong de white folks. Niggers had no say in it. Heap ob them went to wait on their masters what went to fight. Niggers didn't know what the fight war bout. Yankey troops come take everything we had made, take it to the Bluff (DeValls Bluff), waste it and eat it. He claim to be friend to the black man an do him jes dater way. De niggers what had any sense tall stuck to the white folks. Niggers what I knowed didn't spec nothin an they sho didn't get nothin but freedom.

"I was sold. Yes mam I sho was. Jes put up on a platform and auctioned off. Sold right here in Des Arc. Nom taint right. My old mistress [Mrs. Snibley] whoop me till I run off and they took me back when they found out where I lef from. I stayed way bout two weeks.

"One man I sho was glad didn't get me cause he whoop me. N[o]'[o]m he didn't get me. I heard him puttin up the prices and I sho hope he didn't get me.

"I don't know whar I come from. Old Missus Snibley kept my hat pulled down over my face so I couldn't see de way to go back. I didn't want to come and I say I go right back. Whar I set, right between old missus and master on de front seat ob de wagon and my ma set between missus Snibley's two girls right behind us. I recken it was a covered wagon. The girls name was Florence and Emma. Old master Snibley never whip me but old Missus sho did pile it on me. Noom I didn't lack her. I run away. He died f[o] the war was over. I did leave her when de war was over.

"I saw a heap ob bushwhackers and carpet bagger but I nebber seed no Ku Klux. I heard battles of the bushwhackers out at the Wattensaw bridge [Iron bridge]. I was scared might near all de time for four years. Noom I didn't want no soldiers to get me.

"I recken I wo long britches when de war started cause when I pulled off dresses I woe long britches. Never wo no short ones. Nigger boys and white boys too wore loose dresses till they was four, five or six years old in them times. They put on britches when they big nough to help at the field.

"I worked at the house and de field. I'se farmed all my life.

"I vote [HW: many] a time. I don't know what I vote. Noom I don't! I recken I votes Democrat, I don't know. It don't do no good. Noom I ain't voted in a long time. I don't know nothin bout votin. I never did.

"Noom I never owned no land, noom no home neither. I didn't need no home. The man I worked for give me a house on his place. I work for another man and he give me a house on his land. I owned a horse one time. I rode her.

"I don't know nuthin bout the young generation. I takes care bout myself. Dats all I'm able to do now. Some ob dem work. Nom they don't work hard as I did. I works now hard as they do. They ought to work. I don't know what going to become ob them. I can't help what they do.

"The times is hard fo old folks cause they ain't able to work and heap ob time they ain't no work fo em to do.

"Noom I lived at Bells, Arkansas for I come to Hickory Plains and Des Arc. I don't know no kin but my mother. She died durin the war. Noom not all de white folks good to the niggers. Some mean. They whoop em. Some white folks good. Jes lak de niggers, deres some ob em mighty good and some ob em mean.

"I works when I can get a little to do and de relief gives me a little.

"I am er hundred years old! Cause I knows I is. White folks all tell you I am."

United States. Work Projects Administration

Interviewer: Miss Irene Robertson
Person interviewed: Katherine Clay, Forrest City, Arkansas
Age: 69

KATHERINE CLAY

"I was born in West Point, Mississippi. My folks' owners was Master Harris and Liddie Harris. My parent's name was Sely Sikes. She was mother of seven children. Papa was name Owen Sikes. He never was whooped. They had different owners. Both my grandparents was dead on both sides. I never seen them.

"Mama said her owners wasn't good. Her riding boss put a scar on her back she took to her grave. It was deep and a foot long. He wanted to whoop her naked. He had the colored men hold her and he whooped her. She run off and when her owner come home she come to him at his house and told him all about it. She had been in the woods about a week she reckon. She had a baby she had left. The old mistress done had it brought to her. She was nursing it. She had a sicking baby of her own. She kept that baby. Mama said her breast was way out and the doctor had to come wait on her; it nearly ruined.

"Mama said her master was so mad he cursed the overseer, paid him, and give him ten minutes to leave his place. He left in a hurry. That was her very first baby. She was raising a family, so they put her a nurse at the house. She had been ploughing. She had big fine children.

They was proud of them. She raised a big family. She took care of all her and Miss Liddie's babies and washed their hippins. Never no soap went on them she said reason she had that to do. Another woman cooked and another woman washed.

"Mama said she was sold once, away from her mother but they let her have her four children. She grieved for her old mama, 'fraid she would have a hard time. She sold for one thousand dollars. She said that was half price but freedom was coming on. She never laid eyes on her mama ag'in.

"After freedom they had gone to another place and the man owned the place run the Ku Klux off. They come there and he told them to go on away, if he need them he would call them back out there. They never came back, she said. They was scared to death of the Ku Klux. At the place where they was freed all the farm bells rung slow for freedom. That was for miles about. Their master told them up at his house. He said it was sad thing, no time for happiness, they hadn't 'sperienced it. But for them to come back he would divide long as what he had lasted. They didn't go off right at first. They was several years getting broke up. Some went, some stayed, some actually moved back. Like bees trying to find a setting place. Seem like they couldn't get to be satisfied even being free.

"I had eleven children my own self. I let the plough fly back and hit me once and now I got a tumor there. I love to plough. I got two children living. She comes to see me. She lives across over here. I don't hear from my boy. I reckon he living. I gets help from the relief on account I can't work much with this tumor."

Interviewer: Miss Irene Robertson
Person interviewed: Maria Sutton Clemments, DeValls Bluff, Ark.
Age: Between 85 and 90 years

[TR: Also reported as Maria Sutton Clements]

MARIA SUTTON CLEMMENTS

I don't know jes how old I is. Yes mum I show do member the war jes lack as if it was yesterday. I was born in Lincoln County, Georgia. My old mistress was named Frances Sutton. She was a real old lady. Her husband was dead. She had two sons Abraham and George. One of them tried to get old missus to sell my ma jes before the war broke out. He wanter sell her cause she too old to bear children. Sell her and buy young woman raise mo children to sell. Put em in the nigger drove and speculate on em. Young nigger, not stunted, strong made, they look at their wrists and ankles and chestes, bout grown bring the owner fifteen hundred dollars. Yea mam every cent of it. Two weeks after baby born see the mother carrin it cross the field fur de old woman what kept all the children and she be going right on wid de hoe all day. When de sun come up the niggers all in the field and workin when de ridin boss come wid de dogs playin long after him. If they didn't chop dat cotton jes right he have em tied up to a stake or a big saplin and beat him till de blood run out the gashes. They come right back and take up whar they lef off work. Two chaps make a hand soon as dey get big nuf to chop out a row.

Had plenty to eat; meat, corncake and molasses, peas and garden stuff. They didn't set out no variety fo the niggers. They had pewter bowls to eat outer and spoons. Eat out in the yard, at the cabins, in the kitchen. Eat different places owin to what you be workin at when the bell rung. Big bell on a high post.

My ma's name was Sina Sutton. She come from Virginia in a nigger traders drove when she was sixteen years old and Miss Frances husband bought er. She had nine childen whut lived. I am de youngest. She died jes before de war broke out. Till that time I had been trained a house girl. My ma was a field hand. Then when the men all went to the army I plowed. I plowed four years I recken, till de surrender. Howd I know it was freedom? A strange woman—I never seed fore, came runnin down where we was all at work. She say loud as she could "Hay freedom. You is free." Everything toe out fer de house and soldiers was lined up. Dats whut they come by fer. Course dey was Yankee soldiers settin the colored folks all free. Everybody was gettin up his clothes and leaving. They didn't know whar des goin. Jes scatterin round. I say give 'em somethin. They was so mad cause they was free and leavin and nobody to work the land. The hogs and stock was mostly all done gone then. White folks sho had been rich but all they had was the land. The smoke houses had been stripped and stripped. The cows all been took off cept the scrubs. Folks plowed ox and glad to plow one.

Sometime we had a good time. I danced till I joined the church. We didn't have no nigger churches that I knowed till after freedom. Go to the white folks church. We danced square dance jess like the white folks long time ago. The niggers baptized after the white folks down at the pond. They joined the white folks church sometimes. The same woman on the place sewed for de niggers, made some things for Miss Frances. I recollects that. She knitted and seed about things. She showed the nigger women how to sew. All the women on the place could card and spin. They sat around and do that when too bad weather to be on the ground. They show didn't teach them to read. They whoop you if they see you have a book. If they see you gang round talkin, they say they talkin bout freedom or equalization. They scatter you bout.

When they sell you, they take you off. See drove pass the house. Men be ridin wid long whips of cow hide wove together and the dogs. The slaves be walkin, some cryin cause they left their folks. They make em stand in a row sometimes and sometimes they put em up on a high place and auction em.

The pore white folks whut not able to buy hands had to work their own land. There shore was a heap of white folks what had no slaves. Some ob dem say theys glad the niggers got turned loose, maybe they could get them to work for them sometimes and pay em.

When you go to be sold you have to say what they tell you to say. When a man be unruly they sell him to get rid of him heap of times. They call it sellin nigger meat. No use tryin run off they catch you an bring you back.

I don't know that there was ever a thought made bout freedom till they was fightin. Said that was what it was about. That was a white mans war cept they stuck a few niggers in front ob the Yankee lines. And some ob the men carried off some man or boy to wait on him. He so used to bein waited on. I ain't takin sides wid neither one of dem I tell you.

If der was anything to be knowed the white folks knowed it. The niggers get passes and visit round on Saturday evening or on Sunday jes mongst theirselves and mongst folks they knowed at the other farms round.

When dat war was done Georgia was jes like being at the bad place. You couldn't stay in the houses fear some Ku Klux come shoot under yo door and bust in wid hatchets. Folks hide out in de woods mostly. If dey hear you talkin they say you talkin bout equalization. They whoop you. You couldn't be settin or standing talkin. They come and ask you what he been tell you. That Ku Klux killed white men too. They say they put em up to hold offices over them. It was heap worse in Georgia after freedom than it was fore. I think the poor nigger have to suffer fo what de white man put on him. We's had a hard time. Some of em down there in Georgia what didn't get into the cities where they could get victuals and a few rags fo cold weather got so pore out in the woods they nearly starved and died out. I heard em talk bout how they died in piles. Niggers have to have meat to eat or he get weak. White folks didn't have no meat, no flour.

The folks was after some people and I run off and kept goin till I took up with some people. The white folks brought them to Tennessee—Covington—I come too. They come in wagons. My father, he got shot and I never seed him no mo. He lived on another farm fo de war. I lived wid them white folks till bout nine years and I married. My old man wanted to come to dis new country. Heard so much talk how fine it was. Then I had run across my brother. He followed me. One brother was killed in the war somehow. My brother liked Memphis an he stayed there. We come on the train. I never did like no city.

We farmed bout, cleared land. Never got much fo the hard work we done. The white man done learned how to figure the black folks out of what was made cept a bare living.

I could read a little and write. He could too. We went to school a little in Tennessee.

When we got so we not able to work hard he come to town and carpentered, right here, and I cooked fo Mr. Hopkins seven years and fo Mr. Gus Thweatt and fo Mr. Nick Thweatt. We got a little ahead then by the hardest. I carried my money right here [bag on a string tied around her waist]. We bought a house and five acres of land. No mum I don't own it now. We got in hard luck and give a mortgage. They closed us out. Mr. Sanders. They say I can live there long as I lives. But they owns it. My garden fence is down and won't nobody fix it up fo me. They promises to come put the posts in but they won't do it and I ain't able no mo. I had a garden this year. Spoke fo a pig but the man said they all died wid the kolerg [cholera]. So I ain't got no meat to eat dis year.

I ain't never had a chile. I ain't got nobody kin to me livin dat I knows bout. When I gets sick a neighbor woman comes over and looks after me.

I thinks if de present generation don't get killed they die cause they too lazy to work. No mum dey don't know nuthin bout work. They ain't got no religion. They so smart they don't pay no tention to what you advise em. I never tries to find out what folks doin and the young generation is killin time. I sho never did vote. I don't believe in it. The women runnin the world now. The old folks ain't got no money an the young ones wastes theirs. Theys able to make it. They don't give the old folks nuthin. The times changes so much I don't know what goiner come next. I jes stop and looks and listens to see if my eyes is foolin me. I can't see, fo de cataracts gettin bad, nohow. Things is heap better now fo de young folks now if they would help derselves. I'm too wo out. I can't do much like I could when I was young. The white folks don't cheat the niggers outen what they make now bad as they did when I farmed.

I never knowed about uprisings till the Ku Klux sprung up. I never heard bout the Nat Turner rebellion. I tell you bout the onliest man I knowed come from Virginia. A fellow come in the country bout everybody called Solomon. Dis long fo the war. He was a free man he said. He would go bout mong his color and teach em fo little what they could slip him along. He teached some to read. When freedom he went to Augusta. My brother seed him and said "Solomon, what you doin here?" and he said "I am er teaching school to my own color." Then he said they run him out of Virginia cause he was learnin his color and he kept going. Some white folks up North learned him to read and cipher. He used a black slate and he had a book he carried around to teach folks with. He was what they called a ginger cake color. They would whoop you if they seed you with books learnin. Mighty few books to get holt of fo the war. We mark on the ground. The passes bout all the paper I ever seed fo I come to Tennessee. Then I got to go to school a little.

Whah would the niggers get guns and shoot to start

a uprisin? Never had none cept if a white man give it to him. When you a slave you don't have nothin cept a big fireplace and plenty land to work. They cook on the fireplace. Niggers didn't have no guns fo the war an nuthin to shoot in one if he had one whut he picked up somewhere after the war. The Ku Klux done the uprisin. They say they won't let the nigger enjoy freedom. They killed a lot of black folks in Georgia and a few white folks whut they said was in wid em. We darkies had nuthin to do wid freedom. Two or three set down on you, take leaves and build a fire and burn their feet nearly off. That the way the white folks treat the darky.

I never knowed nobody to hold office. Them whut didn't want to starve got someplace whut he could hold a plow handle. You don't know whut hard times is. Dem was hard times. They used to hide in big cane brakes, nearly wild and nearly starved. Scared to come out. I ain't wanted to go back to Georgia.

The folks I lived wid fo I come to Tennessee, he tanned hides down at the branch and made shoes and he made cloth hats, wool hats. He sold them. We farmed but I watched them up at the house minu a time.

One thing I recollect mighty well. Fo de war a big bellied great monster man come in an folks made a big to do over him. He eat round and laughed round havin a big time. His name was Mr. Wimbeish (?). He wo white britches wid red stripes down the sides and a white shad tail coat all trimmed round de edges wid red and a tall beaver hat. He blowed a bugle and marched all the men every Friday ebening. He come to Miss Frances. They fed him on pies and cakes and me brushin the flies off im and my mouth fairly waterin for a chunk ob de cake. When de first shot of war went off no more could be heard ob old Mr. Wimbeish. He lef an never was heard tell ob no mo. He said never was a Yankee had a hart he didn't understand! I never did know whut he was. He jess said that right smart.

I gets the Old Age Pension and meets the wagon and gets a little commodities. I works my garden and raises a few chickens round my house. I trusts in de Lord and try to do right, honey, dat way I lives.

Interviewer: Miss Irene Robertson
Person interviewed: Maria Sutton Clements, De Valls Bluff, Ark.
Age: Between 85 and 90

[TR: Also reported as Maria Sutton Clemments]

MARIA SUTTON CLEMENTS

"Miss, I don't know a whole heap bout Mr. Wimbeish. I don't know no other name that what they all call him. Some I heard say it like Wimbush. He was a great big man, big in here [chest], big in here [stomach]. He have hair bout color youn [light]. He have big blue eyes jes' sparklin' round over the victuals on the table. He was a lively man. He had a heap to tell and a heap to talk bout. He had fair skin and rosy jaws—full round face. He laughed out loud pretty often. He looked fine when he laughed too. They all was foolish bout him. He was a newcommer in there. I don't know whah he stay. He come down the road regular as Friday come, going to practice em marchin'. Looked like bout fifty fellows. I never seed Mr. Wimbeish on a horse all time he passed long that road. He miter jes' et round mong the people while he stayed there. He wore red 'appletts' on his shoulders. I never seed him outer that fresh starched white suit. It was fishtail coat and had red bands stitched all round the edge and white breetches [britches] [TR: 'britches' is marked out by hand] with red bands down the side. He sure was a young man. They had him bout different places eatin'. Old mistress said, 'Fix up a good dinner today we gwiner have company.'

That table was piled full. It was fine eatin'. He say so much I couldn't forgit. Never was a Yankee what have a heart he couldn't understand. I don't know what he was. He was so different. He muster been a Southerner 'cause white folks would not treated him near that good. It was fo de war. They say when the first bugle blowed fo war he was done gone an' nebber been heard of till dis day. I heard some say last they seed him, he was rollin' over an' over on the ground and the men run off to find em nother captain. I don't know if they was tellin' like it took place. I know I never seed him no more.

Slave Times

"The servants take up what they eat in bowls and pans—little wooden bowls—and eat wid their fingers and wid spoons and they had cups. Some had tables fixed up out under the trees. Way they make em—split a big tree half in two and bore holes up in it and trim out legs to fit. They cooked on the fireplaces an' hearth and outerdoors. They cooked sompin to eat. They had plenty to eat. But they didn't have pies and cake less they be goiner have company. They have so much milk they fatten the pigs on it.

"The animals eat up the gardens and crops. The man kill coon and possum if they didn't get nough meat up at the house. I say it sure is good. It is good as pork. The men prowl all night in the winter huntin'. If you be workin' at the field yo dinner is fetched down thar to you in a bucket that high [2 ft.], that big er round [1-1/2 feet wide]. The hands all come an' did they eat. That be mostly fried meat and bread and baked taters, so they could work.

"Old mistress say she first married Mr. Abraham Chenol. Then she married Mr. Joel Sutton and they both died. She had two sons. She had a nephew what come there from way off. She said he was her sister's boy. Couse they had doctors and good ones. Iffen a doctor come say one thing the matter he better stick to it and cure one he come thar to see. Old mistress had three boys till one died. I was brushin' flies offen him. She come and cry and go way cryin'. He callin' her all time. He quit callin' her then he was dead. Made a sorter gurglin' sound. That the first person I seed die. When they say he dead I got out and off I was gone. I was usin' a turkey wing to brush flies offen him. I don't know what was the matter wid em. They buried him on her place whah the grave yard was made. Both her husbands buried down there. She had a fine marble put over his grave. It had things wrote on it. She sent way off an' got it. They hauled it to here in a wagon. The Masons burled him. It was the prettiest sight I ever seed.

"Her son John had some peafowls. She had geese—a big drove—turkeys, guineas, ducks, and geese.

"She had feather beds and wheat straw mattresses, clean whoopee! They used cotton baggin' and straw and some of the servants had a feather bed. Old mistress get up an' go in set till they call her to breakfast. They had a marble top table and a big square piano. That was the parlor furniture. They made rugs outen sheep an' goat skins.

"When she want the cook go wid her she dress her up in some her fine dresses—big white cap like missus slep in an' a white apron tied round her waist. We wore 5¢ calico and gingham dresses for best. She'd buy three and four bolts at Augusta [Georgia] and have it made up to work in. We didn't spin and weave till the war come on. Some old men come round making spinnin' wheels. They was very plain too nearly bout rough. Rich folks had fine silk dresses—jes' rattle when they walked—to wear to preachin'. They sho did have preachin' an' fastin' too durin' the war but folks didn't have fine clothes when it ended like when the war started.

Ku Klux Klan

"It started outener the bushwhackers. Some say they didn't get what was promised em at Shiloh Battle. They didn't get their rights. I don't know what they meant by it. The bushwhackers ketch the men in day goiner work—ketch em this way [by the shoulders or collar]. Such hollerin' and scramblin' then you never heard. They hide behind big pine trees till he come up then step out behind and grab him. They first come an' call fer water. Plenty water in the well or down at the spring. They knowed it too. Then they waste all you had brought up and say—'Ah! First drink I had since I come from hell.' They all knowed ain't nobody come from hell. They had hatchets an' they burst in your house. Jes' to scare you. They shoot under your house. They wore their wives big wide nightgowns and caps and ugliest faces you eber seed. They looked like a gang from hell—ugliest things you ebber did see. It was cold—ground spewed up wid ice and men folks so scared they run out in woods, stay all night. Old mistress died at the close of de war an' her son what was a preacher, he put on a long preacher coat and breeches (britches) [TR: 'britches' is marked out by hand] all black. He put a navy six in his belt and carried carbeen [carbine] on his shoulder. It was a long gun shoot sixteen times. He was a dangerous man. He made the Ku Klux let his folks alone. He walk all night bout his place. He say, 'Forward March!' Then they pass by. He was a dangerous man. So much takin' place all time I was scared nearly to death all time."

United States. Work Projects Administration

Interviewer: Miss Irene Robertson
Person interviewed: Maria Sutton Clements
De Valls Bluff, Arkansas
Age:
[Dec 31 1937]

[TR: Also reported as Maria Sutton Clemments]

MARIA SUTTON CLEMENTS

"Missus, I thought if I'd see you agin I'd tell you this song:

>'Jeff Davis is President
>Abe Lincoln is a fool
>Come here, see Jeff ride the gray horse
>And Abe Lincoln the mule.'

"They sang all sich songs durin' of the war.

"Five wagons come by. They said it was Jeff Davise's wagons. They was loaded wid silver money—all five—in Lincoln County, Georgia. Somehow the folks got a whiz of it and got the money outen one the wagons. Abraham, my old mistress' son had old-fashion saddle bag full. Sho it was white folks all but two or three slaves. Hogs tore up sacks money, find em hid in the woods. They thought it was corn. They found a leather trunk full er money—silver money—down in the creek. Money buried all round. The way it all started one colored man throwed down a bright dime to a Yankee fo sompin he wanter buy. That started it all. They tied their thumbs this way (thumbs crossed) behind em, then strung em up in trees by their wrists behind em. It put heep of em in bed an' some most died never did get over it. The Yankee soldiers come down that [HW: then?] and got all the money nearly. They say the war last four years, five months. Seemed like twenty years."

Interviewer: Pernella Anderson
Person Interviewed: Fannie Clemons
940 N. Washington
El Dorado, Ark.
Age: 78

FANNIE CLEMONS

"I was born down in Farmerville, Louisiana in the year of 1860. Now my ma lived with some white people, but now the name of the people I do not know. You see, child, I am old and I can't recollect so good. I didn't know my pa cause my ma quit him when I was little. My ma said she worked hard in the field like a black stepchild. My ma had nine chilluns and I was the oldest of the nine. She said her old miss wouldn't let her come to the house to nurse me, so she would slip up under the house and crawl through a hole in the floor. She took and pulled a plank up so she could slip through.

"I would drink any kind of water that I saw if I wanted a drink. If the white folks poured out wash water and I wanted a drink that would do me. It just made me fat and healthy. Most we played was tussling, and couldn't no boy throw me. Nobody tried to whip me cause they couldn't.

"We always cooked on fireplaces and our cake was always molasses cakes. At Christmas time we got candy and apples, but these oranges and bananas and stuff like that wasn't out then. Bananas and oranges just been out a few years. And sugar—we did not know about that.

We always used sugar from molasses. I don't think sugar been in session long. If it had I did not get it.

"I got married when I was pretty old, I lived with my husband eight years and he died. I had some children, but I stole them. The biggest work I ever done was farm and we sure worked."

Interviewer: Watt McKinney
Person interviewed: Joe Clinton, Route 2, Marvell, Arkansas
Age: 86

JOE CLINTON

"Uncle Joe" Clinton, on ex-Mississippi slave, lives on a small farm that he owns a few miles north of Marvell, Arkansas. His wife has been dead for a number of years and he has only one living child, if indeed his boy, Joe, who left home fifteen years ago for Chicago and from whom no word has been received since, is still alive. Due to the infirmities of age "Uncle Joe" is unable to work and obtains his support from the income received off the small acreage he rents each year to the Negro family with whom he lives. Seated in an old cane-bottomed chair "Uncle Joe" was dozing in the warm sunshine of on afternoon in early October as I passed through the gate leading into the small yard enclosing his cabin. Arousing himself on my approach, the old Negro offered me a chair. I explained the purpose of my visit and this old man told me the following story:

"I'se now past eighty-six year ole an' was borned in Panola County, Mississippi 'bout three miles from Sardis. My ole mars was Mark Childress, en he sure owned er heap of peoples, womens an' mens bofe, en jus' gangs of chillun. I was real small when us lived in Panola County; how-some-ever I riccolect it well when us all lef' dar and ole mars sold out his land and took us all to de delta where he had bought a big plantation 'bout two or three miles wide in Coahoma County not far from Friar Point. De very place dat my mars bought and dat us moved to is what dey call now, de 'Clover Hill Plantation'. De fust year dat us lived in de delta, us stayed on de place what dey called de 'Swan Lake Place'. Dat place is over dere close to Jonestown and de very place dat Mr. Billy Jones and his son John bought, en dats zackly how come dat town git its name. It was named for Mr. John Jones.

"My mars, Mark Childress, he never was married. He was a bachelor, en I'se tellin' you dis, boss, he was a good, fair man and no fault was to be found wid him. But dem overseers dat he had, dey was real mean. Dey was cruel, least one of them was 'bout de cruelest white man dat I is ever seen. Dat was Harvey Brown. Mars had a nephew what lived with him named Mark Sillers. He was mars' sister's son and was named for my mars. Mr. Mark Sillers, he helped with de runnin' of the place en sich times dat mars 'way from home Mr. Mark, he the real boss den.

"Mr. Harvey Brown, the overseer, he mean sure 'nough I tell you, and de onliest thing that keep him from beatin' de niggers up all de time would be old mars or Mr. Mark Sillers. Bofe of dem was good and kind most all de time. One time dat I remembers, ole mars, he gone back to Panola County for somepin', en Mr. Mark Sillers, he attendin' de camp meeting. That was de day dat Mr. Harvey Brown come mighty nigh killin' Henry. I'll tell you how dat was, boss. It was on Monday morning that it happened. De Friday before dat Monday morning, all of de hands had been pickin' cotton and Mr. Harvey Brown didn't think dat Henry had picked enough cotton dat day en so he give Henry er lashin' out in de field. Dat night Henry, he git mad and burn up his sack and runned off and hid in de canebrake 'long de bayou all of de nex' day. Mr. Harvey, he missed Henry from de field en sent Jeff an' Randall to find him and bring him in. Dey found Henry real soon en tell him iffen he don't come on back to de field dat Mr. Harvey gwine to set de hounds on him. So Henry, he comed on back den 'cause de niggers was skeered of dem wild bloodhounds what they would set on 'em when dey try to run off.

"When Henry git back Mr. Harvey say, 'Henry, where your sack? And how come you ain't pickin' cotton stid runnin' off like dat?' Henry say he done burnt he sack up. Wid dat Mr. Harvey lit in to him like a bear, lashin' him right and left. Henry broke en run den to de cook house where he mammy, 'Aunt Mary', was, en Mr. Harvey right after him wid a heavy stick of wood dat he picked up offen de yard. Mr. Harvey got Henry cornered in de house and near 'bout beat dat nigger to death. In fact, Mr. Harvey, he really think too dat he done kilt Henry 'cause he called 'Uncle Nat' en said, 'Nat, go git some boards en make er coffin for dis nigger what I done kilt.'

"But Henry wasn't daid though he was beat up terrible en they put him in de sick house. For days en days 'Uncle Warner' had to 'tend to him, en wash he wounds, en pick de maggots outen his sores. Dat was jus' de way dat Mr. Harvey Brown treated de niggers every time he git a chanct. He would even lash en beat de wimmens.

"Ole mars had a right good size house in dar 'mongst de quarters where dey kept all de babies en right young chillun whilst dey mammies workin' in de fields pickin' en hoein' time. Old 'Aunt Hannah', an old granny woman, she 'tend to all dem chillun. De chillun's mammies, dey would come in from de fields about three times er day to let de babies suck. Dere was er young nigger woman name Jessie what had a young baby. One day when Jessie come to de house to let dat baby suck, Mr. Harvey think she gone little too long. He give her a hard lashin'.

"Ole mars had a big cook house on de plantation right back in behind he own house en twix his house en de nigger's quarters. Dat was where all de cookin' done for all de niggers on de entire place. Aunt Mary, she de head cook for de mars en all of de niggers too. All of de field hands durin' crop time et dey breakfast en dey dinners in de field. I waited on de table for mars en sort er flunkyed 'round da house en de quarters en de barns, en too I was one of de young darkies what toted de buckets of grub to de field hands.

"Ole mars had a house on de place too dat was called de 'sick house'. Dat was where dem was put dat was sick. It was a place where dey was doctored on en cared for till dey either git well er die. It was er sort er hospital like. 'Uncle Warner', he had charge of de sick house, en he could sure tell iffen you sick er not, or iffen you jus' tryin' to play off from work.

"My pappy, he was named Bill Clinton en my mammy was named Mildred. De reason how come I not named Childress for my mars is 'cause my pappy, he named Clinton when mars git him from de Clintons up in Tennessee somewhere. My mars, he was a good man jus' like I'm tellin' you. Mars had a young nigger woman named Malinda what got married to Charlie Voluntine dat belonged to Mr. Nat Voluntine dat had a place 'bout six miles from our place. In dem days iffen one darky married somebody offen de place where dey lived en what belonged to some other mars, dey didn't git to see one annudder very often, not more'n once a month anyway. So Malinda, she got atter mars to buy Charlie. Sure 'nough he done that very thing so's dem darkies could live togedder. Dat was good in our mars.

"When any marryin' was done 'mongst de darkies on de place in dem days, dey would first hab to ask de mars iffen dey could marry, en iffen he say dat dey could git married den dey would git ole 'Uncle Peyton' to marry 'em. 'Course dere wasn't no sich thing as er license for niggers to marry en I don't riccolect what it was dat 'Uncle Peyton' would say when he done de marryin'. But I 'members well dat 'Uncle Peyton', he de one dat do all of de marryin' 'mongst de darkies.

"My mars, he didn't go to de War but he sure sent er lot er corn en he sent erbout three hundred head er big, fat hogs one time dat I 'members. Den too, he sent somepin like twenty er thirty niggers to de Confedrites in Georgia. I 'members it well de time dat he sent dem niggers. They was all young uns, 'bout grown, en dey was skeered to death to be leavin' en goin' to de War. Dey didn't know en cose but what dey gwine make 'em fight. But mars tole 'em dat dey jus' gwine to work diggin' trenches en sich; but dey didn't want to go nohow en Jeff an' Randall, they runned off en come back home all de way from Georgia en mars let 'em stay.

"Boss, you has heered me tellin' dat my mars was er good, kine man en dat his overseer, Mr. Harvey Brown, was terrible cruel, en mean, en would beat de niggers up every chance he git, en you ask me how come it was dat de mars would have sich a mean man er working for him. Now I'se gwine to tell you de reason. You know de truth is de light, boss, an' dis is de truth what I'se gwine to say. Mars, he in love with Mr. Harvey Brown's wife, Miss Mary, and Miss Mary's young daughter, she was mars' chile. Yas suh, she was dat. She wasn't no kin er tall to Mr. Harvey Brown. Her name was Miss Markis, dats what it was. Mars had done willed dat chile er big part of his property and a whole gang of niggers. He was gwine give her Tolliver, Beckey, Aunt Mary, Austin, an' Savannah en er heap more 'sides dat. But de War, it come on en broke mars up, en all de darkies sot free, en atter dat, so I heered Mr. Harvey Brown en Miss Mary, and de young lady Miss Markis, dey moved up North some place en I ain't never heered no more from dem.

"Mr. Clarke and Mrs. Clarke what de town of Clarksdale is named for, dey lived not far from our place. I knowed dem well. Albert, one of mars' darkies, married Cindy, one of Mr. Clarke's women. General Forrest, I know you is heered of him. I speck he 'bout de bes' general in de War. He sure was a fine looking man en he wore a beard on he face. De general, he had a big plantation down dere in Coahoma County where he would come ever so offen. A lot of times he would come to our place en take dinner wid ole mars, en I would be er waitin' on de table er takin' dem de toddies on de front gallery where dey talkin' 'bout day bizness.

"Boss, you axed me if dey was any sich thing in slavery times as de white men molestin' of de darky wimmen. Dere was a heap of dat went on all de time an' 'course de wimmens, dey couldn't help deyselves and jus' had to put up wid it. Da trouble wasn't from de mars of de wimmens I'se ever knowed of but from de overseers en de outside white folks. Of course all dat couldn't have been goin' on like it did without de mars knowin' it. Dey jus' bound to know dat it went on, but I'se never heered 'bout 'em doin' nothin' to stop it. It jus' was dat way, en dey 'lowed it without tryin' to stop all sich stuff as dat. You know dat niggers is bad 'bout talkin' 'mongst demselves 'bout sich en sich er goin' on, and some of mars' darkies, dey say dat Sam and Dick, what was two real light colored boys, dat us had was mars' chillun. Dat was all talk. I nebber did believe it 'cause dey nebber even looked like mars en he nebber cared no more for dem dan any of the rest of de hands."

United States. Work Projects Administration

Interviewer: Mrs. Bernice Bowden
Person interviewed: Betty Coleman
1112-1/2 Indiana Street, Pine Bluff, Arkansas
Age: 80
Occupation: Cotton Picker
[Dec 31 1937]

BETTY COLEMAN

"My father belonged to Mr. Ben Martin and my mother and me belonged to the Slaughters. I was small then and didn't know what the war was about, but I remember seein' the Yankees and the Ku Klux.

"Old master had about fifteen or twenty hands but Mr. Martin had a plenty—he had bout a hundred head.

"I member when the war was goin' on we was livin' in Bradley County. We was goin' to Texas to keep the Yankees from gettin' us. I member Mr. Gil Martin was just a young lad of a boy. We got as far as Union County and I know we stopped there and stayed long enough to make two crops and then peace was declared so we cane back to Warren.

"While the war was goin' on, I member when my mother took a note to some soldiers in Warren and asked em to come and play for Miss Mary. I know they stood under a sycamore and two catawba trees and played. There was a perty big bunch of em. Us chillun was glad to hear it. I member just as well as if 'twas yesterday.

"I member when the Yankees come and took all of Miss Mary's silver—took every piece of it. And another time they got three or four of the colored men and made em get a horse apiece and ride away with em bareback. Yankees was all ridin' iron gray horses, and lookin' just as mad. Oh Lord, yes, they rid right up to the gate. All the horses was just alike—iron gray. Sho was perty horses. Them Yankees took everything Miss Mary had.

"After the war ended we stayed on the place one year and made a crop and then my father bought fifty acres of Mr. Ben Martin. He paid some on it every year and when it was paid for Mr. Ben give him a deed to it.

"I'm the only child my mother had. She never had but me, one. I went to school after the war and I member at night I'd be studyin' my lesson and rootin' potatoes and papa would tell us stories about the war. I used to love to hear him on long winter evenings.

"I stayed right there till I married. My father had cows and he'd kill hogs and had a peach orchard, so we got along fine. Our white folks was always good to us."

Interviewer: Thomas Elmore Lucy
Person interviewed: Lucy Cotton
Russellville, Arkansas
Age: 72
[Jan 7 1938]

LUCY COTTON

"Lucy Cotton's my name, and I was born on the tenth day of June, 1865, jist two months after the surrender. No suh, I ain't no kin to the other Cottons around here, so far as I knows. My mother was Jane Hays, and she was owned by a master named Wilson.

"I've belonged to the Holiness Church six years. (They call us 'Holiness,' but the real name is Pentecostal.)

"Yes suh, there's a heap of difference in folks now 'an when I was a girl—especially among the young people. I think no woman, white or black, has got any business wastin' time around the votin' polls. Their place is at home raisin' a family. I hear em sometimes slinging out their 'damns' and it sure don't soun' right to me.

"Good day, mistah. I wish you well—but the gov'ment ain't gonna do nothing. It never has yit."

United States. Work Projects Administration

Interviewer: Miss Irene Robertson
Person interviewed: T.W. Cotton, Helena, Arkansas
Age: 80
[May 11 1938]

T.W. COTTON

"I was born close to Indian Bay. I belong to Ed Cotton. Mother was sold from John Mason between Petersburg and Richmond, Virginia. Three sisters was sold and they give grandma and my sister in the trade. Grandma was so old she wasn't much account fer field work. Mother left a son she never seen ag'in. Aunt Adeline's boy come too. They was put on a block but I can't recollect where it was. If mother had a husband she never said nothing 'bout him. He muster been dead.

"Now my papa come from La Grange, Tennessee. Master Bowers sold him to Ed Cotton. He was sold three times. He had one scar on his shoulder. The patrollers hit him as he went over the fence down at Indian Bay. He was a Guinea man. He was heavy set, not very tall. Generally he carried the lead row in the field. He was a good worker. They had to be quiet wid him to get him to work. He would run to the woods. He was a fast runner. He lived to be about a hundred years old. I took keer of him the last five years of his life. Mother was seventy-one years old when she died. She was the mother of twenty-one children.

"Sure, I do remember freedom. After the Civil War ended, Ed Cotton walked out and told papa: 'Rob, you are free.' We worked on till 1866 and we moved to Joe Lambert's place. He had a brother named Tom Lambert. Father never got no land at freedom. He got to own 160 acres, a house on it, and some stock. We all worked and helped him to make it. He was a hard worker and a fast hand.

"I farmed all my life till fifteen years ago I started trucking here in Helena. I gets six dollars assistance from the Sociable Welfare and some little helpouts as I calls it—rice and potatoes and apples. I got one boy fifty-five years old if he be living. I haven't seen him since 1916. He left and went to Chicago. I got a girl in St. Louis. I got a girl here in Helena. I jus' been up to see her. I had nine children. I been married twice. I lived with my first wife thirteen years and seven months. She died. I lived with my second wife forty years and some over—several weeks. She died.

"I was a small boy when the Civil War broke out. Once I got a awful scare. I was perched up on a post. The Yankees come up back of the house and to my back. I seen them. I yelled out, 'Yonder come Yankees.' They come on cussing me. Aunt Ruthie got me under my arms and took me to Miss Fannie Cotton. We lived in part of their house. Walter (white) and me slept together. Mother cooked. Aunt Ruthie was a field hand. Aunt Adeline must have been a field hand too. She hung herself on a black jack tree on the other side of the pool. It was a pool for ducks and stock.

"She hung herself to keep from getting a whooping. Mother raised (reared) her boy. She told mother she would kill herself before she would be whooped. I never heard what she was to be whooped for. She thought she would be whooped. She took a rope and tied it to a limb and to her neck and then jumped. Her toes barely touched the ground. They buried her in the cemetery on the old Ed Cotton place. I never seen her buried. Aunt Ruthie's grave was the first open grave I ever seen. Aunt Mary was papa's sister. She was the oldest.

"I would say anything to the Yankees and hang and hide in Miss Fannie's dress. She wore long big skirts. I hung about her. Grandma raised me on a bottle so mother could nurse Walter (white). There was something wrong wid Miss Fannie. We colored children et out of trays. They hewed them out of small logs. Seven or eight et together. We had our little cups. Grandma had a cup for my water. We et with spoons. It would hold a peck of something to eat. I nursed my mother four weeks and then mama raised Walter and grandma raised me. Walter et out of our tray many and many a time. Mother had good teeth and she chewed for us both. Henry was younger than Walter. They was the only two children Miss Fannie had. Grandma washed out our tray soon as ever we quit eating. She'd put the bread in, then pour the meat and vegetables over it. It was good.

"Did you ever hear of Walter Cotton, a cancer doctor? That was him. He may be dead now. Me and him caused Aunt Sue to get a whooping. They had a little pear tree down twix the house and the spring. Walter knocked one of the sugar pears off and cut it in halves. We et it. Mr. Ed asked 'bout it. Walter told her Aunt Sue pulled it. She didn't come by the tree. He whooped her her declaring all the time she never pulled it nor never seen it. I was scared then to tell on Walter. I hope eat it. Aunt Sue had grown children.

"The Ku Klux come through the first and second gates to papa's house and he opened the door. They grunted around. They told papa to come out. He didn't go and he was ready to hurt them when they come in. He told them when he finished that crop they could have his room. He left that year. They come in on me once before I married. I was at my girl's house. They wanted to be sure we married. The principal thing they was to see was that you didn't live in the house wid a woman till you be married. I wasn't married but I soon did marry her. They scared us up some.

"I don't know if times is so much better for some or not. Some folks won't work. Some do work awful hard. Young folks I'm speaking 'bout. Times is mighty fast now. Seems like they get faster and faster every way. I'll be eighty years old this May. I was born in 1858."

Interviewer: Samuel S. Taylor
Person interviewed: Ellen Cragin
815-1/2 Arch Street, Little Rock, Arkansas
Age: Around 80 or more
[May 31 1939]

ELLEN CRAGIN

[HW: Escapes on Cow]

"I was born on the tenth of March in some year, I don't know what one. I don't know whether it was in the Civil War or before the Civil War. I forget it. I think that I was born in Vicksburg, Mississippi; I'm not sure, but I think it was.

"My mother was a great shouter. One night before I was born, she was at a meeting, and she said, 'Well, I'll have to go in, I feel something.' She said I was walkin' about in there. And when she went in, I was born that same night.

"My mother was a great Christian woman. She raised us right. We had to be in at sundown. If you didn't bring it in at sundown, she'd whip you,—whip you within an inch of your life.

"She didn't work in the field. She worked at a loom. She worked so long and so often that once she went to sleep at the loom. Her master's boy saw her and told his mother. His mother told him to take a whip and wear her out. He took a stick and went out to beat her awake. He beat my mother till she woke up. When she woke up, she took a pole out of the loom and beat him nearly to death with it. He hollered, 'Don't beat me no more, and I won't let 'em whip you.'

"She said, 'I'm goin' to kill you. These black titties sucked you, and then you come out here to beat me.' And when she left him, he wasn't able to walk.

"And that was the last I seen of her until after freedom. She went out and got on an old cow that she used to milk—Dolly, she called it. She rode away from the plantation, because she knew they would kill her if she stayed.

"My mother was named Luvenia Polk. She got plumb away and stayed away. On account of that, I was raised by my mother. She went to Atchison, Kansas—rode all through them woods on that cow. Tore her clothes all off on those bushes.

"Once a man stopped her and she said, 'My folks gone to Kansas and I don't know how to find 'em.' He told her just how to go.

"My father was an Indian. 'Way back in the dark days, his mother ran away, and when she came up, that's what she come with—a little Indian boy. They called him 'Waw-hoo'che.' His master's name was Tom Polk. Tom Polk was my mother's master too. It was Tom Polk's boy that my mother beat up.

"My father wouldn't let nobody beat him either. One time when somethin' he had did didn't suit Tom Polk—I don't know what it was—they cut sores on him that he died with. Cut him with a raw-hide whip, you know. And then they took salt and rubbed it into the sores.

"He told his master, 'You have took me down and beat me for nothin', and when you do it again, I'm goin' to put you in the ground.' Papa never slept in the house again after that. They got scared and he was scared of them. He used to sleep in the woods.

"They used to call me 'Waw-hoo'che' and 'Red-Headed Indian Brat.' I got in a fight once with my mistress' daughter,—on account of that.

"The children used to say to me, 'They beat your papa yesterday.'

"And I would say to them, 'They better not beat my papa,' and they would go up to the house and tell it, and I would beat 'em for tellin' it.

"There was an old white man used to come out and teach papa how to read the Bible.

"Papa said, 'Ain't you 'fraid they'll kill you if they see you?'

"The old man said, 'No; they don't know what I'm doing, and don't you tell 'em. If you do, they will kill me.'

Signs of the War

"One night my father called me outside and told me that he saw the elements opened up and soldiers fighting in the heavens.

"'Don't you see them, honey?' he said; but I couldn't see them. And he said there was going to be a war.

"I went out and told it. The white people said they ought to take him out and beat him and make him hush his mouth. Because if they got such talk going 'round among the colored people, they wouldn't be able to do nothin' with them. Dr. Polk's wife's father, Old Man Woods, used to say that the niggers weren't goin' to be free. He said that God had showed that to him.

Mean Masters

"Dr. Polk and his son, the one my mother beat up and left lying on the ground, were two mean men. When the slaves didn't pick enough cotton for them, they would take them down the field, and turn up their clothes, till they was naked, and beat them nearly to death.

"Mother was a breeder. While she did that weaving, she had children fast. One day, Tom Polk hit my mother. That was before she ran away. He hit her because she didn't pick the required amount of cotton. When there was nothin' to do at the loom, mother had to go in the field, you know. I forget how much cotton they had to pick. I don't know how many times he hit her. I was small. I heard some one say, 'They got Clarisay Down, down there!' I went to see. And they had her down. She was stout, and they had dug a hole in the ground to put her belly in. I never did get over that. I'm an old woman, but Tom Polk better not come 'round me now even.

"I have heard women scream and holler, 'Do pray, massa, do pray.' And I was sure glad when she beat up young Tom and got away. I didn't have no use for neither one of 'em, and ain't yet.

"It wasn't her work to be in the field. He made her breed and then made her work at the loom. That wasn't nothin'. He would have children by a nigger woman and then have them by her daughter.

"I went out one day and got a gun. I don't know whose gun it was. I said to myself, 'If you whip my mother today, I am goin' to shoot you.' I didn't know where the gun belonged. My oldest sister told me to take it and set it by the door, and I did it.

How Freedom Came

"Dr. Polk had a fine horse. He came riding through the field and said, 'All you all niggers are free now. You can stay here and work for me or you can go to the next field and work.'

"I had an old aunt that they used to make set on a log. She jumped off that log and ran down the field to the quarters shouting and hollering.

"The people all said, 'Nancy's free; they ain't no ants biting her today.' She'd been setting on that log one year. She wouldn't do no kind of work and they make her set there all day and let the ants bite her.

"Big Niggers"

"They used to call my folks 'big niggers.' Papa used to get things off a steamboat. One day he brought a big demi-john home and ordered all the people not to touch it. One day when he went out, I went in it. I had to see what it was. I drunk some of it and when he came home he said to me, 'You've been in that demi-john.' I said, 'No, I haven't.' But he said, 'Yes, you have; I can tell by the way you look.' And then I told him the truth.

"He would get shoes, calico goods, coffee, sugar, and a whole lot of other things. Anything he wanted, he would get. That he didn't, he would ask him to bring the next trip.

"It was a Union gunboat, and ran under the water. You could see the smoke. The white people said, 'That boat's goin' to carry some of these niggers away from here one of these days.'

"And sure enough, it did carry one away.

Buried Treasure and a Runaway

"I went to the big gate one morning and there was a nigger named Charles there.

"I said, 'What you doing out here so early this morning?'

"He said to me, 'You hush yo' mouth and get on back up to the house.'

"I went back to the house and told my mother, 'I saw Charles out there.' That was before my mother ran away.

"My mother said, 'He's fixing to run away. And he's got a barrel of money. And it belongs to the Doctor. 'Cause he and the Dr. went out to bury it to keep the Yankees from getting it.'

"He ran away, and he took the money with him, too. He went out to Kansas City and bought a home. We didn't think much of it, because we knew it was wrong to do it. But Old Master Tom had done a heap of wrong too. He was the first one spotted the boat that morning—Charles was. And he went away on it.

Plenty to Eat

"My father would kill a hog and keep the meat in a pit under the house. I know what it is now. I didn't know then. He would clean the hog and everything before he would bring him to the house. You had to come down outside the house and go into the pit when you wanted to get meat to eat. If my father didn't have a hog, he would steal one from his master's pen and cut its throat and bring it to the pit.

"My folks liked hog guts. We didn't try to keep them long. We'd jus' clean 'em and scrape 'em and throw 'em in the pot. I didn't like to clean 'em but I sure loved to eat 'em. Father had a great big pot they called the wash pot and we would cook the chit'lins in it. You could smell 'em all over the country. I didn't have no sense. Whenever we had a big hog killin', I would say to the other kids, 'We got plenty of meat at our house.'

"They would say back, 'Where you got it?'

"I would tell 'em. And they would say, 'Give us some.'

"And I would say to them, 'No, that's for us.'

"So they called us 'big niggers.'

Marriages Since Freedom

"My first baby was born to my husband. I didn't throw myself away. I married Mr. Cragin in 1867. He lived with me about fifteen years before he died. He got kicked. He was a baker. During the War, he was the cook in a camp. He went to get some flour one morning. He snatched the tray too hard and it kicked him in his bowels. He never did get over it. The tray was full of flour and it was big and heavy. It was a sliding tray. It rolled out easy and fast and you had to pull it careful. I don't know why they called it a kick.

"I married a second husband—if you can call it that—a nigger named Jones. He had a spoonful of sense. We didn't live together three months. He came in one day and I didn't have dinner ready. He slapped me. I had never been slapped by a man before. I went to the drawer and got my pistol out and started to kill him. But I didn't. I told him to leave there fast. He had promised to do a lot of things and didn't do them, and then he used to use bad language too.

Occupation

"I've always sewed for a living. See that sign up there?" The sign read:

> ALL KINDS OF BUTTONS SEWED ON
> MENDING TOO

"I can't cut out no dress and make it, but I can use a needle on patching and quilting. Can't nobody beat me doin' that. I can knit, too. I can make stockings, gloves, and all such things.

"I belong to Bib Bethel Church, and I get most of my

support from the Lord. I get help from the government. I'm trying to get moved, and I'm just sittin' here waiting for the man to come and move me. I ain't got no money, but he promised to move me."

INTERVIEWER'S COMMENT

There it was—the appeal to the slush fund. I have contributed to lunch, tobacco, and cold drinks, but not before to moving expenses. I had only six cents which I had reserved for car fare. But after you have talked with people who are too old to work, too feeble to help themselves in any effective fashion, hemmed up in a single room and unable to pay rent on that, odds and ends of broken and dilapidated furniture, ragged clothes, and not even plenty of water on hand for bathing, barely hanging on to the thread of life without a thrill or a passion, then it is a great thing to have six cents to give away and to be able to walk any distance you want to.

United States. Work Projects Administration

Interviewer: Samuel S. Taylor
Person interviewed: Sallie Crane
See first paragraph in interviewer's comment
for residences
Age: 90, or more

SALLIE CRANE

[HW: Whipped from Sunup to Sundown]

"I was born in Hempstead County, between Nashville and Greenville, in Arkansas, on the Military Road. Never been outside the state in my life. I was born ninety years ago. I been here in Pulaski County nearly fifty-seven years.

"I was born in a old double log house chinked and dobbed. Nary a window and one door. I had a bedstead made with saw and ax. Chairs were made with saw, ax, and draw knife. My brother Orange made the furniture. We kept the food in boxes.

"My mother's name was Mandy Bishop, and my father's name was Jerry Bishop. I don't know who my grand folks were. They was all Virginia folks—that is all I know. They come from Virginia, so they told me. My old master was Harmon Bishop and when they divided the property I fell to Miss Evelyn Bishop.

Age

"The first man that came through here writing us up for the Red Cross, I give him my age as near as I could. And they kept that. You know peace was declared in 1865. They told me I was free. I got scared and thought that the speculators were going to put me in them big droves and sell me down in Louisiana. My old mistress said, 'You fool, you are free. We are going to take you to your mammy.' I cried because I thought they was carrying me to see my mother before they would send me to be sold in Louisiana. My old mistress said she would whip me. But she didn't. When we got to my mother's, I said, 'How old is I?' She said, 'You are sixteen.' She didn't say months, she didn't say years, she didn't say weeks, she didn't say days; she just said, 'You are sixteen.' And my case worker told me that made me ninety years old.

"I was in Hempstead County on Harmon Bishop's plantation. It was Miss Polly, Harmon's wife, that told me I was free, and give me my age.

"I know freedom come before 1865, because my brothers would tell me to come home from Nashville where I would be sent to do nursing by my old mistress and master too to nurse for my young mistress.

"When my old master's property was divided, I don't know why—he wasn't dead nor nothin'—I fell to Miss Evelyn, but I stayed in Nashville working for Miss Jennie Nelson, one of Harmon's daughters. Miss Jennie was my young mistress. My brothers were already free. I don't know how Miss Polly came to tell me I was free. But my brothers would see me and tell me to run away and come on home and they would protect me, but I was afraid to try it. Finally Miss Polly found that she couldn't keep me any longer and she come and told me I was free. But I thought that she was fooling me and just wanted to sell me to the speculators.

Family

"My mother was the mother of twenty children and I am the mother of eighteen. My youngest is forty-five. I don't know whether any of my mother's children is living now or not. I left them that didn't join the militia in Hempstead County fifty-seven years ago. Them that joined the militia went off. I don't know nothin' about them. I have two girls living that I know about. I had two boys went to France and I never heard nothin' 'bout what happened to them. Nothing—not a word. Red Cross has hunted 'em. Police Mitchell hunted 'em—police Mitchell in Little Rock. But I ain't heard nothin' 'bout 'em.

Work

"The first work I did was nursing and after that I was water toter. I reckon I was about seven or eight years old when I first began to nurse. I could barely lift the baby. I would have to drag them 'round. Then I toted water to the field. Then when I was put to plowing, and chopping cotton, I don't know exactly how old I was. But I know I was a young girl and it was a good while before the War. I had to do anything that come up—thrashing wheat, sawing logs, with a wristband on, lifting logs, splitting rails. Women in them days wasn't tender like they is now. They would call on you to work like men and you better work too. My mother and father were both field hands.

Soldiers

"Oo-oo-oo-ee-ee-ee!! Man, the soldiers would pass our house at daylight, two deep or four deep, and be passing it at sundown still marching making it to the next stockade. Those were Yankees. They didn't set no slaves free. When I knowed anything about freedom, it was the Bureaus. We didn't know nothing like young folks do now.

"We hardly knowed our names. We was cussed for so many bitches and sons of bitches and bloody bitches, and blood of bitches. We never heard our names scarcely at all. First young man I went with wanted to know my initials! What did I know 'bout initials? You ask 'em ten years old now, and they'll tell you. That was after the War. Initials!!!

Slave Sales

"Have I seen slaves sold! Good God, man! I have seed them sold in droves. I have worn a buck and gag in my mouth for three days for trying to run away. I couldn't eat nor drink—couldn't even catch the slobber that fell from my mouth and run down my chest till the flies settled on it and blowed it. 'Scuse me but jus' look at these places. (She pulled open her waist and showed scars where the maggots had eaten in—ed.)

Whippings

"I been whipped from sunup till sundown. Off and on, you know. They whip me till they got tired and then they go and res' and come out and start again. They kept a bowl filled with vinegar and salt and pepper settin' nearby, and when they had whipped me till the blood come, they would take the mop and sponge the cuts with this stuff so that they would hurt more. They would whip me with the cowhide part of the time and with birch sprouts the other part. There were splinters long as my finger left in my back. A girl named Betty Jones come over and soaped the splinters so that they would be softer and pulled them out. They didn't whip me with a bull whip; they whipped me with a cowhide. They jus' whipped me 'cause they could—'cause they had the privilege. It wasn't nothin' I done; they just whipped me. My married young master, Joe, and his wife, Jennie, they was the ones that did the whipping. But I belonged to Miss Evelyn.

"They had so many babies 'round there I couldn't keep up with all of them. I was jus' a young girl and I couldn't keep track of all them chilen. While I was turned to one, the other would get off. When I looked for that one, another would be gone. Then they would whip me all day for it. They would whip you for anything and wouldn't give you a bite of meat to eat to save your life, but they'd grease your mouth when company come.

Food

"We et out of a trough with a wooden spoon. Mush and milk. Cedar trough and long-handled cedar spoons. Didn't know what meat was. Never got a taste of egg. Oo-ee! Weren't allowed to look at a biscuit. They used to make citrons. They were good too. When the little white chilen would be comin' home from school, we'd run to meet them. They would say, 'Whose nigger are you?' And we would say, 'Yor'n!' And they would say, 'No, you ain't.' They would open those lunch baskets and show us all that good stuff they'd brought back. Hold it out and snatch it back! Finally, they'd give it to us, after they got tired of playing.

Health

"They're burying old Brother Jim Mullen over here today. He was an old man. They buried one here last Sunday—eighty some odd. Brother Mullen had been sick for thirty years. Died settin' up—settin' up in a chair. The old folks is dyin' fas'. Brother Smith, the husband of the old lady that brought you down here, he's in feeble health too. Ain't been well for a long time.

"Look at that place on my head. (There was a knot as big as a hen egg—smooth and shiny—ed.) When it first appeared, it was no bigger then a pea, I scratched it and then the hair commenced to fall out. I went to three doctors, and been to the clinic too. One doctor said it was a busted vein. Another said it was a tumor. Another said it was a wen. I know one thing. It don't hurt me. I can scratch it; I can rub it. (She scratched and rubbed it while I flinched and my flesh crawled—ed.) But it's got me so I can't see and hear good. Dr. Junkins, the best doctor in the community told me not to let anybody cut on it. Dr. Hicks wanted to take it off for fifty dollars. I told him he'd let it stay on for nothin'. I never was sick in my life till a year ago. I used to weigh two hundred ten pounds; now I weigh one hundred forty. I can lap up enough skin on my legs to go 'round 'em twice.

"Since I was sick a year ago. I haven't been able to get 'round any. I never been well since. The first Sunday in January this year, I got worse settin' in the church. I can't hardly get 'round enough to wait on myself. But with what I do and the neighbors' help, I gets along somehow.

Present Condition

"If it weren't for the mercy of the people through here. I would suffer for a drink of water. Somebody ran in on old lady Chairs and killed her for her money. But they didn't get it, and we know who it was too. Somebody born and raised right here 'mongst us. Since then I have been 'fraid to stay at home even.

"I had a fine five-room house and while I was down sick, my daughter sold it and I didn't get but twenty-nine dollars out of it. She got the money, but I never seed it. I jus' lives here in these rags and this dirt and these old broken-down pieces of furniture. I've got fine furniture that she keeps in her house.

"I get some help from the Welfare. They give me eight dollars. They give me commodities too. They give me six at first, and they increased it. My case worker said she would try to git me some more. God knows I need it. I have to pay for everything I get. Have to pay a boy to go get water for me. There's people that gits more 'n they need and have plenty time to go fishin' but don't have no time to work. You see those boys there goin' fishin'; but that's not their fault. One of the merchants in town had them cut off from work because they didn't trade with him.

"You gets 'round lots, son, don't you? Well; if you see anybody that has some old shoes they don't want, git 'em to give 'em to me. I don't care whether they are men's shoes or women's shoes. Men's shoes are more comfortable. I wear number sevens. I don't know what last. Can't you tell? (I suppose that her shoes would be seven E—ed.) I can't live off eight dollar. I have to eat, git help with my washing, pay a child to go for my water, 'n everything. I got these dresses give to me. They too small, and I got 'em laid out to be let out.

"You just come in any time; I can't talk to you like I would a woman; but I guess you can understand me."

Interviewer's Comment

Sallie Crane lives near the highway between Sweet Home and Wrightsville. Wrightsville post office, Lucinda Hays' box. McLain Birch, 1711 Wolfe Street, Little Rock, knows the way to her house.

Her age is not less than ninety, because she hoed cotton and plowed before the War. If anything, it is more than the ninety which she claims. Those who know her well say she must be at least ninety-five.

She has a good memory although she complains of her health. She seems to be pretty well dependent on herself and the Welfare and is asking for old clothes and shoes as you will note by the story.

Interviewer: Miss Irene Robertson
Person Interviewed: Isaac Crawford
Brinkley, Ark.
Age: 75

ISAAC CRAWFORD

"I was born the first year of the Civil War. I was born and raised and married in Holmes County, Mississippi. My parents was named Harriett and James Crawford. They belong to a widow woman, Miss Sallie Crawford. She had a girl named Bettie and three sons named Sam, Mack, Gus. Mack and Gus was heavy drinkers. Moster Sam would drink but he wasn't so bad. They wasn't mean to the Negroes on the place. They had eight or nine families scattered around over their land.

"I farmed till I was eighteen then they made me foreman over the hands on the place I stayed till after I married.

"I know Sam was in the war and come home cripple. He was in the war five years. He couldn't get home from the war. I drove his hack and toted him to it. I toted him in the house. He said he never rode in the war; he always had to walk and tote his baggage. His feet got frost bit and raw. They never got well. He lived. They lived close to Goodman, Mississippi.

"I heard my mother say she was mixed with Creole

Indian. She was some French. My father was pure African. Now what am I?

"Ole mistress wasn't mean to none of us. She wrung my ears and talked to me. I minded her pretty good.

"The children set on the steps to eat and about under the trees. Some folks kept their children looking good. Some let em go. They fed em—set a big pot and dip em out greens. Give em a cup of milk. We all had plenty coarse victuals. We all had to work. It done you no good to be fraid er sweat in them days.

"I didn't know bout freedom and I didn't care bout it. They didn't give no land nor no mules away as I ever know'd of.

"The Ku Klux never come on our place. I heard about em all the time. I seen em in the road. They look like hants.

"I been farming all my life. I come here to farm. Better land and no fence law.

"I come to 'ply to the P.W.A. today. That is the very reason you caught me in town today."

Interviewer: Mrs. Bernice Bowden
Person interviewed: Mary Crosby
1216 Oak Street, Pine Bluff, Arkansas
Age: 76

MARY CROSBY

"Good morning. I don't know anybody 'round here that was born in slavery times 'cept me. I don't know exactly when I was born in Georgia but I can remember my mama said her old master, Mat Fields, sent my father and all the other men folks to Arkansas the second year of the war. After the war, I remember there was a colored man named Mose come from Mississippi to Georgia and told the colored folks they could shake money off the trees in Mississippi. Of course they was just ignorant as cattle and they believed him. I know I thought what a good time I would have. I can remember seeing old master crying cause his colored folks all leaving, but Mose emigrated all of us to Mississippi.

"He kept emigrating folks over there till he like to got killed. The white people give him a stayaway and told him not to come back, but he sure did get some colored folks out of Georgia.

"I 'member they said the war was to free the niggers. They called it the Civil War. I never did know why they called it that. I can't 'member things like I used to.

"My mother's old master's granddaughter, Miss

Anne, had a baby that was six months old when I was born and mama said old master come in and tell Miss Ann, 'I've got a new little nigger for Mary Lou.' He said he was goin' to give her ten and that I was her first little nigger. When we was both grown Mary Lou used to write to me once a year and say 'I claim you yet, Mary.'

"I 'member when Garfield was shot. That was the first time I ever heard of gangrene.

"Yes'm I have worked hard all my life. When I was in Mississippi I used to make as much as ten dollars a week washin' and ironin'. But I'm not able to work now. The Welfare helps me some."

[HW: (COPY)]
El Dorado Division
FOLKLORE SUBJECTS (Ex-Slave)
Mrs. Mildred Thompson
Federal Writers' Project
Union County, Arkansas.
[TR: Hand dated Nov. 6, 1936]

[TR: Ellen Crowley]

MRS. MILDRED THOMPSON

Ellen Crowley an old Negress of Jefferson county, known as "old Aunt Ellen" to both white and colored people. She was quite a character; a slave during Civil War and lived in Mississippi. She later married and moved to Arkansas.

Aunt Ellen was much feared and also respected by the colored race owing to the fact that she could foretell the future and cast a spell on those she didn't like. This unusual talent "come about" while on a white plantation as a nurse. She foretold of a great sorrow that would fall on her white folks and in the year two children passed away. One day soon after she was being teased by a small negro boy to whom she promptly put the 'curse' on and in later years he was subject to "fits."

She said she was "purty nigh" 200 when asked her age, always slept in the nude, and on arising she would say: "I didn't sleep well last night, the debil sit at my feet and worried my soul" or vice versa "I had a good rest the Lord sit at my head and brought me peace."

She was immaculate about her person and clothes and always wore a red bandana around her head.

Her mania was to clean the yard. When asked about her marriage she would say: "I been married seven times" but Jones, Brown and Crowley were the only husbands she could remember by name. She said the other "four no count Negroes wasn't worth remembering."

She was ever faithful to those she worked for, and was known to walk ten and twelve miles to see her white folks with whom she had work. Would come in and say: "Howdy, I'se come to stay awhile. I'll clean the yard for my victuals and I can sleep on the floor." She would go on her way in a few days leaving behind a clean yard and pleasant memories of a faithful servant.

Interviewer: Samuel S. Taylor
Person interviewed: Richard Crump
1801 Gaines Street, Little Rock, Arkansas
Age: 82

RICHARD CRUMP

[HW: Father Takes a "Deadening"]

"I was born right here in Aberdeen, Mississippi about five miles from the town on the east side of the Tom Bigbee River in Monroe County, Mississippi.

"My father's name was Richard Crump. My mother was named Emily Crump. My grandmother on my father's side was named Susan Crump. My mother came from Middleton, Tennessee. But I don't know nothing about any of her people. My father said he come from South Carolina when he was a boy eight or ten years old. That was way before I was born. They brought him to Mississippi from South Carolina.

"My father's master was old man Johnnie Crump. My mistress was named Nina Crump. That was Johnnie Crump's wife. My mars had four boys to my remembrance. One was named Wess, one was named Rufe, one was named Joe, and one was named Johnnie. He had a girl named Annie and one named Lulu.

"My mother was the mother of thirteen children. I am the onliest one living, that I know of. The way they gwine with us now, I ain't goin' a be here long. Just got four dollars to pay rent and bills and git somethin' to eat for a month. You don't git nothin' much when you git the commodities—no grease to cook with.

"We never had no trouble much when I was coming along. My mars was a pretty good old man. He didn't allow no overseer to whip his slaves. The overseer couldn't whip my old mother anyhow because she was a kind of bully and she would git back in a corner with a hoe and dare him in. And he wouldn't go in neither.

"My grandmother had three or four sons. One was name Nels Crump, another was named Miles and another was named Henry and another Jim. She had two or three more but I can't think of them. They died before I was old enough to know anything. Then she had two or three daughters. One was named Lottie. She had another one but I can't think of her name. I was so little. All of them are dead now. All of my people are dead but me. They are trying to find a sister of mine, but I ain't found her yet. She oughter be down here by Forrest City somewheres. But there ain't nobody here that I know about but me. And the way they're carryin' them now I ain't goin' to be here long. All of them people you hear me talk about, they're supposed to be dead.

"I was born in 1858. At least the old man told me that. I mean my father of course. The first thing I knowed anything about was picking cotton. I was a little bitty old fellow with a little sack hangin' at my side. I was pickin' beside my mother. They would grab us sometimes when we didn't pick right. Shake us and pull our ears.

"I didn't know anything about sellin' and buying. I never was sold.

"The next thing I remember was being told I was free. My daddy said old mars told them they were free. I didn't hear him tell it myself. They come 'round on a Monday morning and told papa and the rest that they were free as he was and that they could go if they wanted to or they could stay, 'cause they were free as he was and didn't have no master no more, didn't have no one to domineer over them no more.

"Right after freedom, my folks worked on old man Jim Burdyne's farm. That is the first place I remember after freedom. Father taken a little deadening. You don't know what a deadening is? That's a lease. He cleaned up some land. We boys were just gettin' so we could pick up brush and tops of trees—and burn it, and one thing and another. Two years after the War was over, I got big enough to plow. I was plowing when I was nine years old. We had three boys and four girls older than me. The balance of them was born after freedom. We made crops on shares for three years after freedom, and then we commenced to rent. Shares were one-third of the cotton and one-fourth of the corn. They didn't pay everything they promised. They taken a lot of it away from us. They said figures didn't lie. You know how that was. You dassent dispute a man's word then. Sometimes a man would get mad and beat up his overseer and run him away. But my daddy wouldn't do it. He said, 'Well, if I owe anything I'll pay it. I got a large family to take care of.'

"I never got a chance to go to school any. There was too much work to do. I married when I was twenty-one. I would go off and stay a month or two and come back. Never left home permanent for a long while. Stayed 'round home till I was forty years old. I come to Arkansas in 1898. I made a living by farming at first.

"I didn't shoot no craps. I belong to the church. I have belonged to the church about forty years or more. I did play cords and shoot craps and things like that for years before I got religion.

"I come to Little Rock in 1918 and been here ever since. I worked 'round here in town first one thing and then another. Worked at the railroad and on like that.

"We used to vote right smart in Mississippi. Had a little trouble sometimes but it would soon die down. I haven't voted since I been here. Do no good nohow. Can't vote in none of these primary elections. Vote for the President. And that won't do no good. They can throw your ballot out if they want to.

"I believe in the right thing. I wouldn't believe in anything else. I try to be loyal to the state and the city. But colored folks don't have much show. Work for a man four or five years and go back to him and he don't know nothin' about you. They soon forget you and a white man's word goes far.

"I was able to work as late as 1930, but I ain't been no 'count since to do much work. I get a pension for old age from the Welfare and commodities and I depend on that for a living. Whatever they want to give me, I'll take it and make out with it. If there's any chance for me to git a slave's pension, I wish they would send it to me. For I need it awful bad. They done cut me way down now. I got heart trouble and high blood pressure but I don't give up.

"My mother sure used to make good ash cake. When

she made it for my daddy, she would put a piece of paper on it on top and another on the bottom. That would keep it clean. She made it extra good. When he would git through, she would give us the rest. Sometimes, she wouldn't put the paper on it because she would be mad. He would ask, 'No paper today?' She would say, 'No.' And he wouldn't say nothin' more.

"There is some of the meanest white people in the United States in Mississippi up there on the Yellow Dog River. That's where the Devil makes meanness.

"There's some pretty mean colored folks too. There is some of them right here in Little Rock. Them boys from Dunbar give me a lot of trouble. They ride by on their bicycles and holler at us. If we say anything to them, they say, 'Shut up, old gray head.' Sometimes they say worse. I used to live by Brother Love. Christmas the boys threw at the house and gave me sass when I spoke to them. So I got out of that settlement. Here it is quiet because it is among the white folks."

United States. Work Projects Administration

Interviewer: Mrs. Carol Graham, El Dorado Division
Person interviewed: Zenia Culp
Age: Over 80
[Jan 29 1938]

ZENIA CULP

"Yas'm, my name is Zenia, Zenia Culp 'tis now since I married. My old master's name was Billy Newton. Him and three more brothers come here and settled in this county years ago and Master Billy settled this farm. I was born and raised here and ain't never lived nowheres else. I used to be nurse girl and lived up at the big house. You know up there where Mr. John Dunbar's widow lives now. And the family burying groun' is jus' a little south of the house where you sees them trees and tomb stones out in the middle of the field.

"Master Billy's folks was so good to me and I sure thought a heap of young Master Billy. Believe I told you I was the nurse girl. Well, young Master Billy was my special care. And he was a live one too. I sure had a time keepin' up wid that young rascal. I would get him ready for bed every night. In summer time he went barefoot like all little chaps does and course I would wash his foots before I put him to bed. That little fellow would be so sleepy sometime that he would say: 'Don't wash em, Zenia, jes' wet em.' Oh, he was a sight, young Master Billy was.

"Does you know Miss Pearl? She live there in El Dorado. She is young master's widow. Miss Pearl comes out to see me sometime and we talks lots bout young Master Billy.

"Yas'm, I'se always lived here where I was born. Never moved way from de old plantation. Course things is changed lots since the days when old Master Billy was livin'. When he went off to the war he took most of the men black folks and the womens stayed home to take care of mistress and the chillun.

"My husban' been dead a long, long time and I live here wid my son. His wife is gone from home dis evenin'. So I thought I'd come out and pick off some peanuts jes' to git out in the sunshine awhile. That's my son out there makin' sorghum. My daughter-in-law is so good to me. She treats me like I was a baby.

"You asks me to tell you something bout slave days, and how we done our work then. Well, as I tell you, my job was nurse girl and all I had to do was to keep up wid young Master Billy and that wasn't no work tall, that was just fun. But while I'd be followin' roun' after him I'd see how the others would be doin' things.

"When they gathered sweet potatoes they would dig a pit and line it with straw and put the tatoes in it then cover them with straw and build a coop over it. This would keep the potatoes from rotting. The Irish potatoes they would spread out in the sand under the house and the onions they would hand up in the fence to keep them from rotting.

"In old Master Newton's day they didn' have ice boxes and they would put the milk and butter and eggs in buckets and let em down in the well to keep em cool.

"Master's niggers lived in log houses down at de quarters but they was fed out of the big house. I members they had a long table to eat off and kept hit scoured so nice and clean with sand and ashes and they scoured the floors like that too and it made em so purty and white. They made their mops cut of shucks. I always eat in the nursery with young Master Billy.

"They had big old fireplaces in Master's house and I never seen a stove till after the war.

"I member bein' down at the quarters one time and one of the women had the sideache and they put poultices on her made out of shucks and hot ashes and that sho'ly did ease the pain.

"The pickaninnies had a time playin'. Seein' these peanuts minds me that they used to bust the ends and put them on their ears for ear rings. Course Master Billy had to try it too, then let out a howl cause they pinched.

"Lan', but them was good old days when Master Billy was alive."

United States. Work Projects Administration

Texarkana District
FOLKLORE SUBJECTS
Name of Interviewer: Mrs. W.M. Ball
Subject: Anecdotes
Story:

Information given by: Albert Cummins
Place of Residence: Laurel St., Texarkana, Ark.
Occupation: None (Ex-Slave)
Age: 86

[TR: Personal information moved from bottom of second page.]

ALBERT CUMMINS

An humble cottage, sheltered by four magnificent oak trees, houses an interesting old negro, Albert Cummins.

Texarkana people, old and young, reverence this character, and obtain from him much valuable information concerning the early life of this country. This ex-slave was freed when he was fifteen years old, but continued to live in the same family until he was a man. He says: "All de training an' advice I evah had come frum mah mistress. She wuz a beautiful Christian; if I am anybody, I owe it to her. I nevah went to school a day in mah life; whut I know I absorbed frum de white folks! Mah religion is De Golden Rule. It will take any man to heaben who follows its teachings.

"Mah mahster wuz kilt in de battle fought at Poison Springs, near Camden. We got separated in de skirmish an' I nevah did see him again. Libin' at that time wuz hard because dere wuz no way to communicate, only to sen' messages by horseback riders. It wuz months befo' I really knew dat mah mahster had been kilt, and where.

"Mr. Autrey bought mah mother when I wuz an infant, and gave us de protection an' care dat all good slave owners bestowed on their slaves. I worshipped dis man, dere has nevah been anudder like him. I sees him often in mah dreams now, an' he allus appears without food an' raiment, jus' as de South wuz left after de war."

"I came heah when Texarkana wuz only three years old, jus' a little kindly village, where we all knew each udder. Due to de location an' de comin' ob railroads, de town advanced rapidly. Not until it wuz too late did de citizens realize whut a drawback it is to be on de line between two states. Dis being Texarkana's fate, she has had a hard struggle overcoming dis handicap for sixty-three years. Still dat State Line divides de two cities like de "Mason and Dixon Line" divides the North an' South.

"Living on the Arkansas side of this city, Albert Cummins is naturally very partial to his side. "The Arkansas side is more civilized", according to his version. "Too easy fo' de Texas folks to commit a crime an' step across to Arkansas to escape arrest an' nevah be heard ob again."

Interviewer: Miss Irene Robertson
Person interviewed: Betty Curlett, Hazen, Arkansas
Age: 66
[-- -- 1938]

BETTY CURLETT

"I can tell you all about my kin folks. My mama's owners was Mars John Moore and Miss Molly Moore. They come from Virginia and brought Grandma Mahaley and Grandpa Tom.

"Mr. Daniel Johnson went to North Carolina and bought Alice and John and their family. When he brought them to Mississippi, they come in a hack. It was snowing and cold. It took em so long to came they take turns walkin'. Grandma was walking long wid the hack and somewhere she cut through and climbed over a railin' fence. She lost her baby outer her quilts and went on a mile fore she knowed bout it. She say, 'Lawd, Master Daniel, if I ain't lost my baby.' They stopped the hack and she went back to see where her baby could be. She knowed where she got out the hack and she knowed she had the baby then. Fore she got to the fence she clum over, she seed her baby on the snow. She said the sun was warm and he was well wrop up. That all what saved em. She shuck him round till she woke him up. She was so scared he be froze. When he let out cryin' she knowed he be all right. She put him in the foot of the hack mong jugs of hot water what they had to keep em warm. She say he never had a cold from it. Well, that was John, my papa, what she lost in de snow. Grandma used to set and tell us that and way I can member it was my own papa she be talkin' bout.

"Papa was raised up by the Johnson family and mama by the Moore family. Den Alice Moore had em marry her and John Johnson. Their plantations joined, and joined Judge Reid's (or Reed's) place. We all had a big time on them three farms. They was good to their niggers but Mr. ---- they said whooped his niggers awful heep.

"Ed Amick was Mars Daniel Johnson's overseer. He told him he wanted his slaves treated mighty good and they was good. Yes ma'am, they was good to em!! We had a plenty to eat. Every Saturday they killed a lamb, a goat or a yearlin' and divided up mong his folks and the niggers. Us childen would kill a peafowl and they let us eat em. White folks didn't eat em. They was tender seem like round the head.

"Miss Evaline was Mars Daniel's sister. She was a old maid. Miss Evaline, Aunt Selie old nigger woman and Brittain old nigger man done nuthin' but raise chickens, geese, guineas, ducks, pigeons. They had a few turkeys and peafowls all the time. When they stewed chicken it was stewed in a big black pot they kept to cook fowls in. They fry chicken in a pot er grease then turn drap sweet biscuit bread in. They put eggs in it, too. They call it marble cakes. Then they pour sweet milk in the bottom grease and make good gravy. When they rendered up lard they always made marble cakes. They cut marble cakes all kind er shapes and twisted em round like knots and rings. They take em up in big pans big as dish pans.

"We had plenty to eat and plenty flannel and cotton check dresses. Regular women done our quiltin' and made our dresses. She made our dresses plain waist, full gathered skirt and buttons down the backs on our waist.

"I was named for Miss Betty Johnson. Mars Daniel bought me books. I slip and tear ABC's outen every book he buy for me. Miss Betty say A-B-C-D; I say after her. She say, 'Betty, you ain't lookin' on the book.' I say, 'Miss Betty, I hear Miss Cornelia's baby woke up. Agin Miss Betty—she was my young mistress—ABC's me sayin' em long wid her. I say, 'Miss Betty, I smell ginger bread, can't I go git a piece?' She say, 'Betty—I'm so sorry I name you fer me. I wish I named Mary.' I say, 'Then you name Mary Betty an' give me nother name.' Miss Betty git me down agin to sayin' the ABC's, I be lookin' off. She say, 'Betty, you goin' to be a idiot.' I say, 'That what I wanter be—zactly what I wanter be.' I didn't know what a idiot was then.

"I took up crocheting. Miss Cornelia cut me some quilt pieces. She say 'Betty that's her talent' bout me. Miss Betty say, 'If she goin' to be mine I want her to be smart.' Miss Mary lernt my sister Mary fast.

"When I was bout fifteen I was goiner to the nigger school. I wanted to go to the white school wid Miss Mag. Miss Betty say, 'Betty, that white woman would whoop you every day.' I take my dinner in a bucket and go on wid Mary. I'd leave fore the teacher have time to have my lesson and git in late. The teacher said, 'Betty, Miss Cornelia and Miss Betty say they want you to be smart and you up an' run off and come in late, and do all sorts er ways. Ain't you shamed?'

"They had a big entertainment. Miss Betty learned me a piece to say—poetry. I could lern it from sayin' it over wid Miss Betty. They bought me and Mary our fust calico dresses. I lack to walked myself to death. I was so proud. It had two ruffles on the bottom of the skirt and a shash tied at the waist behind. We had red hats wid streamers hanging down the back. The dresses was red and black small checks. Mary lernt her piece at school. We had singing and speeches and a big dinner at the school closin'.

"Mr. John Moore went to war and was killed at the beginnin' of the first battle soon as he got there. They had a sayin, 'You won't last as long as John Moore when he went to war.'

"Mr. Criss Moore was kickin' a nigger boy. Old Miss say, 'Criss, quit kickin' him, you hurt him.' He say, 'I ain't hurtin' him, I'm playin' wid him!' White boys played wid nigger boys when they come round the house. Glad to meet up to get to play.

"Mr. Criss Moore, Jr. (John Moore's grandson) is a doctor way up North and so is Mr. Daniel Johnson, Jr. One of em in Washington I think. I could ask Miss Betty Carter when I go back to Mississippi.

"When I left Mississippi Mr. Criss hated to see me go. Mr. Johnson say, 'I wanted all our niggers buried on our place.' He say to Jim, my husband, 'Now when she die you let me know and I'll help bring her back and bury her in the old graveyard.' When my papa died Mr. Johnson had the hearse come out and get him and take him in it to the graveyard. He was buried by mama and nearly all the Johnson, Moore, and Reed (or Reid) niggers buried there. My husband is buried here (Hazen, Arkansas) but he was a Curlett.

"Papa set out apple trees on the old Johnson place, still bearin' apples. The old farm place is forty-eight miles from Tupelo and three miles from Houlka, Mississippi.

"My mother had eighteen children and I had sixteen but all mine dead now but three. Mama's ma and grandpapa Haley had twenty-two children. Yes ma'am, they sho did have plenty to eat. Mars Daniel say to his wife, 'Cornelia, feed my niggers.' That bout last he said when he went off to war. Mars Green, Daniel, and Jimmie three brothers. Three Johnson brothers buried their gold money in stone jars and iron cookin' pots fore they left and went to war.

"When the fightin' stopped, people was so glad they rung and rung the farm bells and blowed horns—big old cow horns. When Mars Daniel come home he went to my papa's house and says, 'John, you free.' He says, 'I been free as I wanter be whah I is.' He went on to my grandpa's house and says, 'Toby, you are free!' He raised up and says, 'You brought me here frum Africa and North Carolina and I goiner stay wid you long as ever I get sompin to eat. You gotter look after me!' Mars Daniel say, 'Well, I ain't runnin' nobody off my place long as they behave.' Purtnigh every nigger sot tight till he died of the old sets. Mars Daniel say to grandpa, 'Toby, you ain't my nigger.' Grandpa raise up an' say, 'I is, too.'

"They had to work but they had plenty that made em content. We had good times. On moonlight nights somebody ask Mars Daniel if they could have a cotton pile, then they go tell Mars Moore and Judge Reid (or Reed). They come, when the moon peep up they start pickin'. Pick out four or five bales. Then Mars Daniel say you come to the house. Ring the bell. Then we have a big supper—pot of chicken, stew and sweet potatoes roasted. Have a wash pot full of molasses candy to pull and all the goobers we could eat.

"Then we had three banjos. The musicians was William Word, Uncle Dan Porter, and Miles Porter. Did we dance? Square dance. Then if somebody been wantin' to marry they step over the broom and it be nounced they married. You can't get nobody—colored folks I mean—to step over a broom; they say it bad luck. If it fall and they step over they step back. They say if somebody sweep under your feet you won't marry that year. Folks didn't visit round much. They had some place to go they went but they had to work. They work together and done mighty little—idle vistin'. Folks took the knitting long visting lest it be Sunday.

"White women wouldn't nurse their own babies cause it would make their breast fall. They would bring a healthy woman and a clean woman up to the house. They had a house close by. She would nurse her baby and the white baby, too. They would feed her everything she wanted. She didn't have to work cause the milk would be hot to give the babies. Dannie and my brother Bradford, and Mary my sister and Miss Maggie nursed my mama. Rich women didn't nurse their babies, never did, cause it would cause their breast to be flat.

"My papa was the last slave to die. Mama died twelve months fore he died. I was born after freedom but times changed mighty little mama and papa said. Grandma learned me to cut doll dresses and Miss Cornelia learned me to sew and learned Aunt Joe (a ex-slave Negro here in town) to play Miss Betty's piano. She was their house girl.

Yes ma'am, when I was small girl she was bout grown. Aunt Joe is a fine cook. Miss Cornelia learnt her how. I could learned to played too but I didn't want to. I wanted to knit and crochet and sew. Miss Cornelia said that was my talent. I made wrist warmers and lace. Sister Mary would spin. She spun yarn and cotton thread. They made feather beds. Picked the geese and sheared the sheep. I got my big feather bed now.

"When I married, Miss Betty made my weddin' dress. We had a preacher marry us at my home. My mama give me to Miss Betty and they raised me. I was the weaslingest one of her children. She give me to Miss Betty. Now she wants me to come back. I think I go back Christmas and stay. Miss Betty is old and feeble now. I got three children living here in Hazen now. All I got left.

"The men folks did all go off, white and black, and vote. I don't know how they voted. Now, honey, you know I don't know nothing bout voting.

"Times is so changed. Conditions so changed that I don't know if the young generation is improved much. They learn better but it don't do em no more good. It seems like it is the management that counts. That is the reason my grandpa didn't want to leave Mars Daniel Johnson's. He was a good manager and Miss Betty is a good manager. We don't know how to manage and ain't got much to manage wid. That the way it looks to me. Some folks is luckier than others."

United States. Work Projects Administration

Little Rock District
FOLKLORE SUBJECTS
Name of Interviewer: Irene Robertson
[HW: Yankees Stole Food]
Subject: History—Slavery Days
Subject: Musical Instrument
Story:—Information
[TR: hand dated 11-14-36]

This information given by: Betty Curlett
Place of Residence: Hazen, Arkansas
Occupation: Washwoman
Age: 67

[TR: Additional topic moved from subsequent page.]
[TR: Personal information moved from bottom of first page.]

BETTY CURLETT

"My mother said during the war and in slavery times they ate out of wooden spoons and bowls they made." They cooked a washpot full of peas for a meal or two and roasted potatoes around the pot in the ashes. They always cooked hams and greens of all kinds in the big iron pots for there were so many of them to eat and in slavery times the cook, cooked for her family in with what she cooked for the Master. They made banks of dirt, sand, leaves and plank and never washed the sweet potatoes till they went to cook them. They had rows of banks in the garden or out behind some of the houses, and had potatoes like that all winter and in the spring to bed.

They saved the ashes and put them in a barrel and poured water over them and saved the drip—lye—and made soap or corn hominy—made big pots of soap and cooked pots full of lye hominy. They carried corn to the mill and had it ground into meal and flour made like that too. The women spun, wove, and knitted. The men would hunt between crop times. If the slaves were caught stealing, the Patty Row would catch him and his master whip him.

My Grandpas and Grandmas and Mamma's Master was John Moore. Mr. John said before his daughter and wife should go to the washtub he would wade blood saddle-skirt deep. He set out to war. Went to Vicksburg and was killed.

His wifes name was Mrs. Elisabeth and his daughters name was Miss Inez. They say thats where the saying "He won't last longer than John Moore did when he went to war" sprang up but I don't know about that part of it for sure.

Grandma Becky said when the Yankees came to Mrs. Moores house and to Judge Rieds place they demanded money but they told them they didn't have none. They stole and wasted all the food clothes, beds. Just tore up what they didn't carry with them and burned it in a pile. They took two legs of the chickens and tore them apart and threw them down on the ground, leaving piles of them to waste.

Song her Mother and Grandmother sang:
    Old Cow died in the fork of the branch
     Baby, Ba, Ba.
    Dock held the light, Kimbo skinned it.
     Ba, Ba, Ba.
    Old cow lived no more on the ranch and

frank no more from
branch, Kinba a pair of shoes, he sewed from
the old cows hide
he had tanned.
 Baby, Ba, Ba.

Musical Instrument

"The only musical instrument we had was a banjo. Some made their banjos. Take a bucket or pan a long strip of wood. 3 horse hairs twisted made the base string. 2 horsehairs twisted made the second string. 1 horse hair twisted made the fourth and the fifth string was the fine one, it was not twisted at all but drawn tight. They were all bees waxed."

United States. Work Projects Administration

Circumstances of Interview
STATE—Arkansas
NAME OF WORKER—Samuel S. Taylor
ADDRESS—Little Rock, Arkansas
DATE—December, 1938
SUBJECT—Ex-Slave

[TR: Repetitive information deleted from subsequent pages.]

J.H. CURRY

1. Name and address of informant—**J.H. Curry**, Washington, Arkansas

2. Date and time of interview—

3. Place of interview—Washington, Arkansas

4. Name and address of person, if any, who put you in touch with informant—

5. Name and address of person, if any, accompanying you—

6. Description of room, house, surroundings, etc.

Personal History of Informant

1. Ancestry—father, Washington Curry; mother, Eliza Douglass; grandmother; Malinda Evans; grandfather, Mike Evans.

2. Place and date of birth—Born in Haywood County, Tennessee in 1862.

3. Family—

4. Places lived in, with dates—Tennessee until 1883. From 1883 until now, in Arkansas.

5. Education, with dates—He took a four-years' course at Haywood after the war.

6. Occupations and accomplishments, with dates— Minister

7. Special skills and interest—Church work.

8. Community and religious activities—Preacher

9. Description of informant—

10. Other points gained in interview—His father was a slave and he tells lots of slavery.

[HW: Master Educates Slave]
Text of Interview (Unedited)

"I was born in 1862, September first. I got that off the Bible. My father, he belonged to a doctor and the doctor, he was a kind of a wait man to him. And the doctor learnt him how to read and write. Right after the War, he was a teacher. He was ready to be a teacher before most other people because he learnt to read and write in slavery. There were so many folks that came to see the doctor and wanted to leave numbers and addresses that he had to have some one to 'tend to that and he taught my father to read and write so that he could do it.

"I was born in Tennessee, in Haywood County. My father was born in North Carolina, so they tell me. He was brought to Tennessee. He was a slave and my mother was a slave. His name was Washington Curry and my mother's name was Eliza Douglass before she married. Her master was named John Douglass and my father's master was named T.A. Curry, Tom Curry some folks called him.

"I don't know just how many slaves Tom Curry owned. Lemme see. There was my daddy, his four brothers, his five sisters. My father's father had ten children, and my father had the same number—five boys and six girls. Ten of us lived for forty years. My mother had ten living children when she died in 1921. Since '21, three girls died. My father died in 1892.

"My father's master had around a hundred slaves. Douglass was a richer man than my father's master. I suspect he had two hundred slaves. He was my mother's father as well as her master. I know him. He used to come to our house and he would give mama anything she wanted. He liked her. She was his daughter.

"My father's father—I can't remember what his name was. I know his mother was Candace. I never did see his father but I saw my grandma. He was dead before I was born. My mother's mother was named Malinda Evans. Only one thing I remember that was remarkable about her. Her husband was a free man named Mike Evans. He come from up North and married her in slave time and he bought her. He was a fine carpenter. They used to hire him out to build houses. He was a contractor in slave time. I remember him well.

"After the War, he used to have white men getting training for the carpenter's training under him. He was Grandma Evans' husband. He wasn't my father's father.

My father was born before Grandma Evans was freed. All the rest of them were born afterward. They sold her to him but the children all belonged to the Douglasses. He probably paid for her on time and they kept the children that was born.

"The doctor was good to my father. Way after freedom, he was our family doctor. He was at my father's bedside when father died. He's dead now.

"My father was a carpenter and a wait man (waiter). He was a finished carpenter. He used to make everything 'round the house. Sometimes he went off and worked and would bring the money back to his master, and his master would give him some for himself.

"My mother worked 'round the house. She was a servant. I don't know that she ever did the work in the field. My daddy just come home every Saturday night. My father and mother always belonged to different masters in slavery time. The Douglasses and the Currys were five or six miles apart. My father would walk that distance on Saturday night and stay there all day Sunday and git up before day in the morning Monday so that he would be back home Monday morning in time for his work. I remember myself when we moved away. That's when my memory first starts.

"I could see that old white woman come out begging and saying, 'Uncle Washington, please don't carry Aunt Lize away.' But we went on away. When we got where we was going, my mother made a pallet on the floor that night, and the three children slept on the pallet on the floor. Nothing to eat—not a bite. I went to bed hungry, and you know how it is when you go to bed hungry, you can't sleep. I jerk a little nod, and then I'd be awake again with the gnawing in my stomach. One time I woke up, and there was a big light in the house, and father was working at the table, and mama reached over and said, 'Stick your head back under the cover again, you little rascal you.' I won't say what I saw. But I'll say this much. We had the finest breakfast the next morning that I ever ate in all my life.

"I used to hear my people talk about pateroles but I don't reckon I can recall now what they said. There is a man in Washington named Bob Sanders. He knows everything about slavery, and politics too. He used to be a regular politician. He is about ninety years old. They came there and got him about two year ago and paid him ten dollars a day and his fare. Man came up and got him and carried him to the capitol in his car. They were writing up something about Arkansas history.

"I have been married fifty-seven years. I married in 1881. My wife was a Lemons. I married on February tenth in Tennessee at Stanton. Nancy Lemons.

"I went to public school a little after the war. My wife and I both went to Haywood after we were married. After we married and had children, we went. I took a four-years' course there when it was a fine institution. It's gone down now.

"I was the oldest boy. We had two mules. We farmed on the halves. We made fifteen bales of cotton a year. Never did make less than ten or twelve.

"I have been in the ministry fifty-three years. I was transferred to Arkansas in 1883 in the conference which met at Humboldt. My first work here was in Searcy in 1884.

"I think the question of Negro suffrage will work itself out. As we get further away from the Civil War and the reconstruction, it will be less and less opposition to the Negro's voting. You can see a lot of signs of that now.

"I don't know about the young people. They are gone wild. I don't know what to say about them.

"I think where men are able to work I think it is best to give them work. A man that is able to work ought to be given work by the government if he can't get it any other way."

Interviewer: Mrs. Bernice Bowden
Person interviewed: Lyttleton Dandridge
2800 W. Tenth Street, Pine Bluff, Arkansas
Age: 80

LYTTLETON DANDRIDGE

"I was told I was born in '57 in East Carroll Parish, Louisiana.

"Oh, I can remember before the War broke out. Yes ma'am, I had good owners. Old master and mistress was named James Railey and Matilda Railey. I called her mistress.

"I remember one time my father carried me to Natchez on Christmas to spend with his people. His parents were servants on a plantation near Natchez.

"I remember two shows I saw. They was the Daniel Rice shows. They was animal shows but they had em on a boat, kind of a flatboat. We didn't have trains and things like that—traveled on the big waters.

"I remember when we refugeed to Texas in '63. They raised tobacco there.

"We got free in '65 and the Governor or somebody ordered all the owners to take all the folks back that wanted to go.

"All the young folks, they had them in Tyler, Texas makin' bullets. My father had the care of about fifty youngsters makin' bullets.

"Old master had two plantations in Louisiana and three in Mississippi. He was a large slaveholder.

"When we got back to Louisiana from Texas, ever'thing was the same except where the levees had been cut and overflowed the land.

"Old master died before the War broke out and my mistress died in '67.

"My father died in Texas. That left my mother a widow. She spent about two weeks at the old home place in Louisiana. She pulled up then and went to Natchez to my father's people. She made two crops with my young master. His name was Otie Railey. Help her? Well, I was comin'. I had one brother and one sister.

"In '68 she worked with a colored man on the shares.

"I started to school in '67. A colored man come in there and established a private school. I went in '67, '68, and '69 and then I didn't go any more till '71 and '72. I got along pretty well in it. I know mine from the other fellows. I can write and any common business I can take care of.

"We had two or three men run off and joined the Yankees. One got drowned fore he got there and the other two come back after freedom.

"My mother worked for wages after freedom. She got three bales of cotton for her services and mine and she boarded herself.

"In '74 she rented. I still stayed with her. She lived with me all her life and died with me.

"I come over to Arkansas the twenty-third day of December in 1916. Worked for Long-Bell Lumber Company till they went down. Then I just jobbed around. I can still work a little but not like I used to.

"I used to vote Republican when I was interested in politics but I have no interest in it now.

"The younger generation is faster now than they was in my time. They was more constrictions on the young people. When I was young I had a certain hour to come in at night. Eight o'clock was my hour—not later than that. I think the fault must be in the times but if the parents started in time they could control them.

"I remember one time a cow got after my father and he ran, but she caught up with him. He fell down and she booed him in the back. My grandfather come up with a axe and hit her in the head. She just shook her head and went off.

"Outside of my people, the best friend I ever met up with was a white man."

United States. Work Projects Administration

Interviewer: Samuel S. Taylor
Person interviewed: Ella Daniels
1223 W. Eleventh Street, Little Rock, Arkansas
Age: 74, or over

ELLA DANIELS

[HW: Food Rationed]

"I was born in North Carolina, in Halifax County, in the country near Scotland Neck. My mother's name was Nellie Doggett. Her name was Hale before she married. My father's name was Tom Doggett. I never did see any of my grand people.

"My mother's master was named Lewis Hale. He was a farmer. He was fairly good himself but the overseers wasn't. They have mistreated my mother. All I know is what I heard, of course; I wasn't old enough to see for myself. My mother was a field hand. She worked on the farm. My father did the same thing.

"My father and mother belonged to different masters. I forgot now who my father said he belonged to. My father didn't live on the same plantation with my mother. He just came and visited her from time to time.

Food

"Sometimes they didn't have any food to eat. The old missis sometimes saw that my mother's children were fed. My mother's master was pretty good to her and her children, but my father's master was not. Food was issued every week. They give molasses, meal, a little flour, a little rice and along like that.

House

"My mother and father lived in old weatherboard houses. I don't know whether all of the slaves lived in weatherboarded houses or not. But I nursed the children and had to go from one house to the other and I know several of them lived in weatherboarded houses. Most of the houses had two rooms. The food that was kept by the slaves, that is the rations given them, was kept in the kitchen part of the house.

Breeding

"I don't know of any cases where slaves were compelled to breed but I have heard of them. I don't know the names of the people. Just remember hearing talk about them.

Freedom Comes

"My mother and father never found out they were free till April 1865. Some of them were freed before then. I don't know how they found it out, but I heard them talking about it.

Right after Freedom

"Right after freedom, my father and mother worked right on in the same place just like they always did. I reckon they paid them, I don't know. They did what they wanted to.

Patrollers, Ku Klux, and Reconstruction

"I remember the Ku Klux. They used to come and whip the niggers that didn't have a pass. I think them was pateroles though. There was some people too who used to steal slaves if they found them away from home, and then they would sell them. I don't know what they called them. I just remember the Ku Klux and the pateroles.

"The Ku Klux were the ones that whipped the niggers that they caught out without a pass. I don't remember any Ku Klux whipping niggers after the War because they were in politics.

Voters and Officeholders

"I have heard of Negroes voting and holding office after the War. I wasn't acquainted with any of them except a man named Kane Gibbs and another named Cicero Barnes. I heard the old people talking about them. I don't know what offices they held. They lived in another county somewhere.

Life Since Emancipation

"I went from North Carolina to Louisiana, and from Louisiana here. They had it that you could shake trees out in Louisiana and the money would fall off. They had some good land out there too. One acre would make all you wanted—corn or anything else. That was a rich land. But I don't know—I don't care what you had or what you owned when you left there, you had to leave it there. Never would give you no direct settlement or pay you anything; that is, pay you anything definite. Just gave you something from time to time. Whatever you had you had to leave it there.

Occupational Experiences

"I used to work in the field when I was able. That was when I was in the country. When I came to the city I usually did washing and ironing. Now I can't do anything. All the people I used to work for is dead. There was one woman in particular. She was a good woman, too. I don't have any help at all now, except my son. He has a family of his own—wife and seven children. Right now, he is cut off and ain't making nothing for himself nor nobody else. But I thank God for what I have because things could be much worse."

Interviewer's Comment

Here again, there is a confusion of patrollers with Ku Klux. It seems to point to a use of the word Ku Klux before the War. Of course, it is clear that the Ku Klux Klan operated after the War.

Ella Daniels' age is given as seventy-four on her insurance policy, and I have placed that age on the first page of this story in the heading. But three children were born after her and before the close of the War. She says they were born two years apart. Allowing that the youngest was born, in 1864, the one next to her would have been born in 1860, and she would have been born in 1858. This seems likely too because she speaks of nursing the children and going from house to house (page two) and must have been quite a child to have been able to do that. Born in 1858, she would have been seven years old in 1865 and would have been able to have been doing such nursing as would have been required of her for two years probably. So it appears to me that her age is eighty, but I have recorded in the heading the same age decided upon for insurance.

United States. Work Projects Administration

Interviewer: Miss Irene Robertson
Person interviewed: Mary Allen Darrow, Forrest City, Arkansas
Age: 74

MARY ALLEN DARROW

"I was born at Monticello, Arkansas at the last of the Cibil (Civil) War. My parents' names was Richard and Ann Allen. They had thirteen children. Mother was a house girl and papa a blacksmith and farmer.

"My great-grandma and grandpa was killed in Indian Nation (Alabama) by Sam and Will Allen. They was coming west long 'fo'e the war from one of the Carolinas. I disremembers which they told me. Great-grandpa was a chief. They was shot and all the children run but they caught my Grandma Evaline and put her in the wagon and brought her to Monticello, Arkansas. They fixed her so she couldn't get loose from them. She was a little full-blood Indian girl then. They got her fer my great-grandpa a wife. He seen her and thought she was so pretty.

"She was wild. She wouldn't eat much else but meat and raw at that. She had a child 'fo'e ever she'd eat bread. They tamed her. Grandpa's pa that wanted the Indian wife was full-blood African. Mama was little lighter than 'gingercake' color.

"My Indian grandma was mean. I was feard of 'er. She run us down and ketch us and whoop us. She was tall slender woman. She was mean as she could be. She'd cut a cat's head off fer no cause er tall. Grandpa was kind. He'd bring me candy back if he went off. I cried after him. I played with his girl. We was about the same size. Her name was Annie Mathis. He was a Mathis. He was a blacksmith too at Monticello and later he bought a farm three and one-half miles out. I was raised on a farm. Papa died there. I washed and done field work all my life. Grandma married Bob Mathis.

"Our owner was Sam and Lizzie Allen. William Allen was his brother. I think Sam had eight children. There was a Claude Allen in Monticello and some grandchildren, Eva Allen and Lent Allen. Eva married Robert Lawson. I lived at Round Pond seventeen or eighteen years, then come to Forrest City. I been away from them Allen's and Mathis' and Gill's so long and 'bout forgot 'em. They wasn't none too good to nobody—selfish. They'd make trouble, then crap out of it. Pack it on anybody. They wasn't none too good to do nothing. Some of 'em lazy as ever was white men and women. Some of 'em I know wasn't rich—poor as 'Jobe's stucky.' I don't know nothing 'bout 'em now. They wasn't good.

"I was a baby at freedom and I don't know about that nor the Ku Klux. Grandpa started a blacksmith shop at Monticello after freedom.

"My pa was a white man. Richard Allen was mama's husband.

"Me and my husband gats ten dollars from the Old Age Pension. He is ninety-six years old. He do a little about. I had a stroke and ain't been no 'count since. He can tell you about the Cibil War."

Interviewer's Comment

I missed her husband twice. It was a long ways out there but I will see him another time.

United States. Work Projects Administration

Interviewer: Mrs. Bernice Bowden
Person interviewed: Alice Davis
1700 Vaugine Street, Pine Bluff, Arkansas
Age: 81

ALICE DAVIS

"I was born in Mississippi. My mistress was Jane Davis. She raised me. She owned my mother too.

"When Miss Jane's husband died, he willed the niggers to his childun and Mandy Paine owned me then. When I was one month old they said I was so white Mandy Paine thought her brother was my father, so she got me and carried me to the meat block and was goin' to cut my head off. When the childun heard, they run and cried, 'Mama's goin' to kill Harriet's baby.' Old mistress, Jane Davis, heard about it and she come and paid Miss Jane forty dollars for me and carried me to her home, and I slep right in the bed with her till the war ceasted."

"Her childun was grown and they used to come by and say, 'Ma, why don't you take that nigger out of your bed?' and she'd reach over and pat me and say, 'This the only nigger I got.'

"I stayed there two or three years after freedom. I didn't know what free meant. Big childun all laugh and say, 'All niggers free, all niggers free.' And I'd say, 'What is free?' I was lookin' for a man to come.

"I worked in the house and in the field. I had plenty chances to go to school but I didn't have no sense.

"My mother was sold to nigger traders and I never did see her again. I always say I never had no mother, and I never did know who my father was.

"I've worked hard since I got to be a women. I never been the mother of but three childun. Me and my boy stay together.

"I had a happy time when I lived with Miss Jane, but I been workin' ever since."

Interviewer: Mrs. Bernice Bowden
Person interviewed: Charlie Davis
100 North Plum, Pine Bluff, Arkansas
Age: 76

CHARLIE DAVIS

"They said I was born in 1862, the second day of March, in Little Rock.

"I 'member the War. I 'member the bluecoats. I knowed they was fightin' but I didn't know what about.

"My old master was killed in the War. I don't know his name, I just heered 'em call him old master.

"I know old missis kept lookin' for him all durin' the War and looked for him afterward. As long as I could understand anything she was still lookin'.

"Far as I know, my parents stayed with old missis after the War.

"I 'member my father hired me out when I was a little boy. They treated, me good.

"Never have done anything 'cept farm work. I'm failin' now. Hate to say so but I found out I am.

"I never did want to go away from here. I could a went, but I think a fellow can do better where he is raised. I have watched the dumb beasts go off with others and see how they was treated, so I never did crave to go off from home. I have knowed people have went away and they'd bring 'em back dead, and I'd say to myself, 'I wonder how he died?' I've studied it over and I've just made myself satisfied.

"I went to school some but I was the biggest help the old folks had and they kept me workin'."

Interviewer: Watt McKinney
Person Interviewed: D. Davis
R.F.D., six miles north of Marvell, Arkansas
Age: 85

D. DAVIS

Uncle D. Davis, an ex-slave, 85 years of age lives some miles north of Marvell, Arkansas with a widowed daughter on a small farm the daughter owns. Uncle D himself also owns a nice little farm some distance further up the road and which he rents out each year since he is no longer able to tend the land. This old negro, now old and bent from years of work and crippled from the effects of rheumatism hobbles about with the assistance of a crutch and a cane. His mind however is very clear and his recollection keen. As I sat with him on the porch of his daughter's home he told me the following story:

"Yes Sir, Mr. McKinney, I has been in Phillips County fer pas forty-five years and I is now pas eighty-five. I wuz a grown en settled man when I fust cum here en hed chillun nigh bout growd. Dats how cum me ter com here on er count of one of my boys. Dis boy he cum befo I did en hed done made one crop en dat boy fooled me ober here from Mississippi. Yo know how dese young bucks is, allus driftin er roun en he hed done drifted rite down dere below Marvell on de Cypress Bayou, en war wukin fer Mr. Fred Mayo when he writ me de letter ter cum ober here. I guess dat yo has heard of Mr. Fred Mayo dat owned de big plantation dere close ter Turner. Well dat is de man whut ay boy wuz wid and atter I cum I jined up wid Mr. Mayo en stayed wid him fer two years en I wud er ben wid him fer good I rekkin iffen I hadn't wanter buy me er place of my own, kase Mr. Fred Mayo he wuz a nathal good man en treted all he hands fair.

"When I cided ter git me er little place of my own, I went en got quainted wid Mr. Marve Carruth kase he hed er great name wid de niggers, en all de niggers in dem days dey went ter Mr. Carruth fer ter git de advice, en Mr. Carruth he hoped me ter git de place up de road whut is mine yit. Dere neber wuz no white man whut wuz no better dan Mr. Marve Carruth. No Sir dat is a fac.

"Yo see, Capn, I wuz borned en raised in de hills of Mississippi, in Oktibbawa County not so fer frum Starkville, en dat wuz a ole country time I hed got grown en de lan hit wuz gittin powful thin, en when I cumed ter dis state en seen how much cotton de folks mekin on de groun, en how rish de lan, I jist went crazy ober dis country en stayed rite here en mobed my fambly rite off. Folkses hed cotton piled up all er round dey houses en I cided rite off dat dis war gwine ter be my home den.

"My ole Marster wuz Tom Davis en Capn dere warnt never no finer man whut ever libed dan Marse Tom. Marse Tom wuz lubed by ebery nigger dat he hed, en Marse Tom sho hed a passel of em. He had bettern two-hundred head en de las one dey crazy bout Marse Tom Davis. He war rather old frum my fust riccolection of im, en he neber libed meny years atter de war. Marse Tom he owned a grete heap er lan. His lan hit stretch out fer God knows how fer en den too he hed de big mill whut runned wid de water wheel whar dey saw de lumber en grine de meal en de flour. Dey neber bought no flour en dem days kase dey raised de wheat on de place, en all de meat en nigh bout ebery thing whut dey hed er need of. Marse Tom he tuk de best kine er care of his slabe people en he neber blebe in buyin er sellin no niggers. Dat he didn't. He neber wud sell er one, en he neber did buy but three. Dat is er fac, Capn, en one of dem three whut he bought wuz "Henry" whut wuz my own pappy, en he buyed Henry frum Mr. Spence kase Henry hed done got married ter Malindy, whut wuz my mammy. Dat is whut my Mammy en Pappy dey bofe tole me.

"Marse Tom he neber jine de army kase he too old when de war brek out, but Marse Phil he jined up. Marse Phil dat war Marse Tom's son, en de onliest boy dat Ole Marster en Ole Mis hed, en dey jist hed one mo chile en dat wuz de girl, Miss Rachel, en atter de war ober Miss Rachel she married Capn Dan Travis whut cum from Alabama. Ole Marster he neber laked Capn Dan er bit, en he jes bucked en rared er bout Miss Rachel gwine ter git married ter dat Capn, but hit neber done him no good ter cut up kase Ole Mis she sided wid Miss Rachel, en den too Miss Rachel she hab er head of her own en she know her Pa aint gwine ter stop her. Marse Tom he didn't lak Capn Dan kase de Capn he er big sport, en mighty wild, en lub he whiskey too well, en den he a gamblin man besides dat, do he sho war a fine lookin gentman.

"Whilst Marse Tom he too old ter jine up wid de army, he hired him er man ter fite fer him in his place jes de same, en him en Ole Mis dey neber want Marse Phil ter jine up, en sey dey gwine ter hire er man fer ter tek Marse Phil's place so he won't hatter go, but Marse Phil he sey he gwine ter do he own fitin, en eben do he Ma en Pa dey cut up right smart bout Marse Phil goin ter de war, he up en jine jes de same. Marse Phil he neber wuz sich a stout, healthy pussen, en he always sorter sikly, en it warnt long fore he tuk down in de camp wid sum kine er bad spell er sikness en died. Dat wuz sho tuf on Marse Tom en de Ole Mis fer dem ter lose Marse Phil, kase dey put er heap er sto by dat boy, him bein de onliest son dat dey got, en day so tached ter im. Hit mighty nigh broke dem ole peoples up.

"No Sir, Capn, I betcha dat dere warnt airy uther er slabe-owning white man ter be foun dat wuz er finer man, er dat was mo good ter he niggers dan Marse Tom Davis. Now jes tek dis, dere wuz "Uncle Joe" whut wuz my grand-pappy, en he wuz jes bout de same age as Marse Tom, en dey growed up ter gedder, en dey tole hit dat Marse Tom's pappy git "Uncle Joe" when he war jes a boy frum de speckle-lady (speculator) fer er red hankerchief, dats how cheap he git im en, dat rite off he gib im ter Marse Tom, en atter Marse Tom git up en growd ter be er man, en he pappy died en lef him all de lan en slabes, en den atter er lot mo years pas, en Uncle Joe done raise Marse Tom seben chillun, den Marse Tom he up en sot Uncle Joe free, en gib him er home en forty acres, en sum stock kase Uncle Joe done been good en fathful all dem years, en raise Marse Tom all dem seben chillun, en one of dem seben wuz my own mammy.

"Capn, aint yo eber heard tell of de speckle-ladies? (speculators) Well, I gwine ter tell yo who dey wuz. Dey wuz dem folkses whut dealed in de niggers. Dat is whut bought em, en sole em, en dey wud be gwine round thru de country all de time wid a grete gang er peoples bofe men en womens, er tradin, en er buyin, en er sellin. Hit wuz jes lak you mite sey dat dey wud do wid er gang er mules. Jist befo dese here speckle-ladies wud git ter er town er plantation whar dey gwine ter try ter do sum bizness lak tradin er sich matter, dey stop de crowd long side er creek er pond er water en mek em wash up en clean up good lak, en comb em up rite nice, en mek de wimmens wrap up dey heads wid some nice red cloth so dey all look in good shape ter de man whut dey gwine try ter do de bizness wid. Dats zackly de way dey do Capn, jes lak curryin en fixin up mules fer ter sell, so dey look bettern dey actually is.

"Whilst Marse Tom Davis hed oberseers hired ter look atter de farmin of de lan, he hed his own way er doin de bizness, kase he know dat all he niggers is good wukkers, en dat he kin pend on em, so de fust of ebery week he gib each en ebery single man er fambly er task fer ter do dat week, en atter dat task is done den dey fru wuk fer dat week en kin den ten de patches whut he wud gib dem fer ter raise whut dey want on, en whut de slabes raise on dese patches dat he gib em wud be deres whut-sum-eber hit wud be, cotton er taters er what, hit wub be, dey own, en dey cud sell hit en hab de money fer demselves ter buy whut dey want.

"Marse Tom he wud ride out ober de place at least once a week en always on er Sattidy mornin, en ginerally he wud pass de word out mongst de folkses fer em all ter cum ter de big house er Sattidy atter noon fer er frolic. Ebery pussen on de place frum de littlest chile ter de oldest man er woman wud clean dey selves up en put on dey best clo's for ter "go befo de King", dats whut us called it. All wud gather in bak of de big house under de big oak trees en Marse Tom he wud cum out wid he fiddle under he arm, yo kno Marse Tom he war a grete fiddler, en sot hisself down in de chere whut Uncle Joe done fotched fer im, en den he tell Uncle Joe fer ter go git de barrel er whiskey en he wud gib em all er gill er two so's dey cud all feel rite good, en den Marse Tom he start dat fiddle playin rite lively en all dem niggers wid dance en hab de bes kin er frolic, en Marse Tom he git jes es much fun outen de party as de niggers demselves. Dats de kine er man whut Marse Tom wuz.

"I tell yo, Capn, my marster he sho treated his slabes fair. Dey all draw er plenty rations once ebery week en iffen dey run out tween times dey cud always git mo, en Marse Tom tell em ter git all de meal en flour at de mill eny time dat dey need hit. Dats rite, Capn, en I sho tells dis fer de truf, en dat is I say dat iffen all de slabe owning white folks lak Marse Tom Davis, den dere wudn't ben no use er freedom fer de darkies, kase Marse Tom's slabes dey long ways better off wid him in dey bondage dan dey wuz wid out im when dey sot free en him dead en gone.

"At Chrismus time on Marse Tom's place dey wud hab de fun fer er week er mo, wid no wuk gwine on at all. De candy pullin, en de dances wid be gwine on nigh bout constant, en ebery one gits er present frum de marster.

"All endurin of de war times, Marse Tom he neber raised no cotton er tall but instid he raised de wheat, en de corn en hogs fer de Confedrits, en de baggage waggins wud cum from time ter time fer de loads of flour, en meal en meat dat he wud sen ter de army. De Yankees sumhow dey missed us place en neber did fin hit, en do de damage er bruning [TR: burning?] en sich dat I is heard dat dey done in places in other parts of de state. We all heard one time dat de Yankees wuz close er roun en wuz on de way ter burn Marse Tom's mill but dey got on de wrong road en day neber did git ter our place, en us sho wuz proud er dat too. Yit en still attar de war ober, Marse Tom, he had bout four hundred bales er cotton on han at de barn en de Yankee govment dey sho tuk dat en didn't pay him er bit fer dat cotton. I knows dat ter be er fac.

"I members de war rail well, kase ye see, I wuz bout twelve year old when hit ober. En de last two er three years of de trubble I wuz big enuf ter be doin sum wuk, so dey tuk me in de big house fer ter be er waitin boy round de house, en I slept in dar too on er pallit on de floor, en er lot er times de Calvary sojers wud stop at Marse Tom's en spen de nite, en I wud be layin on de pallit but wudn't be sleep, en I cud hear dem talkin ter Marse Tom, en Marster he wud ax dem how de fite cumin on, en iffen dey whippin de Yankees, en de Calvary sojers dey say dat dey whippin de Yankees ebery day en killin em out, en Marse Tom he sey "Yo is jes er big lie, how cum yo runnin er way iffen yo whippin dem Yankees? Dem Yankees is atter yo, en yo is runnin frum em dats whut yo doin. Yo know yo aint whippin no Yankees kase if yo wuz yo wud be atter dem rite now stid dem atter yo". No Sir, dem Calvary sojers cudn't fool Marse Tom.

"Yes sir, I tell yo, Capn, de slabes dey fared well wid Marse Tom Davis, en dere wudn't neber ben no war ober de slabery question iffen every body ben lak Marse Tom. All his peoples wuz satisfied en dey didn't eben know what de Yankees en de Southern white folks wuz fitin er bout, kase dey wuzn't worried bout no freedom, yit en still atter de freedom cum dey wuz glad ter git hit, but atter dey git hit dey don't know whut ter do wid hit. En atter de bondage lifted, Marse Tom he called em all up en tell em dat dey free es he is, en dey kin lebe if dey want to, but dere wuzn't nairy nigger lef de place. Dey ebery one stayed, en I spect dat er lot of dem Davis niggers is rite dere till yit on dat same lan wid whoever hit belongs to.

"When er slabe man en woman got married in dose days dere wuzn't no sich thing as er license fer dem. All dey hed ter do wuz ter git de permit frum de Marster en den ter start in ter libbin wid each udder. Atter de freedom do, all er dem whut wuz married en libbin wid one er nudder wuz giben er slip ter sho dat dey married, en ter mek dey marriage legal.

"Atter freedom cum ter de darkies, en de trubble all ober in de fitin, en atter de surrender, Marse Tom he hed his whole place lined out by de surveyor en marked off in plots er groun, en he sell er plot er forty acres ter ebery fambly dat he hed, on de credik too, en sell em de stock wid de place so dey kin all hab er home, en dey all set in ter buy de lan frum Marse Tom, but hit warnt long atter dat till Marse Tom en ole Mis bofe died, en dat wuz when Capn Dan Travis, Miss Rachel's husband, he taken charge of de bizness en broke all de contracts dat de darkies hed made wid Marse Tom, an dat wuz de las of de lan buyin on dat place, en dat wuz de startin of de niggers er leavin de Davis place, wid Capn Dan Travis in charge, en Marse Tom gone. But Capn Dan he en Miss Rachel didn't keep dey place long atter her Pa dead, kase de Capn he too wild, en he soon fooled all de money en lan off wid he drinkin en gamblin.

"Capn, did yo eber hear of de "Chapel Hill" fight dat de colored folks en de white folks hed in Mississippi? I will tell yo bout dat fight en de leadin up ter de trubble.

"Atter de war dey hed de carpet-baggers en de Klu Klux bofe, en de white folks dey didn't lak de carpet-baggers tolerable well, dat dey didn't. I don't know who de carpet-baggers wuz but dey wuz powful mean, so de white folks say. You know sum way er udder de Yankees er de carpet-baggers er sum ob de crowd, dey put de niggers in de office at de cote house, en er makein de laws at de statehouse in Jackson. Dat wuz de craziest bizness dat dey eber cud er done, er puttin dem ignorant niggers whut cudn't read er write in dem places. I tell yo, Capn, dem whut put dose niggers in de office dey mus not had es much since es de niggers, kase dey mought know dat hit wudn't wuk, en hit sho didn't wuk long. Dey hed de niggers messed up in sum kind er clubs whut dey swaded dem to jine, en gib em all er drum ter beat, en dey all go marchin er roun er beatin de drums en goin ter de club meetins. Dem ignorant niggers wud sell out fer er seegar er a stick er candy. Hit wasn't long do till de trubble hit broke out en de fite tuk place. De Klu Klux dey wuz er ridin de country continual, en de niggers dey skeered plum sick by dem tall white lookin hants wid dey hosses all white wid de sheets, en sum sey dey jes cum outen dey grabe en er lookin fer er niggers ter tek bak wid em when de day light cum. All de time de niggers habin dey club meetins in er ole loose house dere at Chapel Hill, en de Klux er gittin more numerous all de time, en de feelin mongst de white en de black wuz er gittin wus en wus, en one night when de niggers habin er grete big meetin, en er beatin dey drums en er carryin on, here cum de Klu Klux er sumpin er shootin right en lef en er pourin de shots in ter dat ole house en at ebery niggers dey see, en de niggers dey start er shootin bak but not fer long, kase mos of em done lit out fer de woods, dats is mos all whut ain't kilt, en dat wuz de bery las of de club meetins en de bery las of de niggers er holdin de office in de cote house. I heard bout de fight de nex morn in kase Chapel Hill hit warn't fer frum whar I libed at dat time. I seed Dr. Marris Gray on de rode on he hoss, en he hoss wuz kivered wid mud frum he tall ter he head. Dr. Marris Gray he pulled up en sed, "Good mornin "D" is ye heard bout de fite whut wuz had last nite at Chapel Hill" en I sey "No Sir Doctor, whut fite wuz dat en whut dey fitin er bout?", en de doctor sey he didn't know whut dey fightin bout lessin dey jes tryin ter brake up de club meetin, en he went on ter say dat er heap er niggers wuz kilt en also sum white folks too, en sum mo wuz shot whut ain't dead yit, en dat he been tendin ter dem whut is shot en still ain't dead. En den I sey "Doctor Morris wuz yo dere when de fightin goin on"?, en de doctor he say "En cose I warn't dere yo don't think I gwine be roun what no shootin tekin place, does yo"?, en I say "Naw Suh" en de doctor he rid on down de rode den, but I knowed in my own mine dat Doctor Morris wuz in dat fightin, kass he hoss so spattered up wid mud, en I seed er long pistol barrel stickin out frum under he coat, en den sides dat I iz knowed de doctor eber since I wuz a chile when Marse Tom uster hab him ter gib de darkies de medicine when dey sik, en I seed him one night er ridin wid de Klu Klux en heard him er talkin when I wuz hid in de bushes lon side de rode when I cumin home frum catchin me er possum in de thicket, en den Doctor Morris he wid General Forrest all throo de war en he know whut fightin is, an he sho wudn't neber go outen his way to miss no shootin."

Interviewer: Mrs. Bernice Bowden
Person interviewed: James Davis
1112 Indiana St. (owner), Pine Bluff, Ark.
Age: 96
Occupation: Cotton farmer

JAMES DAVIS

"This is what's left of me. How old? Me? Now listen and let me tell you how 'twas. Old mistress put all our ages in the family Bible, and I was born on Christmas morning in 1840 in Raleigh, North Carolina.

"My old master was Peter Davis and he was old Jeff Davis' brother. There was eight of them brothers and every one of em was as rich as cream.

"Old master was good to us. He said he wanted us singin' and shoutin' and workin' in the field from morning to night. He fed us well and we had plenty good clothes to wear—heavy woolen clothes and good shoes in the winter time. When I was a young man I wore good clothes.

"I served slavery about twenty-four years before peace was declared. We didn't have a thing in God's world to worry bout. Every darky old master had, he put woolen goods and good heavy shoes every winter. Oh, he was rich—had bout five or six thousand slaves. Oh, he had darkies aplenty. He run a hundred plows.

"I went to work when I was seven pullin' worms off

tobacco, and I been workin' ever since. But when I was comin' up I had good times. I had better times than I ever had in my life. I used to be one of the best banjo pickers. I was good. Played for white folks and called figgers for em. In them days they said 'promenade', 'sashay', 'swing corners', 'change partners'. They don't know how to dance now. We had parties and corn shuckin's, oh lord, yes.

"I'll sing you a song

> 'Oh lousy nigger
> Oh grandmammy
> Knock me down with the old fence rider,
> Ask that pretty gal let me court her
> Young gal, come blow the coal.'

"When I was twenty-one I was sold to the speculator and sent to Texas. They started me at a thousand and run me up to a thousand nine hunnerd and fifty and knocked me off. He paid for me in old Jeff Davis' shin plasters.

"I runned away and I was in Mississippi makin' my way back home to North Carolina. I was hidin' in a hollow log when twenty-five of Sherman's Rough Riders come along. When they got close to me the horses jumped sudden and they said, 'Come out of there, we know you're in there!' And when I come out, all twenty-five of them guns was pointin' at that hole. They said they thought I was a Revel and 'serted the army. That was on New Years day of the year the war ended. The Yankees said, 'We's freed you all this mornin', do you want to go with us?' I said, 'If you goin' North, I'll go.' So I stayed with em till I got back to North Carolina.

"After surrender, people went here and yonder and

that's how come I'm here. I emigrated here. I left Raleigh, North Carolina Christmas Eve 1883. I've seen ninety-six Christmases.

"I member the folks said the war was to keep us under bondage. The South wants us under bondage right now or they wouldn't do us like they do.

"When I come to this country of Arkansas I brought twelve chillun and left four in North Carolina. I've had six wives and had twenty-nine chillun by the six wives.

"I've seen them Ku Klux in slavery times and I've cut a many a grapevine. We'd be in the place dancin' and playin' the banjo and the grape vine strung across the road and the Ku Klux come ridin' along and run right into it and throw the horses down.

"Cose I believe in hants. They're in the air. Can't everybody see em. Some come in the shape of a cat or a dog—you know, old folks spirits. I ain't afeared of em—ain't afeared of anything cept a panter. Cose I got a gun—got three or four of em. You can't kill a spirit cept with silver.

"I was in the road one time at night next to a cemetery and I see somethin' white come right up side of me. I didn't run then. You know you can git so scared you can't run, but when I got so I could, I like to killed myself runnin'.

"I'm not able to work now, but I just go anyhow. I got a willin' mind to work and a strong constitution but I ain't got nothin' to back it. I never was sick but twice in my life.

"Since I been in Pine Bluff I worked sixteen years at night firing up and watchin' engines, makin' steam, and never lost but one night. I worked for the Cotton Belt forty-eight years. I worked up until the fust day of this last past May, five years ago, when they laid me off.

"I'm disabled wif dis rheumatism now but I works every day anyway.

"I'll show you I haven't been asleep atall. I worked for the railroad company forty-eight years and I been tryin' to get that railroad pension but there's so much Red Cross (tape) to these things they said it'd be three months before they could do anything."

Interviewer: Mrs. Bernice Bowden
Person interviewed: Jim Davis
1112 Indiana Street
Pine Bluff, Arkansas
Age: 98

[TR: Same as previous informant despite age difference.]

JIM DAVIS

"Well, I've broke completely down. I ain't worth nothing. Got rheumatism all over me.

"I never seen inside a schoolhouse—allus looked on the outside.

"The general run of this younger generation ain't no good. What I'm speakin' of is the greatest mass of 'em. They ain't healthy either. Why, when I was comin' along people was healthy and portly lookin'. Why, look at me. I ain't never had but two spells of sickness and I ain't never had the headache. The only thing—I broke these three fingers. Hit a mule in the head. Killed him too.

"Yes'm, that was in slavery times. Why, they passed a law in Raleigh, North Carolina for me never to hit a man with my fist. That was when I was sold at one thousand nine hundred dollars.

"Ever' time they'd make me mad I'd run off in the woods.

"But they sure was good to their darkies. Plenty to eat

and plenty good clothes. Sam Davis was my owner. And he wouldn't have no rough overseer."

FOLKLORE SUBJECTS
Name of interviewer: Mrs. Bernice Bowden
Subject: Slavery Time Songs
Subject: Superstitions
Story:—Information

This information given by: Jim Davis
Place of residence: 1112 Indiana Street, Pine Bluff, Arkansas
Occupation: None
Age: 98

[TR: Additional topic moved from subsequent page.]
[TR: Personal information moved from bottom of first page.]
[TR: Some word pronunciation was marked in this interview. Letters surrounded by [] represent long vowels.]

JIM DAVIS

"I used to be a banjo picker in Civil War times. I could pick a church song just as good as I could a reel.

"Some of 'em I used to pick was 'Amazing Grace', 'Old Dan Tucker,' Used to pick one went like this

>'Farewell, farewell, sweet Mary;
>I'm ruined forever
>By lovin' of you;
>Your parents don't like me,
>That I do know
>I am not worthy to enter your d[o].'

I used to pick

>'Dark was the night

> Cold was the ground
> On which the Lord might lay.'

I could pick anything.

> 'Amazing grace
> How sweet it sounds
> To save a wretch like me.'

> 'Go preach my Gospel
> Says the Lord,
> Bid this whole earth
> My grace receive;
> Oh trust my word
> Ye shall be saved.'

I used to talk that on my banjo just like I talked it there."

Superstitions

"Oh, yes ma'am, I believe in all the old signs.

"You can take a rabbit foot and a black cat's bone from the left fore shoulder, and you take your mouth and scrape all the meat offin that bone, and you take that bone and sew it up in a red flannel—I know what I'm talkin' 'bout now—and you tote that in your pocket night and day—sleep with it—and it brings you good luck. But the last one I had got burnt up when my house burnt down and I been goin' back ever since.

"And these here frizzly chicken are good luck. If you

have a black frizzly chicken and anybody put any poison or anything down in your yard, they'll scratch it up."

United States. Work Projects Administration

Interviewer: Mrs. Bernice Bowden
Person interviewed: Jeff Davis
1100 Texas Street, Pine Bluff, Arkansas
Age: 85
[May 31 1938]

JEFF DAVIS

"What's my name? I got a good name. Name's Jeff Davis. Miss Mary Vinson was some of my white folks.

"Oh Lord yes, I was here in slavery times—runnin' around like you are—ten years old. I'm eighty-five even.

"Soldiers used to give me dimes and quarters. Blue coats was what they called 'em. And the Rebs was Gray.

"Yankees had a gun as long as from here to there. Had cannon-balls weighed a hundred and forty-four pounds.

"I'm a musician—played the fife. Played it to a T. Had two kinds of drums. Had different kinds of brass horns too. I 'member one time they was a fellow thought he could beat the drum till I took it.

"Had plenty to eat. Old master fed us plenty.

"Oh, I used to do a heap of work in a day.

"I was 'bout ten when freedom come. Yes ma'am."

United States. Work Projects Administration

Interviewer: Watt McKinney
Person interviewed: Jeff Davis
R.F.D. five miles south, Marvell, Arkansas
Age: 78

JEFF DAVIS

"I'se now seventy-eight year old an' gwine on seventy-nine. I was borned in de Tennessee Valley not far from Huntsville, Alabama. Right soon atter I was borned my white folks, de Welborns, dey left Alabama an' come right here to Phillips County, Arkansas, an' brung all the darkies with 'em, an' that's how come me here till dis very day. I is been here all de time since then an' been makin' crops er cotton an' corn every since I been old enough. I is seen good times an' hard times, Boss, all endurin' of those years followin' de War, but de worst times I is ever seen hab been de last several years since de panic struck.

"How-some-ever I is got 'long first rate I reckon 'cause you know I owns my own place here of erbout eighty acres an' has my own meat an' all such like. I really ain't suffered any for nothin'. Still they has been times when I ain't had nary a cent an' couldn't get my hands on a dime, but I is made it out somehow. Us old darkies what come up with de country, an' was de fust one here, us cleared up de land when there wasn't nothin' here much, an' built de log houses, an' had to git 'long on just what us could raise on de land an' so on. Couldn't mind a panic bad as de young folks what is growed up in de last ginnyration.

"You see, I was borned just three years before de darkies was sot free. An' course I can't riccolect nothin' 'bout de slavery days myself but my mammy, she used to tell us chillun 'bout dem times.

"Like I first said, us belonged to de Welborns an' dey was powerful loyal to de Souf an' er heap of de young ones fit in de army, an' dey sont corn an' cows an' hogs an' all sich like supplies to de army in Tennessee an' Georgia. Dat's what my mammy tole me an' I know dey done dem things, an' dey crazy 'bout Mr. Jefferson Davis, de fust an' only President of de Confedracy, an' dat's how come me got dis name I got. Yas suh, dat is how come me named 'Jeff Davis.' An' I always has been proud of my name, 'cause dat was a sure great one what I is named after.

"My pappy was a white man, dat's what my mammy allus told me. I knows he bound to been 'cause I is too bright to not have no white blood in me. My mammy, she named 'Mary Welborn'. She say dat my pappy was a white man name 'Bill Ward' what lived back in Alabama. Dat's all my mammy ever told me about my pappy. She never say iffen he work for de Welborns er no, er iffen he was an overseer er what. I don't know nothin' 'bout him scusin' dat he er white man an' he named 'Bill Ward'. My steppappy, he was name John Sanders, an' he married my mammy when I 'bout four year old, an' dat was atter de slaves taken outen dey bondage.

"My steppappy, he was a fine carpenter an' could do most anything dat he want to do with an axe or any kind of a tool dat you work in wood with. I riccolect dat he made a heap of de culberts for de railroad what was built through Marvell from Helena to Clarendon. He made dem culberts outen logs what would be split half in two. Then he would hew out de two halves what he done split open like dey used to make a dug-out boat. Dey would put dem two halves together like a big pipe under de tracks for de water to run through.

"There was several white mens dat I knowed in dis part of de county what raised nigger famblys, but there wasn't so many at dat. I will say this for them mens though. Whilst it wasn't right for dem to do like dat, dem what did have 'em a nigger woman what dey had chillun by sure took care of de whole gang. I riccolect one white man in particular, an' I knows you is heered of him too. How-some-ever, I won't call no names. He lived down on de ribber on de island. Dis white man, he was a overseer for a widder woman what lived in Helena an' what owned de big place dat dis man oberseer was on. Dis white man, he hab him dis nigger woman for de longest. She have five chillun by him, three boys an' two gals.

"After a while dis man, he got him a place up close to Marvell where he moved to. He brought his nigger fambly with him. He built dem a good house on his farm where he kept them. He give dat woman an' dem chillun dey livin' till de chillun done grown an' de woman she dead. Then he married him a nice white woman after he moved close to Marvell. He built him a house in town where his white wife live an' she de mammy of a heap of chillun too by dis same man. So dis man, he had a white fambly an' a half nigger fambly before. De most of de chillun of dis man is livin' in this county right now.

"Yas suh, Boss, I is sure 'nough growed up with dis here county. In my young days most all de west end of this county was in de woods. There wasn't no ditches or no improvements at all. De houses an' barns was most all made of logs, but I is gwine to tell you one thing, de niggers an' de white folks, dey get erlong more better together then dan dey does at dis time. De white folks then an' de darkies, dey just had more confidence in each other seems like in dem days. I don't know how 'twas in de other states after de War, but right here in Phillips County de white folks, dey encouraged de darkies to buy 'em a home. Dey helped dem to git it. Dey sure done dat. Mr. Marve Carruth, dat was really a good white man. He helped me to get dis very place here dat I is owned for fifty years. An' then I tell you dis too, Boss, when I was coming up, de folks, dey just worked harder dan dey do these days. A good hand then naturally did just about three er four times as much work in a day as dey do now. Seems like dis young bunch awful no 'count er bustin' up and down de road day and night in de cars, er burnin' de gasoline when dey orter be studyin' 'bout makin' er livin' an' gettin' demselves er home.

"Yas suh, I riccolect all 'bout de time dat de niggers holdin' de jobs in de courthouse in Helena, but I is never took no part in that votin' business an' I allus kept out of dem arguments. I left it up to de white folks to 'tend to de 'lectin' of officers.

"De darkies what was in de courthouse dat I riccolect was: Bill Gray, he was one of de clerks; Hense Robinson, Dave Ellison, an' some more dat I don't remember. Bill Gray, he was a eddycated man, but de res', dey was just plain old ex-slave darkies an' didn't know nothing. Bill

Gray, he used to be de slave of a captain on a steamboat on de ribber. He was sorter servant to he mars on de boat where he stayed all the time. The captain used to let him git some eddycation. Darkies, dey never last long in de courthouse. Dey soon git 'em out.

"I gwine tell you somepin else dat is done changed er lot since I was comin' up. Dat is, de signs what de folks used to believe in dey don't believe in no more. Yet de same signs is still here, an' I sure does believe in 'em 'cause I done seen 'em work for all dese years. De Lawd give de peoples a sign for all things. De moon an' de stars, dey is a sign for all them what can read 'em an' tells you when to plant de cotton an' de taters an' all your crops. De screech owls, dey give er warnin' dat some one gwine to die. About de best sign dat some person gwine die 'round close is for a cow to git to lowin' an' a lowin' constant in de middle of de night. Dat is a sign I hardly is ever seen fail an' I seen it work out just a few weeks ago when old Aunt Dinah died up de road. I heered dat cow a lowin' an' a lowin' an' a walkin' back an' forth down de road for 'bout four nights in a row, right past Aunt Dinah's cabin. I say to my old woman dat somepin is sure gwine to take place, an' dat some pusson gwine die soon cause dat cow, she givin' de sign just right. Dere wasn't nobody 'round sick a tall an' Aunt Dinah, she plumb well at de time. About er week from then Aunt Dinah, she took down an' start to sinkin' right off an' in less than a week she died. I knowed some pusson gwine die all right, yet an' still I didn't know who it was to be. I tell you, Boss, I is gittin' uneasy an' troubled de last day or two, 'cause I is done heered another cow a lowin' an' a lowin' in de middle of de night. She keeps a walkin' back an' forth past my house out there in de road. I is really troubled 'cause me an' de old woman both is gittin' old. We is both way up in years an' whilst both of us is in real good health, Aunt Dinah was too. Dat cow a lowin' like she do is a bad sign dat I done noticed mighty nigh allus comes true."

Interviewer: Mrs. Bernice Bowden
Person interviewed: Jordan Davis
306 Cypress Street, Pine Bluff, Arkansas
Age: 86

JORDAN DAVIS

"I was a boy in the house when the war started and I heard the mistress say the abolitionists was about to take the South. Yes ma'm. That was in Natchez, Mississippi. I was about nine or ten.

"Mistress' name was Eliza A. Hart and master's name was Dave A. Hart.

"I guess they was good to me. I lived right there in the house with then. Mistress used to send me to Sunday School and she'd say 'Now, Jordan, you come right on back to the house, don't you go playin' with them nigger chillun on the streets.'

"My daddy belonged to a man named Davis way down the river in the country and after the war he came and got me. Sure did. Carried me to Davis Bend. I was a good-sized boy about twelve or fifteen. He took me to Mrs. Leas Hamer and you know I was a good-sized boy when she put me in the kitchen and taught me how to cook. Yes'm, I sure can cook. She kept me right in the house with her children. I did her cooking and cleaned up the house. I never got any money for it, or if I did I done forgot all about it. She kept me in clothes, she sure did. I didn't need any money. I stayed five or six years with her, sure did. I thought a lot of her and her children—she was so kind to me.

"Yes ma'm, I went to school one or two years in Mississippi.

"When I come here to Arkansas on the steamboat and got off right here in Pine Bluff, there was a white man standin' there named Burks. He kept lookin' at me and directly he said 'Can you cook?' I was married then and had all my household goods with me, so he got a dray and carried me out to his house. His wife kept a first-class boarding house. Just first-class white folks stayed there. After the madam found out I had a good idea 'bout cookin' she put me in the dining room and turned things over to me.

"Miss, it's been so long, I don't study 'bout that votin' business. I have never bothered 'bout no Republican or votin' business—I never cared about it. I know one thing, the white people are the only ones ever did me any good.

"Mrs. J.B. Talbot has been very good to me. My wife used to work for her and so did I. She sure has been a friend to me. Mrs. J.B. Talbot has certainly stuck to me.

"Oh I think the colored folks ought to be free but I know some of 'em had a mighty tight time of it after the war and now too.

"Ain't nothin' to this here younger generation. I see 'em goin' down the street singin' and dancin' and half naked—ain't nothin' to 'em.

"My wife's been dead five or six years and I live here alone. Yes ma'm! I don't want nobody here with me."

United States. Work Projects Administration

Interviewer: Mrs. Bernice Bowden
Person interviewed: Mary Jane Drucilla Davis
1612 W. Barraque, Pine Bluff, Arkansas
Age: 73

MARY JANE DRUCILLA DAVIS

"'Little baby's gone to heaven
To try on his robe
Oh, Lord, I'm most done toiling here
Little baby, m-m-m-m-m-m.'

"Oh, it was so mournful. And let me tell you what they'd do. They'd all march one behind the other and somebody would carry the baby's casket on their shoulder and sing that song. That's the first song I remember. I was three years old and now I'm seventy-three and crippled up with rheumatism.

"My mother had a garden and they went 'round that way to the graveyard and I thought they was buryin' it in the garden. That was in Georgia.

"In the old days when people died they used to sit up and pray all night, but they don't do that now.

"I was married young. I don't love to tell how old but I was fifteen and when I was seventeen I was a widow. I tried and tried to get another husband as good as my first one but I couldn't. I didn't marry then till I was thirty some.

"My parents brought me from Georgia when I was five years old and now I ain't got no blood kin in Pine Bluff.

"Do I believe in signs? Well, let me tell you what I do know. Before my house burned in 1937, I was sittin' on my porch, and my mother and sister come up to my house. They come a distance to the steps and went around the house. They was both dead but I could see 'em just as plain. And do you know in about two or three weeks my house burned. I think that vision was a sign of bad luck.

"And another time when I was havin' water put in my house, I dreamed that my sister who was dead told a friend of mine to tell me not to sign a contract and I didn't know there was a contract. And that next day a man come out for me to sign a contract and I said, 'No.' He wanted to know why and finally I told him, and he said, 'You're just like my mother.' It was two days 'fore I'd sign. The men had quit work waitin' for me to sign. But let me tell you when they put the water in and when they'd flush the pipes my tub overflowed. The ground was too low and I never could use the commode. Now don't you think that dream was a warning?

"Just before I had this spell of sickness I dreamed my baby—he's dead—come and knocked and said. 'Mama.' And I said, 'Yes, darlin', God bless your heart, you done been here three times and this time mama's comin'. I really thought I was goin' to die. I got up and looked in the glass. You know you can see death in the eyes, but I didn't see any sign of death and I haven't gone yet.

"Last Saturday I was prayin' to God not to let me get out of the heart of the people. You see, I have no kin people and I wanted people to come to my rescue. The next day was Sunday and more people come to see me and brought me more things.

"I been in the church fifty-seven years. I'm the oldest member in St. John's. I joined in May 1881.

"I went to school some. I went as far as the fourth grade."

United States. Work Projects Administration

Interviewer: Miss Irene Robertson
Person interviewed: Minerva Davis, Biscoe, Arkansas
Age: 56

MINERVA DAVIS

"My father was sold in Richmond, Virginia when he was eighteen years old to the nigger traders. They had nigger traders and cloth peddlers and horse traders all over the country coming by every few weeks. Papa said he traveled to Tennessee. His job was to wash their faces and hands and fix their hair—comb and cut and braid their hair and dress them to be auctioned off. They sold a lot of children from Virginia all along the way and he was put up in Tennessee and auctioned off. He was sold to the highest bidder. Bill Thomas at Brownsville, Tennessee was the one bought him. Papa was a large strong man.

"He run off and went to war. He had learned to cook and he was one-eyed and couldn't fight. All the endurin' time he cooked at the camps. Then he run off from war when he got a chance before he was mustered out and he never got a pension because of that. He said he come home pretty often and mama was expecting a baby. He thought he was needed at home worse. He was so tired of war. He didn't know it would be valuable to him in his old days. He was sorry he didn't stay till they got him mustered out. He said it was harder in the war than in slavery. They was putting up tents and moving all the time and he be scared purt nigh to death all the time. Never did know when they would be shot and killed.

"Mama said the way they bought grandma was at a well. A drove of folks come by. It was the nigger traders. She had pulled up her two or three buckets. She carried one bucket on her head and one in each hand. They said, 'Draw me up some water to drink.' She was so smart they bragged on her. They said, 'She such a smart little thing.' They went to see her owner and bought her on the spot. They took her away from her people and she never heard tell of none of them no more. She said there was a big family of them. They brought her to Brownsville, Tennessee and Johnny Williams bought her. That was my grandma.

"Mother was born there on Johnny Williams' place and she was heired by his daughter. His daughter married Bill Thomas, the one what done bought my papa. Her young mistress was named Sallie Ann Thomas. Mama got married when she was about grown. She said after she married she'd have a baby about the same time her young mistress had one. Mama had twelve children and raised eleven to be grown. Four of us are living yet. My sister was married when I was born. White folks married young and encouraged their slaves to so they have time to raise big families. Mama died when I was a year old but papa lived on with Johnny Williams where he was when she died. I lived with my married sister. I was the baby and she took me and raised me with her children.

"The Ku Klux wanted to whoop my papa. They all called him Dan. They said he was mean. His white folks protected him. They said he worked well. They wouldn't let him be whooped by them Ku Kluxes.

"Miss Sallie Ann was visiting and she had mama along to see after the children and to help the cook where she visited. They was there a right smart while from the way papa said. The pattyrollers whooped somebody on that farm while she was over there. They wasn't many slaves on her place and they was good to them. That whooping was right smart a curiosity to mama the way papa told us about it.

"When mama and papa married, Johnny Williams had a white preacher to read out of a book to them. They didn't jump over no broom he said.

"They was the biggest kind of Methodist folks and when mama was five years old Johnny Williams had all his slaves baptized into that church by his own white preacher. Papa said some of them didn't believe niggers had no soul but Johnny Williams said they did. (The Negroes must have been christened—ed.)

"Papa said folks coming through the country would tell them about freedom. Mama was working for Miss Sallie Ann and done something wrong. Miss Sallie Ann says, 'I'm a good mind to whoop you. You ain't paying 'tention to a thing you is doing the last week.' Mama says, 'Miss Sallie Ann, we is free; you ain't never got no right to whoop me no more care what I do.' When Bill come home he say, 'How come you to sass my wife? She so good to you.' Mama say, 'Master Bill, them soldiers say I'm free.' He slapped her. That the first time he laid hands on her in his life. In a few days he said, 'We going to town and see is you free. You leave the baby with Sallie Ann.' It was the courthouse. They questioned her and him both. Seemed like he couldn't understand how freedom was to be and mama didn't neither. Then papa took mama on Johnny Williams' place. He come out to Arkansas and picked cotton after freedom and then he moved his children all out here.

"Uncle Albert and grandpa take nights about going out. Uncle Albert was courting.

"They put potatoes on fire to cook when next morning they would be warm ready to eat. The fire popped out on mama. She was in a light blaze. Not a bit of water in the house. Her sisters and brothers peed (urinated) on her to put out the fire. Her stomach was burned and scarred. They was all disappointed because they thought she would be a good breeder. Miss Sallie Ann took her and cured her and when Miss Sallie Ann was going to marry, her folks didn't want to give her Minerva. She tended (contended) out and got her and Agnes both. Agnes died at about emancipation.

"I'm named for my mother. I'm her youngest child.

"I recollect my grandmother and what she told, and papa's mind went back to olden times the older he got to be. When folks would run down slavery he would say it wasn't so bad with them—him and mama. He never seen times bad as times is got to be now. Then he sure would wanted slavery back some more. He was a strong hard laboring man. He was a provider for his family till he got so no 'count.

"Times is changing up fast. Folks is worse about cutting up and carousing than they was thirty years ago to my own knowledge. I ain't old so speaking."

Interviewer: Miss Irene Robertson
Person interviewed: Rosetta Davis, Marianna, Arkansas
Age: 55

ROSETTA DAVIS

"I was born in Phillips County, Arkansas. My folks' master was named Dr. Jack Spivy. Grandma belong to him. She was a field woman. I don't know if he was a good master er not. They didn't know it was freedom till three or four months. They was at work and some man come along and said he was going home, the War was over. Some of the hands asked him who win and he told them the Yankees and told them they was free fer as he knowed. They got to inquiring and found out they done been free. They made that crap I know and I don't recollect nothing else.

"I farmed at Foreman, Arkansas for Taylor Price, Steve Pierce, John Huey. I made a crap here with Will Dale. I come to Arkansas twenty-nine years ago. I come to my son. He had a cleaning and pressing shop here (Marianna). He died. I hired to the city to work on the streets. I never been in jail. I owned a house here in town till me and my wife separated. She caused me to lose it. I was married once.

"I get ten dollars a month from the gover'ment.

"The present time is queer. I guess I could git work if I was able to do it. I believe in saving some of what you make along. I saved some along and things come up so I had to spend it. I made so little.

"Education has brought about a heap of unrest somehow. Education is good fer some folks and not good fer some. Some folks git spoilt and lazy. I think it helped to do it to the people of today."

Interviewer: Miss Irene Robertson
Person interviewed: Virginia (Jennie) Davis
Scott Street, Forrest City, Arkansas
Age: 45 or 47

JENNIE DAVIS

"This is what my father, Isaac Johnson, always told us:

'I was born in Raleigh, North Carolina. Mama died and left three of us children and my papa. He was a blacksmith.' I don't recollect grandpa's name now.

'A man come to buy me. I was a twin. My sisters cried and cried but I didn't cry. I wanted to ride in the surrey. I was sold and taken to Montgomery, Alabama.'

"Angeline was his oldest sister and Emmaline was his twin sister. He never seen any of his people again. He forgot their names. His old master that bought him died soon after he come back from North Carolina.

"His young master didn't even know his age. He tried to get in the army and he did get in the navy. They said he was younger than he told his age. He enlisted for three years. He was in a scrimmage with the Indians once and got wounded. He got twenty dollars then fifty dollars for his services till he died.

"He wasn't old enough to be in the Civil War. He said he remembered his mistress crying and they said Lincoln was to sign a freedom treaty. His young master told him he was free. The colored folks was having a jubilee. He had nowheres to go. He went back to the big house and sot around. They called him to eat, and he went on sleeping where he been sleeping. He had nowheres to go. He stayed there till he joined the navy. Then he come to Mississippi and married Sallie Bratcher and he went back to Alabama and taught school. He went to school at night after the Civil War till he went to the navy. He was a light-brown skin.

"Grandma, Jane Cash, was one brought from Huntingdon, Tennessee in a gang and sold at auction in Memphis, Tennessee. She said her mother, father, the baby, her brother and two sisters and herself was sold, divided out and separated. Grandma said one of her sisters had a suckling baby. She couldn't keep it from crying. They stopped and made her give it away.

"Then grandma fell in the hands of the Walls at Holly Springs, Mississippi. She was a good breeder, so she didn't have to work so hard. They wouldn't let her work when she was pregnant.

"Mrs. Walls buried her silver in the front yard. She had an old trusty colored man to dig a hole and bury it. No one ever found it. The soldiers took their meat and let the molasses run out on the ground. They ransacked her house. Mr. Walls wasn't there.

"My auntie, Eliza Williamson, was half white. She was one of her master's son's children. Her first master put her and her husband together. She lives near Conway, Arkansas now and is very old.

"Grandma was living at Menifee, Arkansas, and a

man from De Valls Bluff, Arkansas come to her house. She saw a scar on his arm. He was marked by gingerbread. She asked him some questions. Epps was his name and he was older than herself. He told her about the sale in Memphis. He remembered some things she didn't. He knowd where they all went. Her sister was Mary Wright at Milan, Tennessee. Grandma was twelve years old when that sale come off. She shouted and they cried. She couldn't eat for a week.

"She said old man Walls was good to them. When my mama was a little girl she was short and fat and light color. Old man Walls would call them in his parlor, all dress up and show them to his company. He was proud of them. He'd give them big dances ever so often. In the evening they had their own preaching in white folks' church. Grandma was good with the needle. She sewed for the mistress and her own family too. She had twelve children I think they said. They said her mistress had a large family too.

"Grandpa belong to Mike Cash. He give her husband what he made on Saturday evening. I think grandpa was sold from the Walls to Mike Cash. He took the Cash name and my mother was a Cash and she married Isaac Johnson. She was raised in Arkansas. Papa was married twice. I was raised around Holly Grove, Arkansas. That is where my folks lived in the last of slavery—that is mama's folks. Papa come to Arkansas at a later time.

"I think times is queer. I work and makes the best of 'em. (Ten dollars a month house rent.) I work all the time washing and ironing. (She has washed for the same families years and years. She is a light mulatto—ed.)

"Young folks is lost respect for the truth. Not dependable. That is their very worst fault, I think.

"No-oom, I wouldn't vote no quicker 'en I'd smoke a cigarette. But I haben never smoked narry one."

Interviewer: Mrs. Bernice Bowden
Subject: Ex-Slaves
Story:—Information

This information given by: Winnie Davis (C)
Place of residence: 304 E. Twenty-First Street
Pine Bluff, Arkansas
Occupation: None
Age: 100

[TR: Personal information moved from bottom of first page.]

WINNIE DAVIS

"Katie Butler was my old missis 'fore I married my husband. His name David Davis. I cooked for Jeff Davis and took care of his daughter, Winnie. I stayed with old missis, Jeff Davis' wife, till she died. She made me promise I'd stay with her. That was in Virginia."

(I have made three trips trying to get information and pictures of Winnie Davis. Her granddaughter said that a good many years ago when Winnie's mind was good, she was down town shopping and that when she gave her name, the clerk said, "Were you named after Jeff Davis' daughter?" and that Winnie replied, "She must have been named after me 'cause I cooked for Jeff Davis 'fore she was born."

Her mind is not very good at times, but the day I took her picture, I asked who she used to cook for and she said, "Jeff Davis."

She is rather deaf, nearly blind and toothless, but can get around the house quite well. The neighbors say that she has been a hard worker and of a very high-strung temperament.

The granddaughter, Mattie Sneed, says her grandmother said she was sold in Virginia when she was eight years old.)

Interviewer: Bernice Bowden
Person interviewed: Leroy Day (c)
Age: 80
Home: 123 N. Walnut Street, Pine Bluff, Ark.

LEROY DAY

"Good Lord yes, lady, I was here in slavery days. I remember my old marster had an overseer that whipped the people pretty rapid.

"I remember when the soldiers—the Yankees—come through, some said they was takin' things.

"Old Marster, his name was Joe Day, he was good to us. He seemed to be a Christian man and he was a Judge. They generally called him Judge Day. I never seen him whip nobody and never seen him have no dispute. I tell you if he wasn't a Christian, he looked like one.

"I was born in Georgia and I can remember the first Governor we had after freedom. His name was Governor Bullock. I heard it said the people raised a lot of sand because they said he was takin' the public money. That was when Milledgeville was the capital of Georgia.

"I used to vote after freedom. I voted Republican. I went to school a little after the war and then emigrated to Louisiana and Arkansas.

"Things has got so now everything is in politics. Some votes cause they want their friends in office and some don't take no interest.

"Some of the younger generation is prospering very well and some are goin' kinda slow. Some is goin' take another growth. The schoolin' they is gittin' is helpin' to build 'em up.

"Yes mam, I use to be strong and I have done a heap of work in my life. Cotton and corn was the business, the white man had the land and the money and we had to work to get some of that money.

"I remember when the Ku Klux was right bad in Louisiana. I never did see any—I didn't try to see 'em. I know I heard that they went to a school house and broke up a negro convention. They called for a colored man named Peck and when he come out they killed him and one white man got killed. They had a right smart little scrummage, and I know the colored people ran off and went to Kansas.

"The fust man I ever seed killed was one time a colored man's dog got in another colored man's field and ate his roasting ears, it made him so mad he shot the dog and then the man what owned the dog killed the other man. I never did know what the punishment was.

"Since I have become afflicted (I'm ruptured) I can't do no work any more. I can't remember anything else. If I had time to study I might think of something else."

Interviewer: Miss Irene Robertson
Person interviewed: Hammett Dell, Brasfield, Arkansas
Age: 90
[-- -- 1937]

[TR: Some word pronunciation was marked in this interview. Letters surrounded by [] represent long vowels.]

HAMMETT DELL

"I was born in Tennessee, 10 miles from Murfreesboro. They call it now Releford. I was born October 12, 1847. I stayed wid old master till he died. I was bout thirty-five years old. He lernt me a good trade, brick layin'. He give me everything I needed and more. After the war he took me by the old brass lamp wid twisted wick—it was made round—and lernt me outer the Blue Back Speller and Rithmetic. The spelling book had readin' in it. Lady ain't you seed one yit? Then I lernt outer Rays Rithmetic and McGuffeys Reader. Old master say it ginst the law to teach slaves foe the war. Dat what he said, it was ginst the law to educate a nigger slave. The white folks schools was pay foe the war.

"My old master had a small farm. His wife died. He never married no more. I caint member her name. She died when I was a little bitter of a boy. They had a putty large family. There was Marion, William, Fletcher, John, Miss Nancy, Miss Claricy, Miss Betsy. I think that all. The older childern raised up the little ones. My master named Mars Pleasant White. Long as I stayed wid him I had a plenty to eat an' wear an' a dollar to spend. I had no sense to save a cent for a old day. Mars White was a good man if ever one lived. He was a good man. Four old darkies all Mars White had. They was my mama, grandma, papa, auntie. My name I would lack it better White but that is where the Dell part come in; papa b'long to the Dells and b'fo the war he talked to me bout it. He took his old master's name. They call him Louis Dell White. He didn't have no brothers but my mama had two sisters. Her name was Mary White. Them was happy days b'fo the war. The happiest days in all my life. Bout at the beginnin' of the war Mama took cole at the loom and died. We all waited on her, white folks too. She didn't lack for waitin' on. Something white folks et, we et. We had plenty good grub all time long as Mars White live.

"How'd I know bout to git in war? I heard white folks talkin' bout it. One time I heard Mars White talkin' to my folks bout takin' us away. We was happy an' doin' well an' I didn't lack the talk but I didn't know what "war" was. No mam that was two years foe they got to fightin' down at Murfreesboro. Mars White was a ruptured man. He never left our place. I never heard bout none of my folks bein' sold. Mars White aired (heired) all us. My papa left and never come back. I d[o]n[o] how he got through the lines in the army. I guess he did fight wid the Yankees.

"Papa didn't speak plain. Grandma couldn't speak plain. They lisp. They talk fast. Sound so funny. Mama and auntie speak well. Plain as I do now. They was up wid Mars White's childern more. Mars White sent his childern to pay school. It was a log house and they had a lady teacher. They had a accordion. Mars Marion's neighbor had one too. All of em could play.

"White women would plat shucks an' make foot mats,

rugs and horse collars. The white women lernt the darkie women. There was no leather horse collars as ever I seed. I lernt to twist shucks and weave chair bottoms. Then I lernt how to make white oak split chair bottoms. I made all kinds baskets. We had all sizes and kinds of baskets. When they git old they turn dark. Shuck bottom chairs last longer but they kinner ruff an' not so fancy.

"Well when they started off fightin' at Murfreesboro, it was a continual roar. The tin pans in the cubbord (cupboard) rattle all time. It was distressful. The house shakin' all time. All our houses jar. The earth quivered. It sound like the judgment. Nobody felt good. Both sides foragin' one bad as the other, hungry, gittin' everything you put way to live on. That's "war". I found out all bout what it was. Lady it ain't nuthin' but hell on dis erth.

"I tole you I was ten miles from the war and how it roared and bout how the cannons shook the earth. There couldn't be a chicken nor a goose nor a year of corn to be found bout our place. It was sich hard times. It was both sides come git what you had. Whole heap of Yankees come in their blue suits and caps on horses up the lane. They was huntin' horses. They done got every horse and colt on the place cepin one old mare, mother of all the stock they had on the place. Young mistress had a furs bout her and led her up the steps and put her in the house.

"Then when they started to leave, one old Yankee set the corner of the house on fire. We all got busy then, white folks and darkies both carry in' water ter put it out. We got it out but while we doin' that, mind out, they went down the lane to the road by the duck pond we had dug out. One old soldier spied a goose settin' in the grass. She been so scared she never come to the house no more.

Nobody knowed there was one on our place. He took his javelin and stuck it through her back. She started hollowin' and flutterin' till the horses, nearly all of em, started runnin' and some of em buckin'. We got the fire bout out. We couldn't help laughin' it look so funny. I been bustin' I was so mad cause they tried take old Beck. Three of em horses throwd em. They struck out cross the jimpson weeds and down through the corn patch tryin' to head off their horses. Them horses throwd em sprawlin'. That was the funniest sight I ever seed.

"We got our water out of a cave. It was good cold limestone water. We had a long pole and a rope with a bucket on the end. We swing the pole round let it down then pull it back and tie it. They go to the other end and git the bucket of water. I toted bout all the water to both places what they used. One day I goin' to the cave after water. I had a habit of throwin' till I got to be prutty exact bout hittin'. I spied a hornets nest in a tree long the lane. I knowd them soldiers be long back fer sompin else, pillagin' bout. It wasn't long show nuff they come back and went up to the house.

"I got a pile of rocks in my hands. I hid down in the hazel nut bushes. When they come by gallopin' I throwd an' hit that big old hornets nest. The way they piled out on them soldiers. You could see em fightin' far as you could see em wid their blue caps. The horses runnin' and buckin'. I let out to the house to see what else they carried off.

"I tole Mars White bout how I hit that hornets nest wid the first rock I throwd. He scolded me, for he said if they had seen me they would killed me. It scared him. He said don't do no more capers like that. That old hornets nest soon come down. It was big as a water bucket. Mars White call me son boy. I tole him what terrible language they used, and bout some of the horses goin' over the lane fence. It was made outer rails piled up. Mars White sho was glad they didn't see me. He kept on sayin' son boy they would killed you right on the spot. Don't do nuthin' to em to aggravate em.

"It look lack we couldn't make a scratch on the ground nowhere the soldiers couldn't find it. We had a ash hopper settin' all time. We made our soap and lye hominy. They took all our salt. We couldn't buy none. We put the dirt in the hopper and simmered the water down to salt. We hid that. No they didn't find it. Our smoke house was logs dobbed wid mud and straw. It was good size bout as big as our cabins. It had somepin in it too. All the time I tell you.

"You ever eat dried beef? It is fine.

"I say I been to corn shuckins. They do that at night. We hurry and git through then we have a dance in front of Mars White's house. We had a good time. Mars White pass round ginger bread and hard cider. We wore a thing on our hands keep shucks from hurtin' our hands. One darkie sit up on the pile and lead the singin'. Old Dan Tucker was one song we lernt. I made some music instruments. We had music. Folks danced then more they do now. Most darkies blowed quills and Jew's harps. I took cane cut four or six made whistles then I tuned em together and knit em together in a row like a mouth harp you see.

Another way get a big long cane cut out holes long down to the joint, hold your fingers over different holes and blow. I never had a better time since freedom. I never had a doctor till since I been 80 years old neither.

"Later on I made me a bow of cedar, put one end in my mouth and pick the string wid my fingers while I hold the other end wid this hand. (Left hand. It was very peculiar shaped in the palm.) See my hand that what caused it. I have been a musician in my time. I lernt to handle the banjo, the fiddle and the mandolin. I played fer many a set, all over the country mostly back home (in Tennessee).

"We had a heap of log rollins back home in slavery times. They have big suppers spread under the trees. We sho know we have a good supper after a log rollin'.

"We most always worked at night in winter. Mama worked at the loom and weaved. Grandma and old mistress carded. They used hand cards. Auntie spun thread. I reeled the thread. I like to hear it cluck off the hanks. Papa he had to feed the stock and look after it. He'd fool round after that. He went off to the war at the first of it and never come home.

"The war broke us up and ruined us all but me. Grandma married old man soon after freedom. He whooped and beat her up till she died. He was a mean old scoundel. They said he was a nigger driver. His name was Wesley Donald. She died soon after the war. Mama was dead. Auntie married and went on off. I was 18 years old. When freedom come on Mars White says you all set free. You can leave or stay on here. I stayed there. Mars White didn't give us nuthin'. He was broke. All he had was land.

"Come a talk bout Lincoln givin' em homes. Some racketed bout what they outer git. That was after freedom. Most of em never got nuthin'. They up and left. Some kept on workin'. They got to stealin' right smart. Some the men got so lazy they woulder starved out their families and white folks too. White folks made em go to work. The darky men sorter quit work and made the women folks do the work. They do thater way now. Some worse den others bout it.

"Me and Mars White went to work. We see droves darkies just rovin' round. Said they huntin' work and homes. Some ask for victuals. Yes they give em something to eat. When they come in droves they couldn't give em much. Some of em oughter left. Some of the masters was mean. Some of em mighty good.

"Me and Mars White and his boys rigged up a high wheel that run a band to a lay (lathe). One man run the wheel wid his hands and one man at the lay (lathe) all time. We made pipes outer maple and chairs. We chiseled out table legs and bed post. We made all sort of things. Anything to sell. We sold a heap of things. We made money. If I'd had sense to keep part of it. Mars White always give me a share. We had a good livin' soon as we got over the war.

"I farmed. I was a brick layer. Mars White lernt me that. When he died I followed that trade. I worked at New Orleans, Van Buren, Jackson, Meridian. I worked at Lake Villiage with Mr. Lasley, and Mr. Ivy. They was fine brick layers. I worked for Dr. Stubbs. Mr. Scroggin never went huntin' without me but once over here on Cache River. He give me land to build my cabins. I got lumber up at the mills here. Folks come to my cabins from 23 states.

J. Dall Long at St. Louis sent me a block wid my picture. I didn't know what it was. Mr. Moss told me it was a bomb like they used in the World War. I had some cards made in Memphis, some Little Rock. I sent em out by the telephone books tellin' em it was good fishin' now.

"J. Dall Long said when I go back home I send you somethin' nice. That what he sent in the mail.

"It was ugliest picture of me in a boat an' a big fish holt my britches leg pullin' me over out the boat. He had me named "Hambones" under it. I still got my block. I got nuther thing—old aunties bonnet she wore in slavery.

"I quit keepin' club house. I kept it 27 years. I rented the cabins, sold minnows and bates. They give me the land but I couldn't sell it. Old woman everybody call "Nig" cook fer me. I wanter live like Nig and go up yonder. I ainter goner be in this world long but I want to go to heben. Nig was not my wife. She was a fine cook. She cooked an' stayed at my cabins. This little chile—orphan chile—I got wid me was Nig's grandchild. When Nig died I took him. I been goin with him to pick cotton. I want er lern him to work. Egercation ain't no good much to darkies. I been tryin' to see what he could do bettern farm. They ain't nuthin'. I set down on the ground and pick some so he will pick. He is six years old. When it rain I caint pick and set on the wet ground.

Ku Klux

"The onlies sperience I had myself wid the Ku Klux was one night fo Grandma and auntie left. Somebody wrap on our cabin door. They opened it. We gat scared when we seed em. They had the horses wrapped up. They had on white long dresses and caps. Every one of em had a horse whoop (whip). They called me out. Grandma and auntie so scared they hid. They tole me to git em water. They poured it some whah it did not spill on the ground. Kept me totin' water. Then they say, "You bin a good boy?" They still drinkin'. One say, "Just from Hell pretty dry." Then they tole me to stand on my head. I turned summer sets a few times. They tickled me round wid the ends of the whoops. I had on a long shirt. They laugh when I stand on my head. Old Mars White laughed. I knowed his laugh. Then I got over my scare. They say, "Who live next down the road?" I tole em Nells Christian. They say, "What he do?" I said, "Works in the field." They all grunt, m-m-m-m. Then they say, "Show us the way." I nearly run to death cross the field to keep outer the way of the white horses. The moon shining bright as day. They say Nells come out here. He say "Holy Moses." He come out. They say "Nells what you do?" "I farms." They say "What you raise?" He say "Cotton and corn." They say "Take us to see yo cotton we jess from Hell. We ain't got no cotton there." He took em out there where it was clean. They got down and felt it. Then they say "What is dat?", feelin' the grass. Nells say "That is grass." They say, "You raise grass too?" He said, "No. It come up." They say "Let us see yo corn." He showed em the corn. They felt it. They say "What this?" Nells say, "It grass." They say, "You raise grass here?" They all grunt m-m-m-m everything Nells say. They give him one bad whoopin' an' tell him they be back soon see if he raisin' grass. They said "You raise cotton and corn but not grass on this farm." They they moan, "m-m-m-m." I herd em say his whole family and him too was out by day light wid their hoes cuttin' the grass out their crop. I was sho glad to git back to our cabin. They didn't come back to Nells no more that I herd bout. The man Nells worked for muster been one in that crowd. He lived way over yonder. No I think the Ku Klux was a good thing at that time. The darkies got sassy (saucy), trifling, lazy. They was notorious. They got mean. The men wouldn't work. Their families have to work an' let them roam round over the country. Some of em mean to their families. They woulder starved the white out and their selves too. I seed the Ku Klux heap a times but they didn't bother me no more. I herd a heap they done along after that. They say some places the Ku Klux go they make em git down an' eat at the grass wid their mouths then they whoop em. Sometimes they make em pull off their clothes and whoop em. I sho did feel for em but they knowd they had no business strollin' round, vistin'. The Ku Klux call that whoopin' helpin' em git rid of the grass. Nells moster lived at what they called Caneville over cross the field.

"The way that Patty Rollers was. The mosters paid somebody. Always somebody round wantin' a job like that. Mars White was his own overseer. All round there was good livers. They worked long wid the slaves. Some of the slaves would race. Papa would race. He wanted to race all time. Grandma cooked for all of us. They had a stone chimney in the kitchen. Big old hearth way out in front. Made outer stone too. We all et the same victuals long as Mars White lived. Then I left."

Interviewer: Miss Irene Robertson
Person interviewed: James Dickey, Marianna, Arkansas
Age: 68
[May 31 1939]

JAMES DICKEY

"I don't know much to tell about my folks. My parents died when I was young. Mother died when I was twelve and father when I was seven years old. Great-grandma was an Indian squaw. My father's pa was his young master. His old master was named George Dickey. The young master was John Dickey. I reckon to start with my mother had a husband. She had twelve children but the last seven was by my pa. He was lighter than I am and paler. This red is Indian in me. I know how he looked and how she looked too. The young master never married. He had some brothers. My father lived with us and his pa was there too some. I don't know what become of John Dickey but my pa was buried at Mt. Tursey Cemetery. It was a sorter mixed burying grown (ground) but at a white church. Mother come here and was buried at Cat Island in a colored church cemetery.

"I farmed in Mississippi, then I come to Miller Lumber Company and I worked with them forty-two years. I worked at Marked Tree, then they sent me here (Marianna).

"I voted in Caruthersville, Missouri last I voted. It

don't do much good to vote. I am too old to vote. I never voted in Arkansas. I voted some in Mississippi but not regular.

"Times is hard. So many white women do their own cooking and washing till it don't leave no work fer the colored folks. The lumber work is gone fer good.

"The present generation is going back'ards. For awhile it looked like they was rising—I'm speaking morally. They going back down in a hurry. Drinking and doing all kinds of devilment. The race is going back'ard now. Seems like everybody could see that when whiskey come back in.

"I got high blood pressure. I do a little work. I watch on Sunday at the mills. I don't get no help from the Gover'ment."

Interviewer: Mrs. Bernice Bowden
Person interviewed: Benjamin Diggs
420 N. Cypress, Pine Bluff, Arkansas
Age: 79

BENJAMIN DIGGS

"I was born in 1859 in North Carolina. Oh, sure, I remember when the Yankees come through. They said they done right smart of damage. I remember goin' by a place where they had burned it down. They didn't do nothin' to my white folks 'cept took the stock.

"The Lyles was my white folks. They called her Polly Lyles. Oh, they was good to us. My mother and her sister and another colored woman and we children all belonged to one set of people—Miss Polly Lyles; and my father belonged to the Diggs.

"After freedom we moved off but they was good to us just the same, and we was glad to pay 'em a visit and they was glad to have us.

"I've heard my mother say she'd ignore the idea of a cold biscuit but my father said he was glad to get one. He said he didn't get 'em but once a week.

"Oh, indeed there was a lot of difference in the way the colored folks was treated. Some of 'em was very good, just like they is now.

"Well, all those old people is dead and gone now 'cause they was old then.

"I come here to Arkansas in '88. That was when they was emigratin' the folks. I was grown and married then. I was twenty-six when I married in '85.

"I went to school a little. I can sorta scribble a little and read a little, but my eyes is failin' now. I started wearin' glasses 'fore I really needed 'em. I got to projectin' with my mother's glasses Looked like they read so good.

"Farmin' is all I know how to do. Never done anything else. I owned some land and farmed for myself.

"Sure, I used to vote—Republican. I never had any trouble. I always tried to conduct my life to avoid trouble. I believe in that policy.

"I joined the church when I was very young, very young. I go by the Golden Rule and by the Bible.

"I first lived in Pope County.

"I learned since I come here to Pine Bluff there's enough churches here to save the world, but there's some mean people here."

Interviewer: Mrs. Bernice Bowden
Person interviewed: Katie Dillon
307 Hazel Street, Pine Bluff, Arkansas
Age: 82
[Dec 31 1937]

KATIE DILLON

"I hope I was here in slavery days—don't I look like it? I was a good big girl after surrender.

"I was born in Rodney, Mississippi in 1855.

"I had a good old master—Doctor Williams. Didn't have no mistress. He never married till after surrender.

"We lived right in town—right on the Mississippi River where the gun boats went by. They shelled the town one day. Remember it just as well as if 'twas now. I hope it was exciting. Everybody moved out. Some run and left their stores. They run to Alcorn University, five miles from there. Some of em come back next day and some never come back till after surrender.

"The old Doctor bought my mother when she was twelve years old. When she got big enough she was the cook. Made a fine one too. I worked around the house and toted in wood and water.

"After surrender, Dr. Williams wanted my mother to give me and my brother to him and he would give her a home, but she wouldn't. I wish she had but you know I wasn't old enough to know what was best. She hired out and took us with her. I hired out too. I reckon I was paid but I never did see it. I reckon my mother collected it. I know she clothed me. I had better clothes than I got now. We stayed there till we come to Arkansas. I was married then. I married when I was seventeen. I was fast wasn't I? I got a good husband. Didn't have to work, only do my own work. Just clean up the house and garden and tend to the chickens. My husband was a picture man. Yes'm, I've lived in town all my life—born and raised up in town.

"After surrender I went to the first free school ever was in Rodney, Mississippi. I went about two sessions. I ought to've learned more'n I did but I didn't see how it would benefit me.

"In slavery days we used to go right to the table and eat after the white folks was through. We didn't eat out of no pots and pans. Whatever was on the table you et it until you got enough.

"When I was comin' up and they was goin' to have a private ball, they sent out invitations and I went, but when they had that kind where everybody could go I wouldn't a gone to one of them for nothin'.

"The way things is goin' now I don't think the end can be very far off.

"I remember when peace was declared I saw the soldiers across the street and they had their guns all stacked. I was lookin' and wonderin' what it was. You know children didn't ask questions in them days. I heard some of the older ones talkin' and I heard em say the war was over.

"I never had but two children and only one livin' now.

Yes'm, I own my home and my son helps me what he can. I'm thankful I got as much as I have."

United States. Work Projects Administration

El Dorado District
FOLKLORE SUBJECTS [HW: Customs]
Name of Interviewer: Pernella Anderson
Subject: Customs—Slavery Days
[Nov 30 1936]

This information given by: Alice Dixon
Place of Residence: Rock Island quarters
Occupation: None
Age: 80 (approx)

[TR: Personal information moved from last page of interview.]

ALICE DIXON

Well honey ah can't tell jes when ah wuz born. De white fokes have mah age. Ah blong tuh de Newtons. As near as ah can get at mah age ahm bout 74 now but ah wuz big nough to member the soldiers comin aroun atter surrender.

Mah mutha had ten chillun but ah can't member but two uv mah sisters and one uv mah bruthes. We staid wid de Newtons till we wuz set free and I nuss fuh de Newtons aftuh we wuz set free. De Newtons wuz awful good ter me and dey wuz good tuh mah ma too. Ah slept up in de big house wid de Newtons. Ah nevah went ter school. Ah didn' have a chance. Ah went ter church jes sometimes. We didn have churches. We jes had meetin in our house we lived in. We cooked on fire places. We cooked our bread in what we called oven bout so high. We had chickens and eggs, peas, tatoes, meat and bread but ah didn know there was no sich thing as cake an pie till ah got to be an oman. Ah can't recollect jes how ole ah wuz in slave time but ah shore can recollect dem Yankees riding dem hosses and ah ask may ma what dey was doin and she said gatherin up cotton dey made in slave time an ah kin recollect an oman a gin. Yo know we had steps made of blocks saved from trees and she wuz a goin ovah em steps er shoutin and singin "Ah am free, at last, ah am free at last, ah'm free at last, thank Gawd a Mighty ah'm free at last." She wuz so glad ter be free.

My ma in huh time would make cloth. She had a loom. Hit wuz a high thing and th thread would go ovah th top and come down jes so in what we call shickle. She'd have a bench so high. The loom was high as dis door and my ma would set on the bench and her foots wuz on somethin like a bicycle and when she put her foots on de pedal dat shickle would come open and make a blum blum an that would make a yard of cloth, an she'd mash the pedal agin and another yard of cloth. Jes so we'd make eight and ten yards of cloth in one day. An when hit wuz made we would carry hit to de white fokes. Dey would make us clo'es outn dat cloth. Ifn dey wanted colored cloth dey would dye de thread. Dey had what we called a loom dat would make, le' me see now, Card would card the cotton, and de looms would make de thread and de shickle would make de cloth, as well as ah can recollect we would make little roll uv cotton on de cards an put it on de loom and make thread. De looms was jes so long. Ever time the wheel would say o-o-o-o-o-o-o-o-o-o we had a spool uv thread. Ah don' know whar dey got the spools, made em tho ah guess. Ah jes caint tell you how hit wuz hits so much.

De Newton's nevah did whup me. She started to whup

me tho one day. Ah kin recollect bout de dogs. There wuz one dog whut wuz called Dinah. But yo know dey had ten uv em. One day ole Uncle Henry Jones done somethin and run off and climbed a tree and de Newton's miss him so dey called de dogs and dey went on to de tree. Dat very tree wha he wuz and stopped. Uncle Henry had been gone all dat mornin and dem dogs track him right dere, to de spot and wouldn let him down till de Newtons come. An chile dem Newtons whip de skin off Uncle Herny's [TR: Henry's] back. Dem dogs would git yo.

Mrs. Newton nevah got outn de bed no time. Ah would lift her from one bed to de utha to make de beds and when she got ready to get dressed ah would bath her and dress huh all de times.

Ah'll tell yo nother funny joke bout Henry Johnson. He had ter clean up mos uv de time. So Mrs. Newton's dress wuz hangin in de room up on de wall and when he come out he said to ole Uncle Jerry, he said: "Jerry guess whut ah done" and Jerry said: "Whut?" And Uncle Henry said: "Ah put mah han undah ole Mistess dress." Uncle Jerry said: "Whut did she say?" Uncle Henry say: "She didn' say nothin." So Uncle Jerry cided he'd try hit. So he went draggin on in de house. Set down on de floor by ole mistess. Ater while he run his han' up under huh dress and old marster jumped up and jumped on Jerry and like to beat him ter death. Jerry went out cryin and got out and called Henry. He said: "Henry ah though yo said yo put yo hand undah ole Mistess's dress and she didn' say nothin." Uncle Henry said: "Ah did and she didn' say nuthin." Jerry said: "Ah put mah han' undah huh dress and ole marster like tuh beat me ter death." Uncle Henry said: "Yo crazy thing huh dress wuz hangin up on de wall when ah put mah han up undah hit."

We didn' eat eggs only on Sunday mornin. Me and mah sis et together in de same plate. We didn know whut knives and forkes wuz den. We et wid our fingahs.

Ah had a good ole pa too. He died a long time ago. Ah member one night he started tuh whoop mah brudder and mah pa and mah brudder had hit. So mah brudder runned off, an de marster called ole Dinah, Dinah wuz a dog yo know but Dinah was a big dog ovah the other dogs yo know and dem dogs went and got me brudder and dem Newtons sho did beat him. But twasnt long befo mah pa taken sick and died aftuh dat. An when we wuz goin ter bury mah pa lamme tell yo what happened: Two turtle doves flew roun the wagon three times, den dey flew right on top uv mah pa's coffin box an hollered three times; and yo know mah sistuh died bout three days aftuh dat. Ah didn' bleave in signs till den. Ah know mah pa always bleaved in signs cause ah know when hit would start lightnin and thunderin round dat place of ourn mah pa would always make us stop. He say twas bad luck. An ah know when evah a dove would holler at night he'd tell us jes tuh tie a knot in th' south cornuh uv de sheet and he would hush. An we would do hit an he would hush. Yo kno hits bad luck fuh dem tuh holler roun yo place.

Oh we use ter have lots o sheep, at least ole mistess did. We made all of our wool clothes from dem sheeps wool and let me tell yo somethin else, ah think ah got some sheep wool in mah trunk now ah had hit fifty years. Hits good fer sores if yo has er cut on yo han' or feet or if blood poison set up jes take a little piece of dat wool an put a piece of fire on hit and [HW: put] some [HW: on] the sore parts and chile, honey, hit will git well right now.

Chile ah had use ter ruther go ter dances than ter eat. Ah'd go ter dances an git early dare and heah dem fiddles. Uh, my! ah jus couldn make mah foots act right. We use ter dance sixteen sets. We'd be er dancing and hit would sound so good. Someone would say swing de one yo love bes but ah wouldn swing de one ah love best cause ah didn want anyone tah know him.

On Sunday mornin dats when we play. Ole marster would put a rope cross fer us ter jump and we'd line up. The rope wuz bout five feet high and chile if we didn' jump it we'd catch hit. O-o-o-o-oooo. We had ter run. He line up two at a time an he say one fuh de money, two fuh de show, three tuh make ready and fo' tuh go. An yo talk bout runnin. We had ter run. He would make us box and de one dat git whooped is de one dat would haft ter box till he got whooped and we had ter whoop three times befo' stoppin. Oh chile, ah had a time when ah miz a chile.

United States. Work Projects Administration

Interviewer: Miss Irene Robertson
Person interviewed: Luke D. Dixon
DeValls Bluff, Ark.
Age: 81

LUKE D. DIXON

"My father's owner was Jim Dixon in Elmo County, Virginia. That is where I was born. I am 81 years old. Jim Dixon had several boys—Baldwin and Joe. Joe took some of the slaves, his pa give him, and went to New Mexico to shun the war. Uncle and pa went in the war as waiters. They went in at the ending up. We lived on the big road that run to the Atlantic Ocean. Not far from Richmond. Ma lived three or four miles from Pa. She lived across big creek—now they call it Farrohs Run. Ma belong to Harper Williams. Pa's folks was very good but Ma's folks was unpleasant.

"Ma lived to be 103 years old. Pa died in 1905 and was 105 years old. I used to set on Grandma's lap and she told me about how they used to catch people in Africa. They herded them up like cattle and put them in stalls and brought them on the ship and sold them. She said some they captured they left bound till they come back and sometimes they never went back to get them. They died. They had room in the stalls on the boat to set down or lie down. They put several together. Put the men to themselves and the women to themselves. When they sold Grandma and Grandpa at a fishing dock called New Port, Va., they had their feet bound down and their hands bound crossed, up on a platform. They sold Grandma's daughter to somebody in Texas. She cried and begged to let them be together. They didn't pay no 'tenshion to her. She couldn't talk but she made them know she didn't want to be parted. Six years after slavery they got together. When a boat was to come in people come and wait to buy slaves. They had several days of selling. I never seen this but that is the way it was told to me.

"The white folks had an iron clip that fastened the thumbs together and they would swing the man or woman up in a tree and whoop them. I seen that done in Virginia across from where I lived. I don't know what the folks had done. They pulled the man up with block and tackle.

"Another thing I seen done was put three or four chinquapin switches together green, twist them and dry them. They would cry like a leather whip. They whooped the slaves with them.

"Grandpa was named Sam Abraham and Phillis Abraham was his mate. They was sold twice. Once she was sold away from her husband to a speculator. Well, it was hard on the Africans to be treated like cattle. I never heard of the Nat Turner rebellion. I have heard of slaves buying their own freedom. I don't know how it was done. I have heard of folks being helped to run off. Grandma on mother's side had a brother run off from Dalton, Mississippi to the North. After the war he come to Virginia.

"When freedom was declared we left and went to Wilmington and Wilson, North Carolina. Dixon never told us we was free but at the end of the year he gave my father a gray mule he had ploughed for a long time and part of the crop. My mother jes picked us up and left her folks now. She was cooking then I recollect. Folks jes went wild when they got turned loose.

"My parents was first married under a twenty-five cents license law in Virginia. After freedom they was re-married under a new law and the license cost more but I forgot how much. They had fourteen children to my knowing. After the war you could register under any name you give yourself. My father went by the name of Right Dixon and mother Jilly Dixon.

"The Ku Klux was bad. They was a band of land owners what took the law in hand. I was a boy. I scared to be caught out. They took the place of pattyrollers before freedom.

"I never went to public school but two days in my life. I went to night school and paid Mr. J.C. Price and Mr. S.H. Vick to teach me. My father got his leg shot off and I had to work. It kept me out of meanness. Work and that woman has kept me right. I come to Arkansas, brought my wife and one child, April 5, 1889. We come from Wilson, North Carolina. Her people come from North Carolina and Moultrie, Georgia.

"I do vote. I sell eggs or a little something and keep my taxes paid up. It look like I'm the kind of folks the government would help—them that works and tries hard to have something—but seems like they don't get no help. They wouldn't help me if I was bout to starve. I vote a Republican ticket."

NOTE: On the wall in the dining room, used as a sitting room, was a framed picture of Booker T. Washington and Teddy Roosevelt sitting at a round-shaped hotel dining table ready to be served. Underneath the picture in large print was "Equality." I didn't appear to ever see the picture.

This negro is well-fixed for living at home. He is large and very black, but his wife is a light mulatto with curly, nearly-straightened hair.

Interviewer: Miss Irene Robertson
Person interviewed: Martha Ann Dixon (mulatto)
DeValls Bluff, Arkansas
Age: 81

MARTHA ANN DIXON

"I am eighty-one years old. I was born close to Saratoga, North Carolina. My mother died before I can recollect and my grandmother raised me. They said my father was a white man. They said Jim Beckton. I don't recollect him. My mother was named Mariah Tyson.

"I recollect how things was. My grandmother was Miss Nancy Tyson's cook. She had one son named Mr. Seth Tyson. He run her farm. They et in the dining room, we et in the kitchen. Clothes and something to eat was scarce. I worked at whatever I was told to do. Grandma told me things to do and Miss Nancy told me what to do. I went to the field when I was pretty little. Once my uncle left the mule standing out in the field and went off to do something else. It come up a hard shower. I crawled under the mule. If I had been still it would been all right but my hair stood up and tickled the mule's stomach. The mule jumped and the plough hit me in my hip here at the side. It is a wonder I didn't get killed.

"After the Civil War was times like now. Money scarce and prices high, and you had to start all over new. Pigs was hard to start, mules and horses was mighty scarce.

Seed was scarce. Everything had to be started from the stump. Something to eat was mighty plain and scarce and one or two dresses a year had to do. Folks didn't study about going so much.

"I had to rake up leaves and fetch em to the barn to make beds for the little pigs in cold weather. The rake was made out of wood. It had hickory wood teeth and about a foot long. It was heavy. I put my leaves in a basket bout so high [three or four feet high]. I couldn't tote it—I drug it. I had to get leaves in to do a long time and wait till the snow got off before I could get more. It seem like it snowed a lot. The pigs rooted the leaves all about in day and back up in the corners at night. It was ditched all around. It didn't get very muddy. Rattle snakes was bad in the mountains. I used to tote water—one bucketful on my head and one bucketful in each hand. We used wooden buckets. It was lot of fun to hunt guinea nests and turkey nests. When other little children come visiting that is what we would do. We didn't set around and listen at the grown folks. We toted up rocks and then they made rock rows [terraces] and rock fences about the yard and garden. They looked so pretty. Some of them would be white, some gray, sometimes it would be mixed. They walled wells with rocks too. All we done or knowed was work. When we got tired there was places to set and rest. The men made plough stocks and hoe handles and worked at the blacksmith shop in snowy weather. I used to pick up literd [HW: lightwood] knots and pile them in piles along the road so they could take them to the house to burn. They made a good light and kindling wood.

"They didn't whoop Grandma but she whooped me a plenty.

"After the war some white folks would tell Grandma one thing and some others tell her something else. She kept me and cooked right on. I didn't know what freedom was. Seemed like most of them I knowed didn't know what to do. Most of the slaves left the white folks where I was raised. It took a long time to ever get fixed. Some of them died, some went to the cities, some up North, some come to new country. I married and come to Fredonia, Arkansas in 1889. I had been married since I was a young girl. But as I was saying the slaves was still hunting a better place and more freedom. The young folks is still hunting a better place and more freedom. Grandma learnt me to set down and be content. We have done better out here than we could done in North Carolina but I don't believe in so much rambling.

"We come on the passenger train and paid our own way to Arkansas. It was a wild and sickly country and has changed. Not like living in the same country. I try to live like the white folks and Grandma raised me. I do like they done. I think is the reason we have saved and have good a living as we got. We do on as little as we can and save a little for the rainy day."

United States. Work Projects Administration

Interviewer: Mrs. Bernice Bowden
Person interviewed: Railroad Dockery
1103 Short 13th, Pine Bluff, Arkansas
Age: 81

RAILROAD DOCKERY

"Railroad Dockery, that's my name. I belonged to John Dockery and we lived at Lamertine, Arkansas where I was born. My mother's name was Martha and I am one of quadruplets, three girls and one boy, that's me. Red River, Ouachita, Mississippi and Railroad were our names. (Mrs. Mary Browning, who is now ninety-eight years of age, told me that her father, John Dockery, was the president of the Mississippi, Red River, Ouachita Railroad, the first one to be surveyed in Arkansas, and that when the directors heard of the quadruplets' birth, they wanted to name them after the railroad, which was done—ed.)

"Yes ma'm, Red River and Ouachita died when they were tots and Mississippi and Railroad were raised. Now that's what my mother said. Mississippi died five or six years ago and I'm the onliest one left.

"I remember mighty little about the war. I never thought anything about the war. All I did then was a crowd of us little chaps would go to the woods and tote in the wood every day for the cook woman. That's what I followed. Never did nothing else but play till after the war.

"After surrender I went with my father and mother to work for General Tom Dockery. He was John Dockery's brother. I was big enough to plow then. I followed the plow all the time. My father and mother were paid for their work. We stayed there about five years and then moved to Falcon, Arkansas. Father died there.

"In the time of the war I heard the folks talkin' about freedom, and I heard my father talk about the Ku Klux but that was all I knowed, just what he said about it.

"I remember the presidents and I voted for some of them but oh Lord, I haven't voted in several years.

"I got along after freedom just as well as I ever did. I never had no trouble—never been in no trouble.

"About the world now—it looks like to me these days things are pretty tight. I could hardly tell you what I think of the younger generation. I think one thing—if the old heads would die all at once they would be out, because it's all you can do to keep em straight now.

"I went to school only three months in my life. I learned to read and write very well. I don't need glasses and I read principally the Bible. To my mind it is the best book in the world. Biggest part of the preachers now won't preach unless they are paid three-fourths more than they are worth.

"The biggest part of my work was farming. I never did delight in cooking. Now I can do any kind of housework, but don't put me to cooking.

"I just can't sing to do no good. Never could sing.

Seems like when I try to sing something gets tangled in my throat.

"Oh Lord, I remember one old song they used to sing

> 'A charge to keep I have
> A God to glorify.'

"I don't remember anything else but now if Mississippi was here, she could tell you lots of things."

United States. Work Projects Administration

Interviewer: Irene Robertson
Subject: Ex-slave
Information given by: Callie Donalson, Biscoe, Arkansas

CALLIE DONALSON

Story

I wasn't born in slavery but I was born in the white folks kitchen. Bob Walker was ma mother's Master and James Austin ma father's Master. They said he wasn't good to none of dem, he was mighty tight. Now ma mothers white folks was sho good to her. When de war was all over me family jined and worked fer people not berry far from ma mother's masters. There was two brothers and a sister older than me. She thought her white folks do better by her than anybody so she went back to em during her pregnancy and thats how come I was born in der kitchen a white mid-wife tended on er. I never will forget her. She was named Mrs. Coffee. There wasn't many doctors in the whole country then. I was born in Haywood county Tennessee in 1866. No'm I tell you when you first come I wasn't born in slavery. My white mistress named me, the young mistress, she named me Callie. Bob Walkers girl married Ben Geeter. I was right in Ben Geeters kitchen when Miss Sallie named me. They seemed proud of the little black babies.

Ma mother was a field hand and she washed and ironed. She was a good spinner. She carded and wove and spun all. She knitted too. She knitted mostly by nite. All the stockings and gloves had to be knit. She sewed and I learned from her. We had to sew with our fingers.

When I was a little girl I just set around, brought in wood. Yes maam we did play and I had some dolls, I was proud of my dolls, just rag dolls. We use to drive the calves up. If they didn't come up they sent the dog fur de cows. One of dem wore a bell. They had shepherd dogs, long haired, gentle dogs, to fetch the cows when they didn't come.

Ma folks farmed in Tennessee till I married and den we farmed. Agents jess kept comin after us to get us to come to this rich country. They say: hogs jess walking round with knife and forks stickin in der backs beggin somebody to eat em over in Arkansas.

No'm I aint seed none lack dat, I seed em down in the swamps what you could saw a good size saplin down wid der backbones. I says I mean I seed plenty raysor back hogs, and long noses and long straight ears. I show have since I come here. The land was so poor in Tennessee and this was uncleared land so we come to a new country. It show is rich land. They use guano back in Tennessee now or they couldn't raise nuthin. Abe Miller an old slave owner what we worked wid come out here. He was broke and he paid our way. We come on the Josie Harry boat. Der was several families sides us come wid him. He done fine out here—we got off the boat at Augusta and I worked up there in Woodruff county till ma husbands brother's wife died and he had a farm his own. We raised his boys and our family till dey was ob age. I left em. They went in big business here in Biscoe and lost de farm and everything. Ma husband died I lives with ma girl. I got one boy married lives in Chicago, and a girl up there too. No'm dey aint rich. Dem his children come home wid ma daughters on a visit—Little Yankees ain't got no manners.

I voted one time in ma life, in 1933, for Hoover. I don't know nothing about voting. I can read. I reads ma Bible. Ma young mistress learnt me to read. I never got to go to school much. Whut my young mistress learnt me was ma A B C's and how to call words. Yes maam I can write ma name but I forgot how to write, been so long since I wrote a letter.

All the songs I ever sung was "In Dixie" "Little Brown Jug" an mostly religious songs, Lawd I forgot em now. I never knowd about no slave uprisings—white folks alway good to us. We misses em now. Times not lack dey use to be.

Dese young generations don't take no interest in nothin no mo. Its kinder kritical. No use trying to tell em nuthin. Dey's getting an education I don't know whut thell do with it. If dey had somebody to manage fur them seem like they kaint kandle no business without getting broke. They work hard and make some seems lack they jes kaint keep nuthin. No'om I don't think they are so bad.

In 1893 me and ma husband worked on our own place till we come down here we sold it and went on his brothers place. I owns ma house thats all. Ma daughters help me and we get a little provisions and clothes along from the relief. If I could work I wouldn't ax nobody for no help. I jess past working much.

I jess don't know what is going to become of the present generation. The conditions are better than they use to be, heap better. They have no education and don't have to work as hard as we use to. They seems so restless and don't take no interest in nothin. They are all right. It is jess the times an the Bible full filling fast as it can.

Interviewer: Samuel S. Taylor
Person interviewed: Charles Green Dortch
804 Victory Street, Little Rock, Arkansas
Age: 81

CHARLES GREEN DORTCH

[HW: Father a Pet]

"I was born June 18, 1857. The reason I don't show my age is because I got Scotch-Irish, Indian, and Negro mixed up in me. I was born in Princeton—that is, near Princeton—in Dallas County. Princeton is near Fordyce. I was born on Hays' farm. Hays was my second master—Archie Hays. Dortch was my first master. He brought my parents from Richmond, Virginia, and he settled right in Princeton.

"My father's name was Reuben Rainey Dortch. He was an octoroon I guess. He looked more like a Cuban than a Negro. He had beautiful wavy hair, naturally wavy. He was tall, way over six feet, closer to seven. His father was Dortch. Some say Rainey. But he must have been a Dortch; he called himself Dortch, and we go in the name of Dortch. Rainey was a white man employed on Dortch's plantation. Rainey's name was Wilson Rainey. My name has always been Dortch.

"My mother was named Martha Dortch. I am trying to think what her maiden name was. My sister can tell you all the details of it. She is five years older than I am.

She can tell you all the old man's folks and my mother's too more easily than I can.

"My father had, as nearly as I can remember—lemme see—Cordelia, Adrianna, Mary, Jennie, Emma, and Dortch. Emma and Dortch were children by a first wife. Cordelia was his stepdaughter. My brothers were Alec and Gabe. There is probably some I have overlooked.

"The Indian blood in me came through my mother's father. He was a full-blooded red Indian. I can't think of his name now. Her mother was a dark woman.

"My father was a carpenter, chair maker, and a farmer too. All the work he did after peace was declared was carpentry and chair and basket making. He made coffins too just after peace was declared. They didn't have no undertakers then. He made the bottoms to chairs too. He could put a roof on a house beautifully and better than any one I know. Nobody could beat him putting shingles on a house.

"My mother was reared to work in the house. She was cook, housekeeper. She was a weaver too. She worked the loom and the spinning wheel. She gardened a little. But her work was mostly in the house as cook and weaver. She never went out in the field as a hand. My father didn't either.

Kind Masters

"My father seemed to have been more of a pet than a slave. He was a kind of boss more than anything else. He had his way. Nobody was allowed to mistreat him in any way. My mother was the same way. I don't think she was ever mistreated in any way by the white folks—not that I ever saw.

Attitude of Slaves Toward Father

"There wasn't any unfriendliness of the other slaves toward my father. My oldest sister can tell you with clearness, but I don't think he ever had any trouble with the other slaves any more than he had with the white folks. He was well liked, and then too he was able to take care of himself. Then again, he had a good master. Hays was a good man. We made a trip down there just a short while ago. We hadn't been there since the Civil War. They made it so pleasant for us! We all set down to the same table and ate together. Frank was down there. He was my young master.

Thirty Acres—not Forty

"They gave us thirty acres of land when we came out of slavery. They didn't give it to us right then, but they did later. I am going down there again sometime. My young master is the postmaster down there now. He thinks the world and all of me and my oldest sister.

"I don't mind telling people anything about myself. I was born in June. They ain't nothing slipping up on me. I understand when to talk. There are two of us, Adrianna Kern—that's her married name. She and I are the ones Mr. Frank gave the thirty acres to. I have a younger sister.

Slave Work

"I don't know how much cotton a slave was expected to pick in a day. The least I ever heard of was one hundred fifty pounds. Some would pick as high as three and four hundred pounds.

"My father was not a field hand. He was what they called the first man 'round there. He was a regular leader on the plantation—boss of the tool room. He was next to the master of them, you might say. He was a kind of boss.

"I never heard of his working for other men besides his master. I believe he drove the stage for a time from Arkadelphia to Camden or Princeton. I don't know just how that come about. My sister though has a more exact remembrance than I have, and she can probably tell you the details of it.

Boyhood Experiences

"My father used to take me to the mill with him when I was a kid. That was in slavery time. He went in a wagon and took me with him.

"The biggest thing I did was to play with the other kids. They had me do such work as pick berries, hunt up the stock, drive the sheep home from the pasture. And as near as I can remember it seems like they had me more picking berries or gathering peaches or something like that.

Food, Houses, Clothes

"Corn bread, buttermilk and bacon and all such as that and game—that was the principal food. The people on our place were fed pretty well. We lived off of ash cakes and biscuits.

"The slaves lived in old log houses. I can almost see them now. Let's see—they usually had just one window. The slaves slept on pallets mostly and wore long cotton shirts.

Patrollers

"I have heard a great deal of talk about the pateroles—how they tied ropes across the road and trapped them. Sometimes they would be knocked off their horses and crippled up so that they had to be carried off from there. Of course, that was sometimes. They was always halting the slaves and questioning them and whipping them if they didn't have passes.

How Freedom Came

"The way I understand it there came a rumor all at once that the Negroes were free. It seems that they throwed up their hands. They had a great fight at Pine Bluff and Helena and De Valls Bluff. Then came peace. The rumor came from Helena. Meade and Thomas winded the thing up some way. Sherman made his march somewhere. The colored soldiers and the white soldiers came pouring in from Little Rock. They come in a rush and said, 'Tell them niggers they're free.' They run into the masters' and notified them they were going to take all the Negroes to Little Rock. It wasn't no time afterwards before here come the teams and the wagons to take us to Little Rock.

"When they brought us here, they put us in soldiers' camps in a row of houses up just west of where the Arch street graveyard is now. They put us all there in the soldiers' buildings. They called them camps. They seemed to be getting us ready for freedom. It wasn't long before they had us in school and in church. The Freedmen's Bureau visited us and gave us rations just like the Government has been doing these last years. They gave us food and clothes and books and put us in school. That was all done right here in Little Rock.

Schooling

"My first teacher was Miss Sarah Henley. I could show you the home she used to live in. It's right up the street. It's on Third Street between Izard and State right in the middle of the block—next to the building on the corner of Izard on the south side of Third Street. There is a brick building there on the corner and her house is a very pretty one right next to it. She was a white woman and was my first teacher. She taught me, as near as I can remember, one session. My next teacher was Mrs. Hunt. She was from Ohio. My first teacher was from Ohio too. Mrs. Hunt taught me about two sessions. Lemme see, Mrs. Clapp came after her. She was from Pennsylvania. Mrs. Clapp taught me one session. I am trying to think of that other teacher. We went over to Union School then. Charlotte Andrews taught us there for a while. That was her maiden name. Her married name is Stephens. She was the first colored teacher in the city. Mrs. Hubbard teached us a while, too. Mrs. Scull taught us right here on Gaines and

Seventh Streets where this church is now. They moved us a long time ago down to the Mess House at the Rock Island for a while but we didn't stay there long. We came back to the Methodist church—the one on Eighth and Broadway, not the Bethel Church on Ninth and Broadway. There was a colored church on Eighth and Broadway then. They kept sweeping us 'round because the schools were all crowded. Woods, a colored man, was one of the teachers at Capitol Hill Public School. We were there when it first opened. That was the last school I went to. I finished eight grades. Me and Scipio Jones went to school together and were in the same class. I left him in school and went to work to take care of my folks.

Occupational Experiences

"Right after the Civil War, I went to school. I did no work except to sell papers and black boots on the corner of Main and Markham on Sunday. After I stopped school I went to work as assistant porter in the railroad office at the Union Station for the St. Louis, Iron Mountain, Southern Railway and Cairo and Fulton. That was one road or system. I stayed with them from 1873 till 1882 in the office as office porter. From that I went train porter out of the office in 1882. I stayed as train porter till 1892. Then right back from 1892 I went in the general superintendent's private car. Then from there I went to the shop here in North Little Rock—the Missouri Pacific Shops—as a straw boss of the storeroom gang. That was in 1893. I stayed in the shop until 1894. Then I was transferred back on this side as coach cleaner. That was in 1895. I stayed as coach cleaner till 1913. From that I went to the State Capitol and stayed there as janitor of the Supreme

Court for three years. In 1917, I went back to the coach cleaning department. That was during the war. I stayed there till 1922. I come out on the strike and have been out ever since. Since then I have done house cleaning all over the city. That brings me up to about two years ago. Now I pick up something here and something there. I have been knocking around sick most of the time and supported by the Relief and the Welfare principally.

Ku Klux Klan

"I don't remember much about the Ku Klux Klan. They never bothered me, and never bothered any one connected with me.

Powell Clayton

"I have stood at the bar and drank with Powell Clayton. He had been 'round here ever since we had. He was a very particular friend of my boss'—the bosses of my work after the war and freedom. They were all Yankees together. They would all meet at the office. That was while I was working my way through school and afterwards too. He was strictly a 'Negroes' Friend'. He was a straight out and out Yankee.

A Broken Thumb in a Political Fight

"I got this thumb broken beating a white man up. No, I'll tell the truth. He was beating me up and I thought he was going to kill me. It was when Benjamin Harrison had been elected President. I was in Sol Joe's saloon and I said, 'Hurrah for Harrison.' A white man standing at the bar there said to me, 'What do you mean, nigger, insulting the guests here?' And before I knew what he was going to do—bop!—he knocked me up on the side of the head and put me flat on the floor. He started to stamp me. My head was roaring, but I grabbed his legs and held them tight against me and then we was both on the floor fighting it out. I butted him in the face with my head and beat him in the face with my fists until he yelled for some one to come and stop me. There was plenty of white people 'round but none of them interfered. A great commotion set up and I slipped out the back door and went home during the excitement.

"When I went back to the saloon again after about a week or so, the fellow had left two dollars for me to drink up. Sol Joe told me that he showed the man he was wrong, that I was one of his best customers. To make Sol and me feel better, he left the two dollars. When I got there and found the money waiting for me, I just called everybody in the house up to the bar and treated it out.

"They claimed I had hit him with brass knucks, but when I showed them my hand—it was swollen double—and then showed them how the thumb was broken, they agreed on what caused the damage. That thumb never did set properly. You see, it's out of shape right now.

Domestic Life

"I met my wife going home. I was a train porter between here and Memphis. She was put in my care to see that she took her train all right out of Memphis, Tennessee, going on farther. I fell in love with her and commenced courting her right from there. She was so white in color that you couldn't tell she was colored by looking at her. After I married her, I was bringing her home, and three white men from another town got on the train and followed us, thinking she was white. Every once in a while they would come back and peep in the Negro coach. Sometimes they would come in and sit down and smoke and watch us. My sister notice it and called my attention to it. I went to the conductor and complained. He called their hand.

"It seems that they were just buying mileage from time to time and staying on the train to be able to get off where I got off. The conductor told them that if they went into Little Rock with the train there would be a delegation of white people there to meet them and that the reception wouldn't be a pleasant one, that I worked on the road, and that all the officials knew me and knew my wife, and that if I just sent a wire ahead they'd find themselves in deep. They got off the train at the next stop, but they gave me plenty of eye, and it looked like they didn't believe what had been told them.

"We were married only three and a half years when she died. Her name was Lillie Love Douglass before she married me. She was a perfect angel. White folks tried to say that she was white. We had two children. Both of them are dead. One died while giving birth to a child and the other died at the age of thirty-three.

"I married the second time. I met my second wife the same way I met the first. I was working on the railroad and she was traveling. I was a coach cleaner. We lived together three years and were separated over foolishness. She had long beautiful hair and an old friend of hers stopped by once and said that he ought to have a lock of her hair to braid into a watch chain. She said, 'I'll give you a lock.' I said, 'You and your hair both belong to me; how are you going to give it away without asking me.' She might have been joking, and I was not altogether serious. But it went on from there in to a deep quarrel. One day, I had been drinking heavily, and we had an argument over the matter. I don't remember what it was all about. Anyway, she called me a liar and I slapped her before I thought.

"For two or three weeks after that we stayed together just as though nothing had happened, except that she never had anything more to say to me. She would lie beside me at night but wouldn't say a word. One day I gave her a hundred dollars to buy some supplies for the store. She was a wonderful hat maker, and we had put up a store which she operated while I was out on the road working. When I came back that evening, the store was wide open and she was gone. She had slipped off and gone home from the station across the river. I didn't find that out till the next day. She hid during part of the night at the home of one of my friends. And another of my friends carried her across the river and put her on the train. I was out with a shotgun watching. I am glad I did not meet them. She is living in Chicago now, married to the man she wanted to give the lock of hair to and doing well the last I heard from her. She was a good woman, just marked with a high temper. There was no reason why we should not have lived together and gotten along well. We loved each other and were making money hand over fist when we separated.

Opinions

"The young people are too much for me. Women are awful now. The young ones are too wild for me. The old ones allow them too much freedom. They are not given proper instruction and training by their elders."

Interviewer's Comment

Dortch's grandfather on the father's side was a white man and either his master or someone closely connected with his master—his first master. His last master was the father of his half-sister, Cordelia, born before any of the other members of his family. These facts account largely for the good treatment accorded his mother and father in slave time and for the friendly attitude toward them subsequent to slavery.

Dortch's whole sister, Adrianna, is living next door to him, and is eighty-five years old going on eighty-six. She has a clearer memory than Dortch, and has also a clear vigorous mentality. She never went to school but uses excellent English and thinks straight. I have not made Dortch's interview any longer because I am spending the rest of this period on his sister's, and there was no need of taking some material which would be common to both and more clearly stated by her. I have already finished ten pages of her story.

Interviewer: Samuel S. Taylor
Person interviewed: Fannie Dorum
423 W. Twenty-Fourth Street
North Little Rock, Arkansas
Age: 94

[TR: Some word pronunciation was marked in this interview. Letters surrounded by [] represent long vowels, and by () short vowels.]

FANNIE DORUM

[HW: Church Holds Old Age Contest]

"I was here in slavery time. Know the years I plowed. Ginned cotton in slavery time. My daddy was the ginner. His name was Hamp High. Stayed down in Lonoke County.

"I was here in slavery time. The third year of the surrender (1868), I married—married Burton Dorum.

"I was born in Franklin, North Carolina. My old master's name was Jack Green, Franklin County. He had five boys—Henry, John, James, Robert, and William Henry. And he had a daughter named Mary. My old mistress' name was Jennie Green. They all came from North Carolina and I think they are still there.

Work

"A slave better pick a hundred pounds of cotton in a day. You better pick a hundred. I couldn't pick a hundred. I never was much on picking cotton.

"I weeded corn, planted corn and cotton, cut up wheat, pulled fodder, and did all such work. I plowed before the War about two years. I used to have to take the horses and go hide when the soldiers would go through. I was about nineteen years old when Lee surrendered. That would make me somewheres about ninety-four years old. The boys figgered it all out when they had the old age contest 'round here. They added up the times I worked and put everything together.

Family

"I raised eight children. Have five living. And I reckon about forty children, grandchildren, great-grandchildren, and great-great-grandchildren. You see I have been here right smart time.

Schooling

"Colored folks didn't get no learning then. I never learned to read or write. Before I married, I learned to spell my name, but I had so much to do I have forgot how to do that.

How Freedom Came

"The Yankees were coming through the place. A great crowd of soldiers. The day the corps of Yankees were to go out, they all went up to the pike and it looked like a dark cloud. There were great big wagons loaded down with everything to eat. They took all the meat, all the whiskey, all the flour. That they didn't take, they give to the slaves or poured on the ground. They took the corn out of the crib.

"The next day, old master called us up to the stand around him. He told us we were all free and that if we would stay with him, he would pay us.

Whipping

"My old master never whipped me but once and never hit me much then. I said, 'Master, if you don't hit me no more, I'll tell you who's been stealing all your eggs.' He said, 'Will, you tell me, sure 'nough.' I said, 'Yes.' But I never done it.

Patrollers

"I heard about the pateroles catching the colored folks. They would catch them on the road as they were going places and whip them. The pateroles was white folks that was supposed to catch colored folks when they were out without a pass. Sometimes the colored folks would stretch ropes across the road and trip them up. You would hear them laughing about it when they got amongst themselves the next day.

House, Etc.

"I was born in a old log house—two rooms. One for the kitchen and one to sleep in. We had homemade furniture. Mighty few of them had bought furniture. Most of then made it themselves. If you had bought furniture, that was called fine. There was no rollers to any bed. Food was kept in the house. Wheat was kept under the bed because they had nowhere else to keep it. Planks were put around it. We children used to jump up and down in it.

Rations

"When the white folks got ready to give us milk, they poured it out in a tub and said, 'Come and git it.'

"They would kill hogs and the colored folks' meat would be put back of the white folks' meat in the smokehouse. They put the white folks' meat in the front and the colored folks' meat in the back. When you wanted something, you would go up to old master and say, 'My meat is out,' and they would give you some more out of the smokehouse.

"Brandy was kept in the storehouse too; but they didn't give that to the colored [TR: corrected from 'cullud'] folks—they didn't give any of it to them. My daddy used to make it and buy it from the white folks and slip and sell it to the colored folks. He didn't tell the white folks who he was gettin' it for.

"You didn't have a regular time to git rations. You didn't on my place. You got things any time you needed them. My master was a good man. My dad got anything he wanted because he was the ginner. When he was working and it came mealtime, he would go right by the white folks' house and git anything he wanted and eat it—brandy, meat, anything.

Slave Wages

"My daddy not only did the ginning on my place; he did the ginning for other folks. He did the ginning for an old rich man named Jack Green, who lived in Franklin County. Jack Green paid wages for my father's, Hampton High's, work and the money was turned over to his mistress. I don't know whether they paid him and he turned it over to his mistress, or whether they told him about it and paid his mistress. They trusted him and I know he did work for pay. On account of the money my father earned he was considered a valuable slave. That's why he could go and eat and drink anything he wanted to.

Life Since Slavery

"My husband married me in May. He went to his uncle and worked an shares for two or three years. Then my husband took a crop to himself. He bought a cow and hog and stayed there twenty-one years. Raised a great big orchard. All my children were born right there. White people owned the farm. Priestley Mangham and his wife were the white people. When we left that place, my children were all big enough to work. That was in North Carolina. The nearest town was College.

"When the white folks tried to take advantage of us and take our crops, then we left and came here. My husband is dead and has been dead over twenty years.

"My daughters do the best they can to help me along, but they're on relief themselves and can't do much for me.

Opinions

"The young people of today are in no good at all, except to eat. They are there on mealtime, but that is about all."

Interviewer's Comment

About three years ago, there was an old age contest in one of the colored churches of North Little Rock. Sister Hatchett was considered the oldest, Fannie Dorum next. Sarah Jane Patterson was among those considered in the nineties also. It is very probable that all of these three are ninety or more. Stories of Dorum and Patterson are already in, and interview with Hatchett will be completed soon.

This paper fails to record Fannie Dorum's accent with any approach to accuracy. She speaks fairly accurately and clearly and with a good deal of attention to grammaticalness. But she pronounces all "er" ending as "uh"; e.g., nigguh, cullud, fathuh, mothuh, m(o)stuh, daughtuhs.

There are a number of variations from correct pronunciation which I do not record because they do not constitute a variation from the normal pronunciation; e.g., "wuz" for "was", "(e)r" for "[e]r".

The slave pronunciation of "m(o)ster" is more nearly correct than the normal pronunciation of "m(a)" Frequent pronunciations are marse, marsa, m(o)ssa, m(o)stuh, and m(a)ssa.

Interviewer: Samuel S. Taylor
Person interviewed: Silas Dothrum
1419 Pulaski Street, Little Rock, Arkansas
Age: 82 or 83
Occupation: Field hand, general work
[May 31 1939]

SILAS DOTHRUM

[HW: Don't Know Nothin']

"The white people that owned me are all dead. I am in this world by myself. Do you know anything that a man can put on his leg to keep the flies off it when it has sores on it? I had the city doctor here, but he didn't do me no good. I have to tie these rags around my foot to keep the flies off the sores.

"I worked with a white man nineteen years—put all that concrete down out there. He is still living. He helps me a little sometimes. If it weren't for him I couldn't live. The government allows me and my wife together eight dollars a month. I asked for more, but I couldn't get it. I get commodities too. They amount to about a dollar and a half a month. They don't give any flour or meat. Last month they gave some eggs and those were nice. What they give is a help to a man in my condition.

"I don't know where I was born and I don't know when. I know I am eighty-two or eighty-three years old. The white folks that raised me told me how old I was. I never saw my father and my mother in my life. I don't know nothin'. I'm just on old green man. I don't know none of my kin people—father, mother, uncles, cousins, nothin'. When I found myself the white people had me.

"That was right down here in Arkansas here on old Dick Fletcher's farm. There was a big family of them Fletchers. They took me to Harriet Lindsay to raise. She is dead. She had a husband and he is dead. She had two or three daughters and they are dead.

Slave Houses

"I can remember what they used to live in. The slaves lived in old wooden houses. They ain't living in no houses now—one-half of them. They were log houses—two rooms. I have forgot what kind of floors—dirt, I guess. Food was kept in a smokehouse.

Relatives

"The whole family of Fletchers is dead. I think that there is a Jef Fletcher living in this town. I don't know just where but I met him sometime ago. He doesn't do nothing for me. Nobody gives me anything for myself but the man I used to work for—the concrete man. He's a man.

How Freedom Came

"All I remember is that they boxed us all up in covered wagons and carried us to Texas and kept us there till freedom came. Then they told us we were free and could go where wanted. But they kept me in bondage and a girl that used to be with them. We were bound to them that we would have to stay with them. They kept me just the same as under bondage. I wasn't allowed no kind of say-so.

"After Dick Fletcher died, his wife and his two children fetched us back—fetched us back in a covered wagon.

"I am a Arkansas man. Was raised here. I am very well known here, too. Some years after that she turned us loose. I can't remember just how many years it was, but it was a good many.

Right After the War

"After Mrs. Fletcher turned us loose, we worked with some families. I was working by the year. If I broke anything they took it out of my wages. If I broke a plow they would charge me for it. I was working for niggers. I can't remember how much they paid, but it wasn't anything when they got through taking out. I'm dogged if I know how much they were supposed to pay; it has been so long. But I know that if I broke anything—a tool or something—they charged me for it. I didn't have much at the end of the year. It would take me a lifetime to make anything if I had to do that.

Patrollers

"I have been out in the bushes when the pateroles would come up and gone into log houses and get niggers and whip their asses. They would surround all the niggers and make them go into the house where they could whip them as much as they wanted to. All that is been years and years ago. I never seen any niggers get away from them. I have heared of them getting away, but if they did I never knowed it.

Ku Klux Klan

"I heared of the Ku Klux, but they never bothered me. I never saw them do anything to anybody.

Recollections Relating to Parents

"I don't know who my parents were, but it seems like I heard them say my father was a white man, and I seen to remember that they said my mother was a dark woman.

Opinions

"The young people today ain't worth a shit. These young people going to school don't mean good to nobody. They dance all the night and all the time, and do everything else. That man across the street runs a whiskey house where they dance and do everything they're big enough to do. They ain't worth nothing."

Interviewer: Pernella M. Anderson
Person interviewed: Sarah Douglas
Route 2, Box 19-A, El Dorado, Arkansas
Age: 82?

[TR: Original interview where photograph inserted notes photograph of "Sarah and Sam Douglas." The Library of Congress photo archive notes "'Tom' written in pencil above 'Sam' in title."]

United States. Work Projects Administration

SARAH DOUGLAS

"I was born in Alabama. I don't know when though. I did not find out when I was born because old miss never told me. My ma died when I was real small and my old miss raised me. I had a hard time of my life. I slept on the floor just like a cat—anywhere I laid down I slept. In winter I slept on rags. If I got sick old miss would give me plenty of medicine because she wanted me to stay well in order to work. My old master was name John Buffett and old misses name was Eddie Buffett. She would fix my bread and licker in a tin lid and shove it to me on the floor. I never ate at the table until I was twelve and that was after freedom.

"To whip me she put my head between the two fence rails and she taken the cow hide whip and beat me until I couldn't sit down for a week. Sometimes she tied our hands around a tree and tie our neck to the tree with our face to the tree and they would get behind us with that cow hide whip with a piece of lead tied to the end and lord have mercy! child, I shouted when I wasn't happy. All I could say was, 'Oh pray, mistress, pray.' That was our way to say Lord have mercy. The last whipping old miss give me she tied me to a tree and oh my Lord! old miss whipped me that day. That was the worse whipping I ever got in my life. I cried and bucked and hollered until I couldn't. I give up for dead and she wouldn't stop. I stop crying and said to her, 'Old miss, if I were you and you were me I wouldn't beat you this way.' That struck old miss's heart and she let me go and she did not have the heart to beat me any more.

"I did every kind of work when I was a little slave; split rails, sprouted, ditched, plowed, chopped, and picked and planted.

"I remember young master going to war and I remember hearing the first gun shoot but I did not see it. I saw the smoke though.

"I never went to school a day in my life. The white folks said we did not need to learn, if we needed to learn anything they could learn us with that cow hide whip.

"We went to the white folks' church, so we sit in the back on the floor. They allowed us to join their church whenever one got ready to join or felt that the Lord had forgiven them of their sins. We told our determination; this is what we said: 'I feel that the Lord have forgiven me for my sins. I have prayed and I feel that I am a better girl. I belong to master so and so and I am so old.' The white preacher would then ask our miss and master what they thought about it and if they could see any change. They would get up and say: 'I notice she don't steal and I notice she don't lie as much and I notice she works better.' Then they let us join. We served our mistress and master in slavery-time and not God.

"I recollect miss died just after the War. Old miss was very strict on us and after she died we was so glad we had a big dance in miss's kitchen and old miss came back and slapped one of the slaves and left the print of her hand on her face. That white hand never did go away and that place was forever haunted after that.

"Now I don't know how to tell you to get after my age but I was twelve years old two years after surrender."

Interviewer: Carol Graham
Subject: Ex-slaves
Information given by: Sarah Douglas, El Dorado, Arkansas

SARAH DOUGLAS

Mornin' honey. I thought you wuz comin' back tuh see me ergin las' summer an' I looked fuh you the longes' time. I'se plum proud tuh see you ergin. Dis other lady ain't de one that wuz wid you las' summer is she?

Now jes lis'en tuh that will yuh, she wants Aunt Sarah tuh tell huh some more 'bout slave'y times. John Bufford wuz mah marster's name. I wuz bo'n in Alabama an' brought to Louisiana by my marster's fambly. Aftuh de wah he freed us an' some of 'em mixed up in politics an' the white folks from the North fooled 'em into makin speeches fuh 'em, but dey soon learnt bettuh.

I ain't been well lately. The doctuh said I had slamatory rheumatis. I'm ol' now end don' have nobody tuh do nothin fuh me. My mistress wuz mammy in de ol' days.

Aftuh I got up fum mah rheumatism I went down tuh that church you sees, I give de lan' fuh hit, me and Tom did and I jes felt good and wanted tuh praise the Lord. I wuz so glad the sperit come once more, I got happy and I got up and went down tuh de fron' and said; "I want to shake hand wid ever' body in dis house. I wanna stroke yo hand." An' I stood down there at the front so happy an' duh yuh know one little chile and two women come down an' shook hands wid me, I jes didn't know whut tuh think. Yoh know when I wuz young and a body got happy evuh body did an' dey made a noise but not so now. An' tuh think dey couldn't turn praises.

You say yo' wants tuh talk tuh Tom? Well he's out dar in de back yard but he aint well and I specks he won't talk tuh but if you mus' come on. Tom here is a lady wants tuh talk tuh you. I'll go back an talk tuh de lady whuts waitin' in de car.

(The above written just as Sarah Douglas expressed it).

(Taken down word for word.)

(August 11, 1937.)

Interviewer: Pernella M. Anderson
Person interviewed: Tom Douglas
Route 2, Box 19-A, El Dorado, Arkansas
Age: 91

TOM DOUGLAS

"I was born in Marion, Louisiana September 15, 1847 at 8 o'clock in the morning. I was eighteen years of age at surrender. My master and missus was B.B. Thomas and Miss Susan Thomas. Old master had a gang of slaves and we all worked like we were putting out fire. Lord child, wasn't near like it is now. We went to bed early and got up early. There was a gang of plow hands, hoe hands, hands to clear new ground, a bunch of cooks, a washwoman. We worked too and didn't mind it. If we acted like we didn't want to work, our hands was crossed and tied and we was tied to a tree or bush and whipped until we bled. They had a whipping post that they tied us to to whip us.

"We was sold just like hogs and cows and stock is sold today. They built nigger pens like you see cow pens and hog pens. They drove niggers in there by the hundred and auctioned them off to the highest bidder. The white folks kept up with our age so when they got ready to sell us they could tell how old we were. They had a 'penetenture' for the white folks when they did wrong. When we done wrong we was tied to that whipping post and our hide busted open with that cow hide.

"We stayed out in the field in a log house and old master would allowance our week's rations out to us and Sunday morning we got one biscuit each. If our week's allowance give out before the week we did not get any more.

"Cooked on fireplaces, wasn't no stoves. We did not have to worry about our clothes. Old missus looked after everything. We wore brogan shoes and homespun clothes. There was a bunch of women that did the spinning and weaving just like these sewing room women are now. I was a shoe maker. I made all the shoes during the time we wasn't farming. We had to go nice and clean. If old missus caught us dirty our hide was busted. I got slavery time scars on my back now. You ought to see my back. Scars been on my back for seventy-five years.

"I never went to school a day in my life. I learned my ABC'S after I was nineteen years old. I went to night school, then to a teacher by the name of Nelse Otom. I was the first nigger to join the church on this side of the Mason and Dixie line. During slavery we all joined the white folk's church set in the back. After slavery in 1866 they met in conference and motioned to turn all of the black sheep out then. There was four or five they turned out here and four or five there, so we called our preacher and I was the first one to join. Old master asked our preacher what we paid him to preach to us. We told him old shoes and clothes. Old master says, 'Well, that's damn poor pay.' Our preacher says, 'And they got a damn poor preacher.'

"I did not know anything about war. Only I know it began in 1861, closed in 1865, and I know they fought at Vicksburg. That was two or three hundred miles from us but we could not keep our dishes upon the table whenever they shot a bomb. Those bombs would jar the house so hard and we could see the smoke that far.

"We was allowed to visit Saturday night and Sunday. If you had a wife you could go to see her Wednesday night and Saturday night and stay with her until Monday morning and if you were caught away any other time the patrollers would catch you. That is where the song come from, 'Run nigger run, don't the patarolls will catch you.' Sometimes a nigger would run off and the nigger dogs would track them. In slavery white folks put you together. Just tell you to go on and go to bed with her or him. You had to stay with them whether you wanted them or not.

"After freedom old master called all us slaves and told us we was free, opened a big gate and drove us all out. We didn't know what to do—not a penny, nowhere to go—so we went out there and set down. In about thirty minutes master came back and told us if we wanted to finish the crop for food and clothes we could, so we all went back and finished the crop and the next year they gave us half. So ever' since then we people been working for half.

"Here is one of my boy songs:

> 'Sadday night and Sunday too,
> A pretty girl on my mind
> As soon as Monday morning come
> The white folks get me gwi-ng.'"

United States. Work Projects Administration

[HW: Regrets End of Slavery]
OLD SLAVE STORIES

[TR: Sarah and Tom Douglas]

SARAH AND TOM DOUGLAS

[TR: Aunt Sarah Douglas]—

Ah wuz baptized de second year of surrender. Wuz twelve years ole at de time an my mistress spoke fuh me when ah j'ined de church. In them days when chillun j'ined de church some grown person had ter speak fuh em an tell if they thought they wuz converted or not. Now when chillun j'in de church if they is big enough ter talk they take em in widout grown fokes speaking fuh em a tall.

Slavery times wuz sho good times. We wuz fed an clothed an had nothin to worry about. Now poar ole niggers go hungry. Sho we wuz whipped in slavery times. Mah ole man has stripes on his back now wha he wuz whipped an ah wuz whipped too but hit hoped me up till now. Coase hit did. Hit keeps me fum goin aroun here tellin lies an stealin yo chickens.

Me an mah ole man is been married sixty-six years an have nevah had no chillun. Yo know little chillun is de sweetest thing in de worl'. Now if we had chillun we would have someone tuh take care of us in our ole days. Mah ole man, Tom, is 89 an I'se 82. Poar ole man. Ah does all ah kin fuh him but I'se ole too. These young niggers is gettin so uppity. They think they is better than we is. A Darkey jes don' love one another an stick t'gether like white fokes does. But ah is goin ter stick ter my ole man. He needs me. He is jes like a little helpless chile widout me ter look after him. Ah used to be mighty frisky an mighty proud when ah wuz young but ah wazn' as good then as ah is now. Ah likes ter go ter church. See that little white church over de hill? That is Douglas Chapel, a Baptist church. Me an mah ole man give de lan' fuh that church. We had plenty them days when Douglas was laid out (meaning Douglas Addition). But now poar ole niggers don' have enough ter eat all de time. None of them church members is missionary enough ter bring us somethin' ter eat. White fokes have good hearts but niggers is grudgeful. De bigges thing among white fokes is they do lie sometime an when they do they kin best a nigger all to pieces.

Niggers don' have as much 'ligion as they use ter. Ah went to a missionary meeting at one sister's house an she said ter me: "Sister Douglas, start us off wid a song" an ah started off with "Amazing Grace." Sang bout half of de first verse an noticed none of them j'ined in but ah kep' right on singin' an wuz gettin full of de sperit when that sister spoke up an said: "Sister Douglas, don' yo know that is done gone out of style?" an selected "Fly Away" an den all of them sisters j'ined in an sung "Fly away, fly away" an hit sounded jes like a dance chune.

Yas'm, that is our ole buggy standin aroun de corner of de house. We use ter ride in hit till hit got so rickety. An that ole horse is our fambly horse. Dolly Jane ah calls her. We've had her forty years an she gits sick sometime jes like ah does an ah thinks sho she is gone this time but she gits ovah hit jes like ah does when ah has a spell. We has lived in this house since 1900 but we is goin ovah on de utha side of de tracks soon wid the res of de niggers. Nobody lef on this side but white fokes now ceptin us. When de railroad come through down there ah had a cotton patch growin there an ah cried cause hit went through mah cotton patch an ruint part of hit. All we got out'n hit wuz damages.

No'm, mah ole man caint talk ter yo all terday; he is sick. Mebby ifn yo all come back he kin talk ter yo then.

(In the meantime we investigated Tom and Sarah Douglas and found that he has a bank account and at one time owned all the land that is now Douglas Addition. In a few days we went back and found Tom sitting on the porch.)

Uncle Tom Douglas—

Yas'm, ah members de wah. Ah wuz fo'teen when de wah began an eighteen when hit closed. Mah marster wuz B.B. Thomas, Union Parish, Louisiana, near Marion, Louisiana. Ah saw de fust soldiers go an saw young marster go. When young marster come back at de close of de wah he brought back a big piece of mule meat ter show us niggers what he done have ter eat while he wuz in de army.

Ah nevah wuz sold but lots of marster's slaves wuz sold. They wuz sold jes like stock. Ah members one fambly. De man wuz a blacksmith, de woman a cook, an one of their chillun wuz waitin boy. They wuz put on de block an sold an a diffunt man bought each one an they went ter diffunt part of de country ter live on nevah did see one nother no moah. They wuz sole jes like cows an horses. No'm, ah didn't like slavery days. Ah'd rather be free an hungry.

(Tom is the only ex-slave who has told us that he had rather be free and we believe that is because he has a bank account and is independent.)

Yo say tell yo about hants. There is such a thing. Yes mam. Some fokes calls it fogyness but hit sho is true fuh me an Sarah has seed em haint we Sarah. Here young missy, what is yo doin wid that pencil?

(After we had put up our notebooks and pencils and assured them that we would not repeat it, they told us the following):

When me an Sarah lived out at de Moore place about three miles east on the main street road we seed plenty of haints. De graveyard wuz in sight of our house an we could see them sperits come up out de groun an they would go past de house down in a grove an we could see them there campin. We could see they campfires. We could hear their dishes rattling an their tincups an knives an forks. An hear em talkin. Den again they would be diggin with shovels. Sometimes in de graveyard we could see de sperits doin de things they did befo they died. Some would be plowing, some blacksmithing an each one doin what he had done while he wuz livin. When day wuz breakin they would go runnin crost our yard an git back in de graves. Yes'm, we seed em as long as we lived there. After we moved from ther somebody dug up some gold that wuz buried at de corner of de chimney. An hit is said that from that day hants have not been seen there.

Yes'm, there is no doubt erbout hit. They is such thin's as hants. Me an Sarah has both seed em but we aint seed any in a long time.

United States. Work Projects Administration

Interviewer: Mrs. Carol Graham
Person interviewed: Tom & Sarah Douglas
Resident: El Dorado, Arkansas
Age: 90 and 83

TOM & SARAH DOUGLAS

NOTE:

This is a second interview with Uncle Tom and Aunt Sarah Douglas. The first was sent to your office in September 1936 from interview by Mrs. Mildred Thompson, El Dorado, Arkansas. Mrs. Thompson is not now with the Project. Mrs. Carol Graham made the second interview.

Tom Douglas—Ex-slave. I was a slave boy till I was eighteen. Was born in 1847, 'mancipated in '65. No, my master did not give me forty acres of land and a mule. When we was 'mancipated my master came took us outside the gate across the road and told us we was freed. "You are free to work for anybody you want to." We set there a while then we went whare ol' master was and he tol' us if we wanted to stay wid him and finish the crop he would provide our victuals and clothes. The next year we worked for him on the halves, and continued to do so for four or five years. 'F we didn' eat an' wear it up he would give us the balance in money an we of'en had as much as fifty dollars when the year was over.

My ol' master was S.B. [TR: in two previous interviews, B.B. Thomas] Thomas. The young master was Emmett Thomas. Mr. Emmett was his son. Dey was near Marion, Louisiana, then I worked fuh his brother-in-law 'Lias George. His wife was Susan George. I tell you the fact, these times is much bettuh than slave times. If I'm hungry an' naked, I'm free. I'm crazy 'bout liberty.

I've heard of the Ku Klux Klan but never did see none of 'em. Have seen where they is been but nevuh did see 'em.

We voted several years. Was considered citizens—voted an' all that sort of thing. I think if we pay taxes we ought to vote for payin' taxes makes us citizens don' it? I used to be a big politics man—lost all I had house, forty acres, a good well an' stock an' ever'thing. I was tol' one day that the Ku Kluxes was comin' to my house that night an' I got on my horse at sundown an left an aint nevuh been back. I was a big politics man then—lost all I had and quit politics. I'm ninety years old and fifteenth of next September. Looks like the old might get pensions if old has anything to do with it I ought to get a pension but us ol' folks that is gettin' long an has a place to stay an' somethin' to eat they say don' get none.

I come to El Dorado January 3, 1893. This place was in the woods then. I bought 120 acres from Mr. Dave Armstrong at five dollars per acre and in nine years I had it all paid for. It was after I got tired of workin' on the halves that I bought me a place.

Worked at a sawmill four years beginnin in 1897 or 98. Than I jobbed aroun' town three years doin' this an' that an' the other. Carried $25 with me when I moved to town and brought $28 back with me. Cleared $1 a year an' got tired of that.

Am livin' off my land. Have sol' some an' am sellin some now but times is hard and folks can't pay. I takes in from $18 to $25 per month.

The young folks is gone to destruction. Aint nothin' but destruction. You is young your self but you can tell times aint the same as they was ten years back. Young folks is goin' to destruction. Me, I'm goin' home. Goin' back 80 years an comin' up to day I is seen a mighty big change. Me, I'm goin' home. Don't know what you young folks going to see eighty years from now. Everybody is trying to get something for nothing.

We use to sing "Gimme this Old Time Religion, It's Good enough for me". An' we sung "I'm a Soldier of the Cross" an lots of others. We don' live right now, don' serve God. Pride, formality an love of money keeps folks from worshipping an' away from the ol' time religion. You know that ol' sayin: "Preacher in the pulpit preachin' mighty bold; All for your money an' none for your soul." Seems like its true now days.

You ask does I have stripes on my back from bein beat in slave'y times? No maam. I was always a good boy and smart boy raised in the same yard with the little white chillun. You says Sarah told you that las' year? Missy you mus' be mistaken. I was whipped once or twice but I needed it then or ol' master wouldn't a whipped me an he never did leave no stripes on me. My old master was good to all his niggers and I'm tellin you I was raised up with his chullun an him and old mistress was good to me. All we little black chillun et out of the boilin' pot an every Sunday mornin' we had hot biscuit and butter for breakfact. No maam my old master was always good to his niggers.

(Above is as exactly told by Tom Douglas with the exception that he used the word Marster, for master; wuz for was, tuh for to; ah for I and other quaint expressions—these were omitted because of instruction in Bulletin received August 7th, 1937.)

Taken down word for word. August 11, 1937.

Interviewer: Mrs. Bernice Bowden
Person interviewed: Sebert Douglas
610 Catalpa Street, Pine Bluff, Arkansas
Age: 82

SEBERT DOUGLAS

"I was born in Lebanon, Kentucky. Gover Hood was my old master. His wife's name was Ann Hood.

"I 'member Morgan's Raid. I don't 'member what year it was but I 'member a right smart about it. Cumberland Gap was where they met.

"The Rebs and Yankees both come and took things from old master. I 'member three horses they taken well. Yankees had tents in the yard. They was right in the yard right in front of the Methodist church.

"My mother was Mrs. Hood's slave, and when she married she took my mother along and I was born on her place.

"I was the carriage boy in slave times. My father did the driving and I was the waitin' boy. I opened the gates.

"I 'member Billy Chandler and Lewis Rodman run off and j'ined the Yankees but they come back after the War was over.

"Paddyrollers was about the same as the Ku Klux. The Ku Klux would take the roof off the colored folks' houses and take their bedding and make 'em go back where they come from.

"We stayed right there with old master for two or three years, then we went to the country and farmed for ourselves.

"I went to school just long enough to read and write. I never seed no use for figgers till I married and went to farmin'.

"Since I been in Pine Bluff I done mill work. I was a sash and door man.

"I used to vote every election till Hoover, but I never held any office.

"The younger generation is bad medicine. Can't tell what's gwine come of 'em!"

Interviewer: Miss Irene Robertson
Person interviewed: Henry Doyl, Brinkley, Arkansas
Age: Will be 74
Feb. 2, 1938

HENRY DOYL

"I was born in Hardeman County near Bolivar, Tennessee. My mother's moster was Bryant Cox and his wife was Miss Neely Cox. My mother was Dilly Cox. Two things I remembers tinctly that took place in my childhood: that was when my mother married George Doyl. I was raised by a stepfather. Miss Neely told my mother she was going to sell me and put me in her pocket. She told her that more'n one time. I recollect that.

"My oldest brother, one older en me, burned to death. My mother was a field hand. She was at work in the field. When she come to the house, the cabin burned up and the baby burned up too. That grieved her mighty bad and when Miss Neely tell her soon as I got big nough she was goner sell me mighty near break her heart.

"The first year after the surrender my father, Buck Rogers, left my mother in her bad condition. She said she followed him crying and begging him not to leave her to Montgomery Bridge, in Alabama. The last she seen him he was on Montgomery Bridge.

"They just expected freedom. My mother left her mistress and moved to the Doyl place. She didn't get nothing but her few clothes. I was born at the Doyl place. She worked for Moster Bob Doyl, a young man. They share cropped. We had a plenty I reckon of what we raised and a little money.

"I worked on Colonel Nuckles place when I got up grown. I worked on the Lunatic Asylum at Bolivar and loaded tires and ditched for the I.C. Railroad a long time.

"I don't recollect that the Ku Klux ever bothered us.

"My stepfather voted Republican ticket. I haven't voted for a good many years—not since Garfield or McKinley was our President.

"I come to Arkansas in 1887. I married in Arkansas. I heard that Arkansas was a rich country. My mother was dead. My stepfather had been out here. I come on the train, paid my own way. Come to Palestine the first night then on to Brinkley. I been close to Brinkley ever since.

"The old man died what learned me how to walk rice levies. I still work on the place. Everybody don't know how to walk levies. It will kill an old man. Your feet stay wet and cold all time. I do wear hip boots but my feet stay cold and damp. I got down with the rheumatism and jes' now got so I can walk.

"I got a wife and three living children. They all married and gone.

"Times is hard for old folks and changed so much. Children used to get jobs and take care of the granny folks and the old parents. They can't take care of themselves no more it look like. I don't know how to take the young generation. They are drifting along with the fast times.

"I applied but don't get no pension."

United States. Work Projects Administration

Interviewer: Miss Irene Robertson
Person interviewed: Willie Doyld (male), Brinkley, Arkansas
Age: 78
[-- -- 1938]

WILLIE DOYLD

"I was born in Grenada, Mississippi. My parents belong to the same family of white folks. My moster was Jim Doyld. His wife was Mistress Karoline Doyld. Well as I recollect they had four childen. My parent's name was Hannah and William Doyld. I'm named for em. They was three of us childen. They belong to same family of white folks for a fact. I heard em say Moster Jim bought em offen the block at the same time. He got em at Galveston, Texas. He kept five families of slaves on his place well as I recollect.

"My pa was Moster Jim's ox driver. He drove five or six yokes at a time. He walk long side of em, wagons loaded up. He toted a long cowhide whoop. He toted it over his shoulder. When he'd crack it you could hear his whoop half a mile. Knowed he was comin' on up to the house. Them oxen would step long, peartin up when he crack his whoop over em. He'd be haulin' logs, wood, cotton, corn, taters, sorghum cane and stuff. He nearly always walked long side of em; sometimes he'd crawl upon the front wagon an' ride a piece.

"He was a very good moster I recken far as I knows. They go up there, get sompin' to eat. He give em a midlin' meat. He give us clothes. Folks wore heep of clothes then. They got whoopin's if they not do lack they tole em to do—plenty whoopin's! He kept ten dogs, they call bear dogs. They hunt fox, wolves, deer, bear, birds. Them dogs died wid black tongue. Every one of em died.

"We et at home mostly. We was lounced wid the rations but had a big plenty. We got the rations every Saturday mornin'. One fellow cut and weighed out the meat, sacked out the meal in pans what they take to git it in. Sometimes we et up at the house. Mama bring a big bucket milk and set it down, give us a tin cup. We eat it up lack pigs lappin' up slop. Mama cooked for old mistress. She bring us 'nough cooked up grub to last us two or three days at er time. Papa could cook when he be round the house too. I recollect all four my grandmas and grandpas. They come from Georgia. Moster Jim muster bought them too but I don't know if he got em all at the same time down at Galveston, Texas.

"Moster Jim show did drink liquor—whiskey. I recken he would. When he got drunk old missus have him on the bed an' she set by him till he sober up. Miss Karoline good as ever drawed a breath to colored and white.

"My grandma, mother's ma, was a light sorter woman. The balance of my kin was pure nigger.

"I kin for a fact recollect a right smart about the war. Papa went off to war wid Jack Hoskins. He was goin' to be his waitin' man. He stayed a good while fore he got home. Jack Hoskins got kilt fore he et breakfast one mornin'. That all I heard him say. I recken he helped bury him but I never heard em say.

"The plainest thing I recollect was a big drove of the Yankee soldiers—some ridin', some walkin'—come up to the moster's house. He was sorter old man. He was settin' in the gallery. He lived in a big log house. He was readin' the paper. He throwed back his head and was dead. Jes' scared to death. They said that was what the matter. In spite of that they come down there and ordered us up to the house. All the niggers scared to death not to go. There lay old Moster Jim stretched dead in his chair. They was backed up to the smoke house door and the horses makin' splinters of the door. It was three planks thick, crossed one another and bradded together wid iron nails. They throwed the stuff out an' say, 'Come an' git it. Take it to your houses.' They took it. It was ours and we didn't want it wasted. Soon as they gone they got mighty busy bringing it back. They built nother door an' put it up. Old Miss Karoline bout somewheres, scared purty near to death. They buried Moster Jim at Water Valley, Mississippi. Miss Karoline broke up and went back to Virginia. My grandma got her feather bed and died on it. Bout two years after that the Yankees sot fire to the house and burned it down. We all had good log houses down close together. They didn't bother us.

"I don't recollect the Ku Klux.

"Our folks never knowed when freedom come on. Some didn't believe they was free at all. They went on farmin' wid what left. What they made they got it. My folks purty nigh all died right there.

"I lives alone. I got two childern in Lulu, Mississippi. I had three childern. My wife come here wid me. She dead.

"I had forty acres land, two mules, wagon. It went for debts. White folks got it. I ain't made nuthin' since.

"I ain't no hand at votin' much. I railly never understood nuthin' bout the run of politics.

"I hates to say it but the young generation won't work if they can get by widout it. They take it, if they can, outen the old folks. I used to didn't ask folks no diffrunce. I worked right long.

"I gets commodities wid this old woman. I come here to build her fires and see after er. I don't git no check."

Interviewer: Miss Irene Robertson
Person interviewed: Wade Dudley, Moro, Ark.
Age: 73

WADE DUDLEY

"Bill Kidd and Miss Nancy Kidd owned my parents. I was born close to Okalona, Chickasha County, Mississippi, about the last year of the Civil War. Mr. Bill was Miss Nancy's boy. He was a nigger trader. They said the overseers treated em pretty rough. They made em work in nearly a run. When Miss Nancy was living they was rich but after she died he got down pretty low. He married. Course I knowd em. I been through his house. He had a fine house. My mother said she was born in Virginia. She belong to Addison and Duley. Her mother come wid her. They sold them but didn't sell her father so she never seed him no more. She walked or come in a ox wagon part of the way. She was with a drove. My father come from North Carolina. His father was free. My father weighed out rations. He was bright color. He worked round the house and then durin' the war he run a refugee wagon. The Yankees got men, mules, meat from Mr. Bill Kidd. My father he was hiding em and hiding the provisions from one place to another to keep the Yankees from starving em all to death. My mother had nine boys. They all belong to Mr. Miller. He died, his widow married Mr. Owen then Mr. Owen sold them to Mrs. Kidd. That was where they was freed. My parents stayed about Mrs. Kidd's till she died. They worked for a third some of the time, I don't know how long. When I was a boy size of that yonder biggest boy my folks was still thinking the government was going to give em something. I was ten years old when they left Mrs. Kidd's. They thought the government was going to give em 40 acres and a mule or some kind of a start. I don't know where they got the notion. My father voted down in Mississippi. I vote. I was working in the car shops in St. Louis in 1923. Me and my wife both voted then. I worked there two years. I come back to Arkansas where I could farm. The land was better here than in Mississippi. I walked part of the way and rode part of the way when I come here from Mississippi. I vote a Republican ticket. Bout all I owns is two little pigs and a few chickens. I did have a spring garden. We work in the field and make a little to eat and wear.

"I find the present times is hard for old folks. Some young folks is doing well I guess. They look like it. I made application twice for help but I ain't never got on. I don't know what to think bout the young folks. If they can get a living they have a good time. They don't worry bout the future. A little money don't buy nothin' much now. It seem like everything is to buy. Money is hard to get."

Interviewer: Miss Irene Robertson
Person interviewed: Isabella Duke
Little Rock, Arkansas (towards Benton)
Visiting in Hazen
Age: 62

ISABELLA DUKE

[HW: Father Wore a Bonnet]

"My own dear mother was born at Faithville, Alabama. She belong to Sam Norse. His wife was Mistress Mai Jane. They moved to Little Rock years after my mother had come there. After seberal months they got trace of one another. I seed two of the Norse girls and a boy. Master Norse was a farmer in Alabama. Mother said he had plenty hands in slavery. She was a field hand. She had a tough time during slavery.

"Pa said he had a good time. 'Bout all he ever done was put on old mistress' shoes and pull her chair about for her to sit in. He built and chunked up the fires. Old mistress raised him and he had to wear a bonnet. He was real light. He said the worse whoopings he ever got was when he would be out riding stick horses with his bonnet on. The hands on the place would catch him and whoop him and say, 'Old mis' thinks he's white sure as de worl'.' The hands on the place sent him to the big house squalling many a time.

"After he got grown he could be took for a white man

easy. He was part French. He talked Frenchy and acted Frenchy. Every one who knowd him in Little Rock called him Pa Frazier and called my mother Ma Frazier, but she was dark. Pa said he et out his mistress' plate more times than he didn't. She raised him about like her own boy.

"Mother had a hard time. Alex Norse bought my mother and a small brother from some people leaving her own dear mother when she was fifteen years old. Her mother kept the baby and the little boy took sick and died. But there had been an older boy sold to some folks near Norse's place before she was sold. The brother that was two years old died. There were other older children sold. My mother never saw her mother after she was sold. She heard from her mother in 1910. She was then one hundred and one years old and could thread her needles to piece quilts. Her baby boy six months old when mother was sold come to visit us. Mother wanted to go back to see her but never was able to get the money ready. Mother had good sight when she died in 1920. She was eighty-seven years old and didn't have to wear glasses to see. Mother's father was on another place. He was said to be part or all Indian.

"Mother said once a cloth peddler come through the country. Her older brother John lived on a place close to the Norse place. John told the peddler that ma took the piece of goods he missed. But John was the one got the goods mind out. The peddler reported it to Master Norse. He give my mother a terrible beating. After that it come out on John. He had stole the piece of cloth. John then took sick, lay sick a long time. Master Norse wouldn't let her go nigh John. She knowd when he died and the day he was to be buried. Master Norse wouldn't let her go nigh there, not even look like she wanted to cry.

"Mother married before freedom, jumped the broom she said. Then after freedom she married my father. My parents named Clara and George Frazier. She had twelve children. Pa was a cripple man. He was a soldier. He said he never was shot and never shot no one. He was on a horse and going this way (reeling from side to side dodging the shooting) all time. A horse throwed him and hurt his hip in the army. After that he limped. He drew a pension. I limps but I'm better as I got grown. I'm marked after him. One of my children I named after him what died was cripple like him. My little George died when he was ten. He was marked at birth after his grandpa. I had ten, jus' got five living children.

"My husband's father's father was in the Civil War. He didn't want to go out on battle-field, so in the camps he cut his eyeball with his fingernail so he could get to go to the horsepital. His eye went out. He hurt it too near the sight. He said he was sorry the rest of his life he done that. He got a pension too. He was blind and always was sorry for his disobedience. He said he was scared so bad he 'bout leave die then as go into the battlefield.

"In some ways times is better. People are no better. Children jus' growing up wild. Their education is of the head and not their heart and hands.

"I was raised around Little Rock is about right. I gets a pension. I'm sixty-two years old but I was down sick with nerve trouble several years. I'm better now. I've been gradually coming on up for over a year now.

"Mr. Ernest Harper of Little Rock takes out truckloads of black folks to work on his place in the country every day. They can get work that way if they can work."

Interviewer: Bernice Bowden
Person interviewed: "Wash" Dukes
2217 E. Barraque
Pine Bluff, Ark.
Age: 83

WASH DUKES

"Yes'm, Wash Dukes is my name. My mother liked Washington so well, she named me General Washington Dukes, but I said my name was Wash Dukes. I'm the oldest one and I'm still here. Me? I was born in the state of Georgia, Howson County. Perry, Georgia was my closest place. I was born and raised on the Riggins place. I was born in 1855, you understand. The first day of March is my birthday. We had it on the Bible, four boys and four girls, and I was the oldest. House caught fire and burned up the Bible, but I always say I'm as old as a hoss.

"I can't see as good as I used to—gettin' too old, I reckon.

"Old master and mistis was good to us.

"My mother plowed just like a man. Had a little black mule named Mollie and wore these big old leggins come up to her knee.

"Old master was a long tall man with black hair.

"You know I was here cause I remember when Lincoln was elected president. He run against George Washington.

"I seen the Yankees but I never talked to em. I was scared of em. Had them muskets with a spear on the end. They give my uncle a hoss. When it thundered and lightninged that old hoss started to dance—thought twas a battle. And when he come to a fence, just jump right over with me on him. I say, 'Where you get that hoss?' and uncle say, 'Yankees give him to me.'

"I know one time they was a fellow come by there walkin'. I guess they shot his hoss. He had plenty money. I tried to get him to give me some but he wouldn't give me a bit.

"At Oglethorpe they had a place where they kep the prisoners. They was a little stream run through it and the Rebels pizened it and killed a lot of em.

"I was so crazy when I was young. I know one time mama sent me to town to get a dress pattern—ten yards. She say, 'Now, Wash, when you go across that bottom, you'll hear somethin' sounds like somebody dyin', but you just go on, it won't hurt you.' But I say, 'I won't hear it.' I went through there so fast and come back, mama say, 'You done been to town already?' I said, 'Yes, here's your dress pattern.' I went through there ninety to nothin'. I went so fast my heart hurt me.

"In slave times I remember if you wanted to go to another plantation you had to have a pass. Paddyrollers nearly got me one night. I was on a hoss. They was shootin' at me. I know the hoss was just stretched out and I was layin' right down on his neck.

"I stayed in Georgia till '74. I heared em say the cotton grow so big here in Arkansas you could sit on a limb and eat dinner. I know when I got here they was havin' that Brooks-Baxter war in Little Rock. I say, 'Press me into the war.' Man say, 'I ain't goin' press no boys.' I say, 'Give me a gun, I can kill em.' I wanted to fight.

"I tell you where I voted—colored folks don't vote now—it was when I was on the Davis place. I voted once or twice since I been up here. I called myself votin' Republican. I member since I been up here you know they had a colored man in the courthouse. When they had a grand jury they had em mixed, some colored and some white. I say now they ain't got no privilege. If they don't want em to vote ought not make em pay taxes.

"Up north they all sits together in the deppo but here in the south they got a 'tition between em.

"When I first went to farmin' I rented the land and the cotton was all mine, but now you work on the shares and don't have nothin'.

"If I keep a livin', I'm goin' away from here. I'm goin' up north. I won't go fore it gets warm though. I seen the snow knee deep in Cleveland, Ohio.

"I was workin' up north once. I had a pretty good job in Detroit doin' piece work, and doin' well, but I come back here cause my wife's mother was too old to move. If I had stayed I might have done well.

"I own this property but I'm bout to lose it on account o' taxes.

"I got grown boys and they ain't no more help to

me than the spit out o' my mouth. None of em has ever give me a dime in their life. This younger generation is goin' to nothin'. They got a good education. I got a boy can write six different kinds a hands. Write enough to get in the pen. I got him pardoned and he's in Philadelphia now. Never sends me a dime.

"I never went to any school but night school a little. I was the oldest and it kep me knockin' around to help take care of the little ones.

"I preach sometimes. I'm not ordained—I'm a floor preacher, just stands in front of the altar."

Interviewer: Miss Irene Robertson
Person interviewed: Lizzie Dunn, Clarendon, Arkansas
Age: 88

LIZZIE DUNN

"I was born close to Hernando, Mississippi. My parents was Cassie Gillahm and Ely Gillahm. My master was John Gillahm. I fell to John Gillahm and Tim bought me from him so I could be with my mother. I was a young baby. Bill Gillahm was our old master. He might had a big farm but I was raised on a small farm. White folks raised me. They put me to sewing young. I sewed with my fingers. I could sew mighty nice. My mistress had a machine she screwed on a table.

"All the Gillahms went to Louisiana in war time and left the women with youngest white master. They was trying to keep their slaves from scattering. They were so sure that the War would be lost.

"The Yankees camped close to us but didn't bother my white folks to hurt them. They et them out time and ag'in. I seen the Yankees every day. I seen the cannons and cavalry a mile long. The sound was like eternity had turned loose. Everything shook like earthquakes day and night. The light was bright and red and smoke terrible.

"Mother cooked and we et from our master's table.

"We was all scared when the War was on and glad

it was over. Mama died at the close. Me and my sister sharecropped and made seven bales of cotton in one year.

"When freedom come on, our master and mistress told us. We all cried. Miss Mollie was next to our own mother. She raised us. We kept on their place.

"I cooked for Joe Campbell at Forrest City. He had one boy I help to raise. They think well of me."

Interviewer's Comment

Very light mulatto. Bed fast and had two rolls and a cup of coffee. Had been alone all day except when Home Aid girls bathed and cleaned her bed. She is paralyzed. She said she was hungry.

Interviewer: Mrs. Bernice Bowden
Person interviewed: Nellie Dunne
3900 W. Sixth Avenue, Pine Bluff, Arkansas
Age: 78

NELLIE DUNNE

"Yes ma'am, I was slavery born but free raised. I was half as big as I is now. (She is not much over four feet tall—ed.) Born in Silver Creek, Mississippi. Yes ma'am. They give ever'body on the place their ages but mama said it wasn't no 'count and tore it up, so I don't know what year I was born.

"Cy Magby—mama was under his control. He would carry us over to the white folks' house every morning to see Miss Becky. When old master come after us, he'd say, 'What you gwine say?' and we'd say, 'One-two-three.' Then we'd go over to old Mis' and courtesy and say, 'Good morning, Miss Becky; good morning, Mars Albert; good morning, Mars Wardly.' They was just little old kids but we had to call 'em Mars.

"What I know I'm gwine tell you, but you ain't gwine ketch me in no tale.

"I 'member they was gwine put us to carryin' water for the hands next year, and that year we got free. My mother shouted, 'Now I ain't lyin' 'bout dat.' I sure 'member when they sot the people free. They was just ready to blow the folks out to the field. I 'member old Mose would blow the bugle and he could blow that bugle.

If you wasn't in, you better get in. Yes ma'am! The day freedom come, I know Mose was just ready to blow the bugle when the Yankees begun to beat the drum down the road. They knowed it was all over then. That ain't no joke.

"I was a full grown woman then I come to Arkansas; I wasn't no baby.

"I went to school one month in my life. That was in Mississippi.

"My Joe" (her husband) "just lack one year bein' a graduate. He went up here to that Branch Normal. That boy had good learnin'. He could a learnt me but he was too high tempered. If I missed a word he would be so crabb'y. So one night I throwed the book across the room and said, 'You don't need try to learn me no more.'"

Interviewer: Samuel S. Taylor
Person interviewed: William L. Dunwoody
2116 W. 24th Street, Little Rock, Arkansas
Age: About 98

WILLIAM L. DUNWOODY

[HW: Remembers Jeff Davis]

"I was born in Charleston, South Carolina, in the year 1840.

"My father was killed in the Civil War when they taken South Carolina. His name was Charles Dunwoody. My mother's name was Mary Dunwoody. My father was a free man and my mother was a slave. When he courted and married her he took the name of Dunwoody.

Houses

"Ain't you seen a house built in the country when they were clearing up and wanted to put up somethin' for the men to live in while they were working? They'd cut down a tree. Then they'd line it—fasten a piece of twine to each end and whiten it and pull it up and let it fly down and mark the log. Then they'd score it with axes. Then the hewers would come along and hew the log. Sometimes they could hew it so straight you couldn't put a line on it and find any difference. Where they didn't take time with the logs, it would be where they were just putting up a little shack for the men to sleep in.

"Just like you box timber in the sawmill, the men would straighten out a log.

"To make the log house, you would saw your blocks, set em up, then you put the sills on the blocks, then you put the sleepers. When you get them in, lay the planks to walk on. Then they put on the first log. You notch it. To make the roof, you would keep on cutting the logs in half first one way and then the other until you got the blocks small enough for shingles. Then you would saw the shingles off. They had plenty of time.

Food

"The slaves ate just what the master ate. They ate the same on my master's place. All people didn't farm alike. Some just raised cotton and corn. Some raised peas, oats, rye, and a lot of different things. My old master raised corn, potatoes—Irish and sweet—, goober peas (peanuts), rye, and wheat, and I can't remember what else. That's in the eating line. He had hogs, goats, sheep, cows, chickens, turkeys, geese, ducks. That is all I can remember in the eating line. My old master's slaves et anything he raised.

"He would send three or four wagons down to the mill at a time. One of them would carry sacks; all the rest would carry wheat. You know flour seconds, shorts and brand come from the wheat. You get all that from the wheat. Buckwheat flour comes from a large grained wheat. The wagons came back loaded with flour, seconds, shorts and brand. The old man had six wheat barns to keep the wheat in.

"All the slaves ate together. They had a cook special

for them. This cook would cook in a long house more than thirty feet long. Two or three women would work there and a man, just like the cooks would in a hotel now. All the working hands ate there and got whatever the cook gave them. It was one thing one time and another another. The cook gave the hands anything that was raised on the place. There was one woman in there cooking that was called 'Mammy' and she seed to all the chilen.

Feeding the Children

"After the old folks among the slaves had had their breakfast, the cook would blow a horn. That would be about nine o'clock or eight. All the children that were big enough would come to the cook shack. Some of them would bring small children that had been weaned but couldn't look after themselves. The cook would serve them whatever the old folks had for breakfast. They ate out of the same kind of dishes as the old folks.

"Between ten and eleven o'clock, the cook would blow the horn again and the children would come in from play. There would be a large bowl and a large spoon for each group of larger children. There would be enough children in each group to get around the bowl comfortably. One would take a spoon of what was in the bowl and then pass the spoon to his neighbor. His neighbor would take a spoonful and then pass the spoon on, and so on until everyone would have a spoonful. Then they would begin again, and so on until the bowl was empty. If they did not have enough then, the cook would put some more in the bowl. Most of the time, bread and milk was in the bowl; sometimes mush and milk.

"There was a small spoon and a small bowl for the smaller children in the group that the big children would use for them and pass around just like they passed around the big spoon.

"About two or three o'clock, the cook would blow the horn again. Time the children all got in there and et, it would be four or five o'clock. The old mammy would cut up greens real fine and cut up meat into little pieces and boil it with corn-meal dumplings. They'd call it pepper pot. Then she'd put some of the pepper pot into the bowls and we'd eat it. And it was good.

"After the large children had et, they would go back to see after the babies. If they were awake, the large children would put on their clothes and clean them up. Then where there was a woman who had two or three small children and didn't have one large enough to do this, they'd give her a large one from some other family to look after her children. If she had any relatives, they would use their children for her. If she didn't then they would use anybody's children.

"About eleven o'clock all the women who had little children that had not been weaned would come in to see after them and let them suck. When a woman had nursing children, she would nurse them before she went to work, again at around eleven o'clock and again when she came from work in the evening. She would come in long before sundown. In between times, the old mammy and the other children would look after them.

War Memories

"I saw Jeff Davis once. He was one-eyed. He had a glass eye. My old mistiss had three girls. They got into the buggy and went to see Jeff Davis when he come through Auburn, Alabama. We were living in Auburn then. I drove them. Jeff Davis came through first, and then the Confederate army, and then the Yankees. They didn't come on the same day but some days apart.

"The way I happened to see the Yanks was like this. I went to carry some clothes to my young master. He was a doctor, and was out where they were drilling the men. I laid down on the carpet in his tent and I heard music playing 'In Dixie Land I'll take my stand and live and die in Dixie.' I got up and come out and looked up ever which way but I couldn't see nothing. I went back again and laid down again in the tent, and I heard it again. I run out and looked all up and around again, and I still couldn't see nothin'. That time I looked and saw my young master talking to another officer—I can't remember his name. My young master said, 'What you looking for?'

"I said, 'I'm looking for them angels I hear playing. Don't you hear em playing Dixie?' The other officer said, 'Celas, you ought to whip that nigger.' I went back into the tent. My young master said, 'Whip him for what?' And he said, 'For telling that lie.' My young master said to him like this, 'He don't tell lies. He heard something somewhere.'

"Then they got through talking and he come on in and I seed him and beckoned to him. He came to me and I said, 'Lie down there.' He laid down and I laid down with him, and he heard it. Then he said, 'Look out there and tell him to come in.'

"I called the other officer and he come in. The doctor (that was my young master) said, 'Lie down there.' When he laid down by my young master, he heard it too. Then the doctor said to him, 'You said William was telling a damn lie.' He said, 'I beg your pardon, doctor.'

"My young master got up and said, 'Where is my spy glasses? Le'me have a look.' He went out and there was a mountain called the Blue Ridge Mountain. He looked but he didn't see nothin'. I went out and looked too. I said, 'Look down the line beside those two big trees,' and I handed the glasses back to him. He looked and then he hollered, 'My God, look yonder' and handed the spy glasses to the other officer. He looked too. Then the doctor said, 'What are we going to do?' He said, 'I am goin' to put pickets way out.' He told me to get to my mule. I got. He put one of his spurs on my foot and told me to go home and tell 'ma' the Yanks were coming. You know what 'ma' he was talking about? That was his wife's mother. We all called her 'mother.'

"I carried the note. When I got to Mrs. Dobbins' house, I yelled, 'The Yanks are coming—Yankees, Yankees, Yankees!' She had two boys. They runned out and said, 'What did you say?'

"I said, 'Yankees, Yankees!'

"They said, 'Hell, what could he see?'

"I come on then and got against Miss Yancy's. She had a son, a man named Henry Yancy. He had a sore leg. He asked me what I said. I told him that the Yanks were coming. He called for Henry, a boy that stayed with him, and had him saddle his horse. Then he got on it and rode up town. When he got up there, he was questioned bout how did he know it. Did he see them. He said he didn't see them, that Celas Neal saw them and the doctor's mother's boy brought the message. Then he taken off.

"Jeff Davis went on. The Confederates went on. They all went on. Then the Yanks passed through.

"The first fight they had there, they cleaned up the Sixty-Ninth Alabama troops. My young master had been helping drill them. He went on and overtook the others.

Right After the War

"I am not sure just what we did immediately after freedom. I don't know whether it was a year or whether it was a year and a half. I can just go by my mother. After freedom, we came from Auburn, Alabama to Opelika, Alabama, and she went to cooking at a hotel until she got money enough for what she wanted to do. When she got fixed, she moved then to Columbus, Georgia. She rented a place from Ned Burns, a policeman. When that place gave out, she went to washing and ironing. Sterling Love rented a house from the same man. He had four children and they were going to school and they took me too.

Schooling

"I fixed up and went to school with them. I didn't get no learning at all in slavery times.

How Freedom Came

"I don't know whether all the whites did it or not; but I know this—when they quit fighting, I know the white children called we little children and all the grown people who worked around the house and said, 'You all is jus' as free as we is. You ain't got no master and no mistiss,' and I don't know what they told them at the plantation.

Occupation

"Right after the War, my mother worked—washed—for an old white man. He took an interest in me and taught me. I did little things for him. When he died, I took up the teaching which he had been doing.

"At first I taught in Columbus, Georgia. By and by, a white man came along looking for laborers for this part of the country. He said money grew on bushes out here. He cleaned out the place. All the children and all the grown folks followed him. Two of my boys came to me and told me they were coming. We hoboed on freights and walked to Chattanooga, Tennessee. We stayed there awhile. Then a white man came along getting laborers. I never kept the year nor nothin'. He brought us to Lonoke County, and I got work on The Bood Bar Plantation. Squirrels, wild things, cotton and corn, plenty of it. So you see, the man told the truth when he said money grew on bushes.

"I taught and farmed all my life. Farming is the greatest occupation. It supports the teacher, the preacher, the lawyer, the doctor. None of them can live without it.

"I can't do much now since that lady knocked me

down with her automobile and made me a cripple. I'd a been all right if so many of them young doctors hadn't experimented on me. Then I can't see good out of one eye. I can't do much now. I don't know why they won't give me a pension."

Interviewer's Comment

William Dunwoody had some of his dates and occurrences mixed up as would be natural for a man ninety-eight years old. But there was one respect in which he was sharper than anyone else interviewed.

At the close of the first day's interview when I arose to go he said to me, "Now you got what you want?" I told him yes and that I would be back for more the next day. Then he said, "Well, if you got what you want, there's one thing I want you to do for me before you go."

"Certainly, Brother Dunwoody," I said, "I'll be glad to do anything you want me to do. Just what can I do for you?"

"Well," he said, "I want you to read me what you been writin' there."

And I read it.

A little grandchild about four years old kept us company while he dictated to me. I furnished pennies for the child's candy and a nickel for the old man's tobacco.

The old man got a kick out of the dictation. After the first day, he became very cautious. He would say, "Now don't write this," and he wouldn't let me take it down the way he said it. Instead, he would make a long statement and then we would work out the gist of it together. He is not highly schooled, and he is not especially prepossessing in appearance; but he is a long way from decrepit—mentally.

He walks with a crutch and has a defect in the sight of one eye. He has good hearing and talks in a pleasant voice.

Interviewer: Miss Irene Robertson
Person interviewed: Lucius Edwards
Age: 72

LUCIUS EDWARDS

Interviewer's Comment

I went to see Lucius Edwards, age seventy-two, twice. He has colitis. He wouldn't tell me anything. He said he was born in Shreveport, Louisiana and his father took him away so young he knew no mother; his aunt raised him. The first day he said he remembered all that about his parents' owners. The next day the nurse had him cleaned up and nice meals were sent in and still he wouldn't tell us anything. He told the nurse he had farmed and worked on the railroad all his life. He was up but wouldn't tell us anything. He told me, "I don't think I ever voted." We decided he might be afraid he'd twist his tales and we'd catch him some way.

United States. Work Projects Administration

Interviewer: Mary D. Hudgins
Person Interviewed: John Elliott
Age: 80
Home: South Border (property of brother's estate)

JOHN ELLIOTT

As told by: John Elliott

"No, ma'am. I ain't got no folks. They've all died out. My son, he may be alive. When I last heard from him, he was in Pine Bluff. But I wrote down lots of times and nobody can't find him. Brother said, that was before he died, that I could stay on in the place as long as I lived. His wife come to see me some years back and she said it was that way.

The comodity gives me milk, and a little beside. I'm expectin' to hear if I get the pension, Tuesday. No ma'am, I ain't worked in three years. Yes, ma'am, I was a slave. I was about 8 years old when they mustered 'em out the last time.

My daddy went along to take care of his young master. He died, and my daddy brought his horse and all his belongings home.

You see it was this way. My mother was a run-away slave. She was from, what's that big state off there—Virginia—yes, ma'am, that's it. There was a pretty good flock of them. They came into North Carolina—Wayne

County was where John Elliott found them. They was in a pretty bad way. They didn't have no place to go and they didn't have nothing to eat. They didn't have nobody to own 'em. They didn't know what to do. My mother was about 13.

By some means or other they met up with a man named John Elliott. He was a teacher. He struck a bargain with them. He pitched in and he bought 200 acres of land. He built a big house for Miss Polly and Bunk and Margaret. Miss Polly was his sister. And he built cabins for the black folks.

And he says 'You stay here, and you take care of Miss Polly and the children. Now mind, you raise lots to eat. You take care of the place too. And if anybody bothers you you tell Miss Polly.' My Uncle Mose, he was the oldest. He was a blacksmith. Jacob was the carpenter. 'Now look here, Mose,' says Mister John, 'you raise plenty of hogs. Mind you give all the folks plenty of meat. Then you take the rest to Miss Polly and let her lock it in the smokehouse.' Miss Polly carried the key, but Mose was head man and had dominion over the smokehouse.

They didn't get money to any extreme. But whatever they wanted, Miss Polly would go along with them and they would buy it. They went to Goldsboro. That was the biggest town near us. The patrollers never bothered any of us. Once or twice they tried it. But Miss Polly wrote to Mr. John. He'd write it all down like it ought to be. Then they didn't bother us any more.

There was no speculation wid 'em like there was with other negro people. They never had to go to the hiring ground. Mr. John built a church for my mother and the other women who was running mates with her. And he built a school for the children. Some other colored children tried to come to the school too. They was welcome. But sometimes the white folks would tear up the books of the colored children from outside that tried to come.

Our folks stayed on and on. Mr. John was off teaching school most of the time. We stayed on and on. Pretty soon there was about 150-200, of us. Some of them was carpenters and some of them was this and some was that. Mr. John even put in a mill. A groundhog saw mill, it was. Some white men put it in. But it was the colored folks who run it. They all stayed right on on the farm. There wasn't any white folks about at all, except Miss Polly and Bunk and Margaret.

No, ma'am, after the war it didn't make much difference. We all stayed on. We worked the place. And when we got a chance, Mr. John let us hire out and keep the money. And if the folks wouldn't pay us, Mr. John would write the Federal and the Federal would see that we got our money for what we had worked. Mr. John was a mighty good man to us.

No ma'am. Nobody got discontented for a long time. Then some men come in and messed them up. Told us that we could make more money other places. And it was true too—if they had let us get the money. By that time Mr. John, had died. Bunk had died too, Miss Margaret had grown up and married. Her husband was managing the farm. He was good, but he wasn't like Mr. John. So lots of us moved away.

But about not making money. Take me. I raised 14-16 bales of cotton. The man who owned the land, I worked on halvers, sold it on the Liverpool market. But he wouldn't pay me but about 1/3 of what he collected on my half. And I says to him, 'You gets full price for your half, why can't I get full price for mine?' And he says, 'It's against the rules.' And I says, 'It ain't fair! And he says, 'It's the rules.' So after about six years I quit farming. You can't make no money that way. Yes—you make it, but you can't get it.

I went to town at Pine Bluff. There I got to mixing concrete. I made pretty good at it, too. I stayed on for some years. Then I came to Hot Springs. My brother was along with me. We both worked and after work we built a house. It took us four years. But it was a good house. It has six rooms in it. It makes a good home. My brother had the deed. But his widow says I can stay on. The folks what lives in the rest of the house are good to me.

When I got to Hot Springs I worked mixing concrete. There was lots of sidewalks being made along about that time. Then I scatter dirt all around where the court house is now. Then I worked at both of the very biggest hotels. I washed. I washed cream pitchers—the little ones with corners that were hard to clean.

No, I ain't worked in three years. It hard to try to get along. Some states, they pays good pensions. I can't be here long—don't look like I can be here long. Seems as if they could take care of me for the few days I'm going to be on this earth. Seems like they could.

Interviewer: Mrs. Carol Graham
Person interviewed: Millie Evans
Age:

United States. Work Projects Administration

MILLIE EVANS

Yo' say yo' is in'rested in the lives of the slaves? Well, Miss, I is one of 'em. Was born in 1849 but I don' know jus' when. My birthday comes in fodder pullin' time cause my ma said she was pullin up till bout a hour 'fore I was born. Was born in North Carolina and was a young lady at the time of surrender.

I don' 'member ol' master's name; all I 'member is that we call 'em ol' master an ol' mistress. They had bout a hundred niggers and they was rich. Master always tended the men and mistress tended to us.

Ev'y mornin' bout fo' 'clock ol' master would ring de bell for us to git up by an yo could hear dat bell ringin all over de plantation. I can hear hit now. Hit would go ting-a-ling, ting-a-ling and I can see 'em now stirrin in Carolina. I git so lonesome when I thinks bout times we used to have. Twas better livin back yonder than now.

I stayed with my ma every night but my mistress raised me. My ma had to work hard so ev'y time ol' mistress thought we little black chilluns was hungry 'tween meals she would call us up to the house to eat. Sometime she would give us johnny cake an plenty of buttermilk to drink wid it. They had a long trough fo' us dat day would keep so clean. They would fill dis trough wid buttermilk and all us chillun would git roun' th' trough an drink wid our mouths an hol' our johnny cake wid our han's. I can jus' see myself drinkin' now. Hit was so good. There was so many black fo'ks to cook fuh that the cookin was done outdoors. Greens was cooked in a big black washpot jus' like yo' boils clothes in now. An' sometime they would crumble bread in the potlicker an give us spoons an we would stan' roun' the pot an' eat. When we et our regular meals the table was set under a chinaberry tree wid a oil cloth table cloth on when dey called us to th' table they would ring the bell. But we didn' eat out'n plates. We et out of gourds an had ho'made wood spoons. An' we had plenty t'eat. Whooo-eee! Jus' plenty t'eat. Ol' master's folks raised plenty o' meat an dey raise dey sugar, rice, peas, chickens, eggs, cows an' jus' ev'ything good t'eat.

Ev'y ev'nin' at three 'clock ol' mistress would call all us litsy bitsy chillun in an we would lay down on pallets an have to go to sleep. I can hear her now singin' to us piccaninnies:

> "Hush-a-bye, bye-yo'-bye, mammy's piccaninnies
> Way beneath the silver shining moon
> Hush-a-bye, bye-yo'-bye, mammy's piccaninnies
> Daddy's little Carolina coons
> Now go to sleep yo' little piccaninnies."

When I got big 'nough I nursed my mistress's baby. When de baby go to sleep in de evenin' I woul' put hit in de cradle an' lay down by de cradle an go to sleep. I played a heap when I was little. We played Susannah Gal, jump rope, callin' cows, runnin', jumpin', skippin', an jus' ev'ythin' we could think of. When I got big 'nough to cook, I cooked den.

The kitchen of the big house was built way off f'om the house and we cooked on a great big ol' fi' place. We had swing pots an would swing 'em over the fire an cook an had a big ol' skillet wi' legs on hit. We call hit a ubben an cooked bread an cakes in it.

We had the bes' mistress an master in the worl' and they was Christian fo'ks an they taught us to be Christianlike too. Ev'y Sunday mornin' ol' master would have all us niggers to the house while he would sing an pray an read de Bible to us all. Ol' master taught us not to be bad; he taught us to be good; he tol' us to never steal nor to tell false tales an not to do anythin' that was bad. He said: Yo' will reap what yo' sow, that you sow it single an' reap double. I learnt that when I was a little chile an I ain't fo'got it yet. When I got grown I went de Baptist way. God called my pa to preach an ol' master let him preach in de kitchen an in the back yard under th' trees. On preachin' day ol' master took his whole family an all th' slaves to church wid him.

We had log school houses in them days an fo'ks learnt more than they does in the bricks t'day.

Down in the quarters ev'y black family had a one or two room log cabin. We didn' have no floors in them cabins. Nice dirt floors was de style then an we used sage brooms. Took a string an tied the sage together an had a nice broom out'n that. We would gather broom sage fo' our winter brooms jus' like we gathered our other winter stuff. We kep' our dirt floors swep' as clean an' white. An our bed was big an tall an had little beds to push under there. They was all little er nough to go under de other an in th' daytime we would push 'em all under the big one an make heaps of room. Our beds was stuffed wid hay an straw an shucks an b'lieve me chile they sho' slep' good.

When the boys would start to the quarters from th'

fiel' they would get a turn of lider knots. I specks yo' knows 'em as pine knots. That was what we use' fo' light. When our fire went out we had no fire. Didn' know nothin' bout no matches. To start a fire we would take a skillet lid an a piece of cotton an a flint rock. Lay de cotton on th' skillet lid an' take a piece of iron an beat the flint rock till the fire would come. Sometime we would beat fo' thirty minutes before the fire would come an start the cotton then we woul' light our pine.

Up at th' big house we didn' use lider knots but used tallow candles for lights. We made the candles f'om tallow that we took f'om cows. We had moulds and would put string in there an leave the en' stickin' out to light an melt the tallow an pour it down aroun' th' string in the mould.

We use to play at night by moonlight and I can recollec' singin wid the fiddle. Oh, Lord, dat fiddle could almos' talk an I can hear it ringin now. Sometime we would dance in the moonlight too.

Ol' master raised lots of cotton and the women fo'ks carded an spun an wove cloth, then they dyed hit an made clothes. An we knit all the stockin's we wo'. They made their dye too, f'om diffe'nt kin's of bark an leaves an things. Dey would take the bark an boil it an strain it up an let it stan' a day then wet the 'terial in col' water an shake hit out an drop in the boilin' dye an let it set bout twenty minutes then take it out an hang it up an let it dry right out of that dye. Then rinse it in col' water an let it dry then it woul' be ready to make.

I'll tell yo' how to dye. A little beech bark dyes slate color set with copperas. Hickory bark and bay leaves dye yellow set with chamber lye; bamboo dyes turkey red, set color wid copperas. Pine straw dyes purple, set color with chamber lye. To dye cloth brown we would take de cloth an put it in the water where leather had been tanned an let it soak then set the color with apple vinegar. An we dyed blue wid indigo an set the color wid alum.

We wo' draws made out of termestic that come down longer than our dresses an we wo' seven petticoats in the winter wid sleeves in dem petticoats in the winter an the boys wo' big ol' long shirts. They didn' know nothin bout no britches till they was great big, jus' wen' roun' in dey shirttails. An we all wo' shoes cause my pa made shoes.

Master taught pa to make shoes an the way he done, they killed a cow an took the hide an tanned it. The way they tanned it was to take red oak bark and put in vats made somethin' like troughs that held water. Firs' he would put in a layer of leather an a layer of oak ashes an a layer of leather an a layer of oak ashes till he got it all in an cover with water. After that he let it soak till the hair come off the hide. Then he would take the hide out an it was ready for tannin'. Then the hide was put to soak in with the red oak bark. It stayed in the water till the hide turned tan then pa took the hide out of the red oak dye an it was a purty tan. It didn' have to soak long. Then he would get his pattern an cut an make tan shoes out'n the tanned hides. We called 'em brogans.

They planted indigo an it growed jus' like wheat. When it got ripe they gathered it an we would put it in a barrel an let it soak bout a week then we woul' take the indigo stems out an squeeze all the juice out of 'em an put the juice back in the barrel an let it stan' bout nother week, then we jus' stirred an stirred one whole day. We let it set three or four days then drained the water off an left the settlings and the settlings was blueing jus' like we have these days. We cut ours in little blocks an we dyed clothes wid it too.

We made vinegar out of apples. Took over ripe apples an ground 'em up an put 'em in a sack an let drip. Didn' add no water an when it got through drippin we let it sour an strained an let it stan for six months an had some of the bes vinegar ever made.

We had homemade tubs and didn' have no wash boa'ds. We had a block an battlin' stick. We put our clo'es in soak then took 'em out of soak an lay them on the block an take the battling stick an battle the dirt out of 'em. We mos'ly used rattan vines for clotheslines an they made the bes clo'es lines they was.

Ol' master raised big patches of tobaccy an when dey gather it they let it dry an then put it in lasses. After the lasses dripped off then they roll hit up an twisted it an let it dry in the sun 10 or 12 days. It sho' was ready for some and chewin an hit was sweet an stuck together so yo' could chew an spit an 'joy hit.

The way we got our perfume we took rose leaves, cape jasmines an sweet bazil an laid dem wid our clo'es an let 'em stay three or fo' days then we had good smellin' clo'es that would las' too.

When there was distressful news master would ring the bell. When the niggers in the fiel' would hear the bell everyone would lis'en an wonder what the trouble was. You'd see 'em stirrin' too. They would always ring the bell at twelve 'clock. Sometime then they would think it was some thin' serious an they would stan up straight but if they could see they shadow right under 'em they would know it was time for dinner.

The reason so many white folks was rich was they made money an didn' have nothin' to do but save it. They made money an raised ev'ything they used, an jus' didn' have no use fo' money. Didn' have no banks in them days an master buried his money.

The floo's in the big house was so pretty an white. We always kep' them scoured good. We didn' know what it was to use soap. We jus' took oak ashes out of the fi'place and sprinkled them on the floo' and scoured with a corn shuck mop. Then we would sweep the ashes off an rinse two times an let it dry. When it dried it was the cleanes' floo' they was. To make it white, clean sand was sprinkled on the floo' an we let it stay a couple of days then the floo' would be too clean to walk on. The way we dried the floo' was with a sack an a rag. We would get down on our knees an dry it so dry.

I 'member one night one of ol' master's girls was goin' to get married. That was after I was big 'nough to cook an we was sho' doin' some cookin. Some of the niggers on the place jus' natchally would steal so we cook a big cake of co'n-bread an iced it all pretty an put it out to cool an some of 'em stole it. This way old master found out who was doin the stealin cause it was such a joke on 'em they had to tell.

All ol' master's niggers was married by the white preacher but he had a neighbor who would marry his niggers hisself. He would say to the man: "Do yo' want this woman?" and to the girl, "Do yo' want this boy?"

Then he would call the ol' mistress to fetch the broom an ol' master would hold one end an ol' mistress the other an tell the boy and girl to jump dis broom and he would say: "Dat's yo' wife." Dey called marryin' like that jumpin the broom.

Now chile I can't 'member everything I done in them days but we didn' have ter worry bout nothin. Ol' mistress was the one to worry. Twasn't then like it is now, no twasn't. We had such a good time an ev'ybody cried when the Yankees cried out: "Free." Tother niggers say dey had a hard time 'fo' dey was free but twas then like tis now. If you had a hard time we don it ourselves.

Ol' master didn' want to part with his niggers an the niggers didn' wan' to part with ol' master so they thought by comin to Arkansas they would have a chance to keep 'em. So they got on their way. We loaded up our wagons an put up our wagon sheet an we had plenty to eat an plenty of horse feed. We traveled bout 15 or 20 miles a day an would stop an camp at night. We would cook enough in the morning to las' all day. The cows was drove t'gether. Some was gentle an some was not an did dey have a time. I mean, dey had a time. While we was on our way ol' master died an three of the slaves died too. We buried the slaves there but we camped while ol' master was carried back to North Carolina. When ol' mistress come back we started on to Arkansas an reached here safe but when we got here we foun' freedom here too. Ol' mistress begged us to stay wid her an we stayed till she died then they took her back to Carolina. There wasn' nobody lef' but Miss Nancy an she soon married an lef' an I los' track of her an Mr. Tom.

El Dorado District
FOLKLORE SUBJECTS
Name of Interviewer: Pernella Anderson
Subjects: Customs related to Slavery Time [HW: Ex Slave Story]
Subject: Food—Particular foods typical and characteristic of certain
localities and certain people (negroes)
[Nov 6 1936]

This information given by: Millie Evans (Negroes pronounce it Irvins)
Place of Residence: By Missouri Pacific Track near MOP Shops
Occupation: None
Age: 87

[TR: Additional topic moved from subsequent page.]
[TR: Personal information moved from bottom of interview.]

MILLIE EVANS

I wuz a young lady in the time of surrender. I am a slave chile. I am one of them. I had a gran' time in slavery time. I wuz born wid de white foks. I stayed wid mah muthah at night but mah mistress raised me. I nussed mah mutha's gran'chile. I churned and sot de table. When de baby go to sleep in de evenin' I put hit in de cradle. An' I'd lay down by the cradle and go to sleep. Every evenin' I'd go git lida knots. I played a lots. I wuz born 1849. We played Susanna Gals, and we just played jump rope. Jes' we gals did. We played calling' cows. Dey'd come to us and we run from um. My [TR: 'I' corrected to 'My'] mistess wuz a millionaire. I went to school a while. I can count only lit bit. One uz de girl made fun uz me. She kotch me nodding and we fit dare in de school house. Old log school house. Dey had two big rooms. Ah went to de ole fokes' church. Young un too. We'd cry if we didn't git ter go ter church wid ma and pa.

Our table was sot under a china berry tree and ooo-eee chile I can see hit now. We et on a loal (oil) table cloth. When dey called us to de table dey would ring a bell. We didn' eat out uz plates. We et outn gourds. We all et outn gourds. When I got big nuff ter cook I cooked den. We had plenty to eat. We raised who-eee plenty meat. We raised our sugar, rice, peas, chikens, eggs, cows. Who-eee chile we had plenty to eat. Our mistess had ovah a hunert (100) niggers. Ole moster nevah did whip none uv us niggers. He tended de men and mistess always tended to us. I wudden (wasn't) quite grown when I wuz married. We cooked out in de yard an' on fireplaces too in dose big ubbens (ovens). We cooked greens in a wash pot jes like you boil clothes, dats de way we cook greens. We cooked ash cakes too an we cooked persimmon braid (bread). An evah thing we had wuz good too. We made our churns in dem days. Made dem outn cypress.

Evahbody cried when dem yankees cried out: "Free." We cried too; we hated hit so bad. We had such a good time. I is gittin so ole I can't member so ever' thin' I done. Now chile ah cain't member evah' thin' I done but in dem days we didn' have ter worry 'bout nothin'. Ole mistress wuz de one ter worry. Twasn't den like hit is now. No Twasn't. Tother niggers say dey had er hard time foe dem Yankee cried "Free" but it waz den jes like hit is now if you had a hard time we done hit ourselves.

[HW: Negro food]

PERSIMMON PIE Make a crust like you would any other pie crust and take your persimmons and wash them. Let them be good and ripe. Get the seed out of them. Don't cook them. Mash them and put cinnamon and spice in and butter. Sugar to taste. Then roll your dough and put in custard pan, and then add the filling, then put a top crust on it, sprinkle a little sugar on top and bake.

PERSIMMON CORNBREAD Sift meal and add your ingredients then your persimmons that have been washed and the seeds taken out and mash them and put in and stir well together. Grease pan well and pour in and bake. Eat with fresh meat.

PERSIMMON BEER Gather your persimmons, wash and put in a keg, cover well with water and add about two cups of meal to it and let sour about three days. That makes a nice drink.

Boil persimmons just as you do prunes now day and they will answer for the same purpose.

ASH CAKE Two cups of meal and one teaspoon of salt and just enough hot water to make it stick together. Roll out in pones and wrap in a corn shuck or collard leaves or paper. Lay on hot ashes and cover with hot ashes and let cook about ten minutes.

CORNBREAD JOHNNY CAKE Two cups of meal, one half cup of flour about a teaspoon of soda, one cup of syrup, one-half teaspoon salt, beat well. Add teaspoon of lard. Pour in greased pan and bake.

[HW: Water or Milk added?]

(Old Mistress wud give us this corn bread johnny cake about four o'clock in de evening and give us plenty of buttermilk to drink wid it. Dey had a long trough. Dey kep' hit so clean fur us. Ev'ry evening about four dey would fill de trough full uv milk and wus abut 100 of us chilluns. We'd all get round de trough and drink wid our mouth and hold our johnny cake in our han's. I can jes see mahself drinkin now. It wus so good.)

BEEF DUMPLINS Take the brough (meaning broth) from boiled beef and season with salt, peper and add you dumplins jus as you would chicken dumplins.

Pick and wash beet tops just as you would turnip greens and cook with meat to season. Season to suit taste. This makes the best vegetable dish.

POTATO BISCUIT Two cups flour. Two teaspoons of baking powder, pinch of soda, teaspoon of salt, tablespoon of lard, two cups of cooked, well mashed sweet potatoes and milk to make a nice dough.

IRISH POTATO PIE Boil potatoes, set off and let cool, then mash well and add one cup sugar, two eggs, butter size of an egg, milk, spice to suit taste, bake in pie crust. Irish potatoes make a better pie than sweet potatoes.

Interviewer: Mary D. Hudgins
Person Interviewed: Mose Evans
Home: 451 Walnut
Aged: 76

MOSE EVANS

Radios from half a dozen houses blared out on the afternoon air. Ben[TR:?] Winslow was popular but ran a poor second to jazz bands in which moaning trombones predominated.

At one or two houses a knock or jangling bell had roused nobody. "They's all off at work," a neighbor usually volunteered. But in this block of comfortable cottages fronting on the paved section of Walnut evidently there were a goodly number of stay-at-homes. A mild prosperity seemed to pervade everything. The Walnut section is in the "old part of town". Some of the houses had evidently been built during the 90s; but they were well kept up and painted.

There was evidence here and there of former dependence on wells for water. One or two had been simply boarded over. One, a front yard affair had been ingeniously converted into a huge flower pot. The well had been filled in, its circular brick walls covered with a thick layer of cement. Into this, while still damp, had been pressed crystals. Even in January the vessel bore evidence of summer blooming.

"PREPARE TO MEET YOUR GOD" admonished the

electrified box sign attatched to the front porch of one dwelling. Its border was of black wood. The sign itself was of white frosted glass. Letters of the slogan were in scarlet.

Next doer was another religious reminder. It was a modest pasteboard window card and announced Bible Study at 2: P.M. daily.

Three blocks up Walnut the pavement ends. Beyond that sidewalks too, listlessly peter out. A young, but enthusiastically growing ditch is beginning to separate path from street. Houses begin to take on a more dilapidated appearance. They lean uncertainly.

A colored woman stops to stare at the white one, plants herself directly in the stranger's path and demands, "Is you the investigator? No? Well who is you looking for? Oh, Mose, he's at his son's. Good thing I stopped you. Cause you would have gone too far. He's at his son's. His grandson just done had his tonsils out. He's over there."

The interviewer climbed the ladder-like steps leading to "his son's house". No Mose wasn't there. He had just left. Maybe he'd gone home. The de-tonsiled child proved to be a bright eyed, saddle-colored youngster of three, enormously interested in the stranger. He wore whip-cord jodphurs—protruding widely on either side of his plump thighs—and knee high leather riding boots. Plump and smiling, he looked for all the world like a kewpie provided with a kink ey crown and blistered to a rich chocolate by a friendly sun.

The child eyed the interviewer's pencil. Since, she was carrying a "spare" she offered it to him. He smiled and accepted with alacrity. Later when the interviewer had found Mose and brought him back to the house to be questioned, the grandson brought forth his long new pencil and showed it with heartfelt pride.

On up the street went the interviewer. Arrived at 451 she approached the house through a yard strewn, with wood chips and piled with cordwood. Nobody answered her knock. Two blocks back toward town she was stopped by the same woman who had accosted her before. "Did you find him?" "No," replied the interviewer. "Well he's somewhere on the street. He's a'carrying a cane. You just stop any man you see with a cane and ask him if he ain't Mose Evans." The advice was sound/ The first elderly man coming north was carrying a cane. He was Mose Evans.

"So you-all got together?" called the officious neighbor. "Mose, you ought of asked her—when you see her coming up the street if she wasn't looking for you." "Maybe," said Mose, "but then I didn't know, and I don't want to butt into other folks business" "Huh," snorted the woman, "spose I hadn't butted in. Where'd you be. You wouldn't have found her and she wouldn't have found you!" Both Mose and the interviewer wore forced to admit that she was right—but from Mose's disapproving expression he, like the interviewer, was sorry of it.

"No, ma'am. I ain't been here long. Just about two weeks. You want to talk to me. Let's go on up to my son's house. We'll stop there. I's tired. Seems like I get tired awful quick. Had to go down to the store to get some coal." (He was carrying a paper sack of about two gallon capacity. "Coal" was probably charcoal—much favored among wash women for use in a small bucket-furnace for heating "flat-irons".) My wife has to work awful hard to earn enough, to buy enough coal and wood.

Did I say I'd been here two weeks? I meant I has been here two years. I's lived all over. Came here from Woodruff county. Yes, ma'am. I can't work no more. My wife she gets 2-3 days washing a week. Then she gets some bundles to bring home and do. She got sick, same as me and her brothers come on down to bring her up here to look after. They provided for me too. They took good care of us. Then one of 'em got sick himself, and the other he lost out in a money way. So she's a washing.

Can't remember very much about the war. I was just a little thing when it was a'going on. Was hardly any size at all. I does remember standing in the door of my mother's house and watching the soldiers go by. Men dressed in blue they was. Wasn't afraid of them—didn't have sense enough to be, I guess. Looked sort of pretty to me, dressed all in blue that way. And they was riding fine horses. Made a big noise they did. They was a'riding by in a sort of sweeping gallop. I won't never forgot it.

Guess Confederates passed too. I was too small to know about them. They was all soldiers to me. Folks told me they was on their way to Vicksburg. I heard tell that there was lots of fighting down around Vicksburg.

I was born on a place which belonged to a man named Thad Shackleford. Don't remember him very well. They took me away from his place when I was little. But I never did hear my mother say anything against him. Awful fine man, she said, awful fine man. I had lots of half sisters—5 of 'em and 6 half brothers. There was just one full sister.

Farm? Not until I was 14. Just stayed around the house and nursed the children. Nursed lots of children. Took care of them and amused them. Played with them. But for four, five, maybe six years I helped my mother farm. Went out into the fields and worked.

Then I went to myself. Yes, ma'am, I share cropped. Share cropped up until about 1908. By that time I had got together a pretty good lot and bought stock and tools. Then I rented—rented thirds and fourths. I liked that way lots best. It's best if a body can get himself stocked up.

But let me tell you, ma'am. It's a lot easier to get behind than it is to catch up. Falling behind is easy. Catching up ain't so simple. I sort of lost my health and then I had to sell my stock. After that it was share-crop again. I share cropped right up until 1935. That's when we come here.

Yes, ma'am we moved around a lot. Longest what I worked for any man was 12 years. He was J.W. Hill, the best man I ever did see. Once I rented from a colored man, but he died. Was with him 6 years before another man came into possession. Rented from Cockerill 4 years and Doss 2 years, and Doyle 3 years. But now I's like an old shoe. I's worn out. Been a good, faithful servant, but I's wore out."

United States. Work Projects Administration

Interviewer: S.S. Taylor
Person interviewed: Rachel Fairley
1600 Brown St.
Little Rock, Ark.
Age: 75
Occupation: General Housework
[Jan 23 1938]

RACHEL FAIRLEY

[HW: Mother Stole to Get Food]

"My mother said she had a hard time getting through. Had to steal half the time; had to put her head under the pot and pray for freedom. It was a large pot which she used to cook in on the yard. She would set it aside when she got through and put it down and put her head under it to pray.

"My father, when nine years old, was put on the speculator's block and sold at Charlottesville, North Carolina. My mother was sold on the same day. They sold her to a man named Paul Barringer, and refugeed her to a place near Sardis, Mississippi, to the cotton country. Before he was sold, my father belonged to the Greers in Charlottesville. I don't know who owned my mother. I never did hear her say how old she was when she was sold. They was auctioned off just like you would sell goods. One would holler one price and another would holler another, and the highest bid would get the slave.

"Mother did not go clear to Sardis but to a plantation ten miles from Sardis. This was before freedom. We stayed there till two years after freedom.

"I remember when my mother moved. I had never seen a wagon before. I was so uplifted, I had to walk a while and ride a while. We'd never seen a wagon nor a train neither. McKeever was the place where she moved from when she moved to Sardis.

"The first year she got free, she started sharecropping on the place. The next year she moved. That was the year she moved to Sardis itself. There she made sharecrops. That was the third year after freedom. That is what my father and mother called it, sharecropping. I don't know what their share was. But I guess it was half to them and half to him.

"I do general housework. I been doing that for eleven years. I never have any trouble. Whenever I want to I get off.

"The slaves used to live in one room log huts. They cooked out in the yard. I have seen them huts many a time. They had to cook out in the yard in the summertime. If they didn't, they'd burn up.

"My mother seen her master take off a big pot of money to bury. He didn't know he'd been seen. She didn't know where he went, but she seen the direction he took. Her master was Paul Barringer. That was on McKeever Creek near Sardis. It was near the end of the war. I never heard my mother say what became of the money, but I guess he got it back after everything was over.

"They had to work all the time. When they went to church on Sunday, they would tell them not to steal their master's things. How could they help but steal when they didn't have nothin'? You didn't eat if you didn't steal.

"My mother never would have been sold but the first bunch of slaves Barringer bought ran away from him and went back to the places where they come from. Lots of the old people wouldn't stay anywheres only at their homes. They would go back if they were sold away. It took a long time because they walked. When my mother and father were sold they had to walk. It took them six weeks,—from Charlottesville, North Carolina to Sardis, Mississippi.

"In Sardis my father was made the coachman, and mother was sent to the field. Master was mean and hard. Whipped them lots. Mother had to pick cotton all day every day and Sunday. When I first seen my father to remember him, he had on a big old coat which was given to him for special days. We called it a ham-beater. It had pieces that would make it set on you like a basque. He wore a high beaver hat too. That was his uniform. Whenever he drove, he had to dress up in it.

"My mother tickled me. She said she went out one day and kill a billygoat, but when she went to get it it was walking around just like the rest of them. My mother couldn't eat hogshead after freedom because they dried them and give them to them in slave time. You had to eat what you could git then.

"My mother said you jumped over a broomstick when you married.

"My father and mother were not exactly sold to Mississippi. My father was but my mother wasn't. When

Paul Barringer lost all of his niggers, what he first had, his sister give him my mother and a whole lot more of them. I don't know how many he had, but he had a great many. My father went alone, but all my mother's people were taken—four sisters, and three brothers. They were all grown when I first seen them. I never seen my mother's father at all.

"There was a world of yellow people then. My mother said her sister had two yellow children; they were her master's. I know of plenty of light people who were living at that time.

"My mother had two light children that belonged to her sister. They were taken from her after freedom, and were made to cook and work for their sister and brother (white). All the orphans were taken and given back to the people what owned them when freedom came. My mother's sister was refugeed back to Charlottesville, North Carolina before the end of the war so that she wouldn't get free. After the war they were set free out there and never came back. The children were with my mother and they had to stay with their master until they were twenty years old. Then they would be free. They wouldn't give them any schooling at all. They were as white as the white children nearly but their mother was a colored woman. That made the difference.

"My mother said that the Ku Klux used to come through ridin' horses. I don't remember her saying what they wore.

"When the Yanks came through, they took everything. Made the niggers all leave. My mother said they just came in droves, riding horses, killing everything, even the babies.

"I was born in Sardis, Mississippi, Panolun (?) County, April 10, 1863."

United States. Work Projects Administration

Interviewer: Miss Irene Robertson
Person interviewed: Pauline Fakes, Brinkley, Arkansas
Age: 74

PAULINE FAKES

"My mama come from Virginia. Her owner was Moses Crawford. He had a bachelor son Prior Crawford. My papa's owner was Step Crawford. They was in Arkansas during the Civil War I know because I was born close to Cotton Plant. Papa's folks had lived in Tennessee but grandma and grandpa was raised in Indian Nation; they called it Alabama afterwards. She was a full blooded Creek and he was part Cherokee.

"Mama had twelve sisters and they was all sold. They took them to Texas. She never seen one of them again. Mama had scrofula and her owners let a woman take her North. She cured her. She wanted to keep her but they didn't let her. They kept her till freedom.

"The owners told them they was free. Stayed on a while. We never have got very fur off from where I was born. I had thirteen children of my own. Three living now.

"I know times was mighty hard when I was a child. Biscuits was big rarity as cake is now. I don't have much cake. Little cornbread and meat, molasses and proud to get that. We didn't have much clothes but we had plenty wood. We had wood to keep up the fire in the fireplace all night. They saw the back sticks in the woods and roll em up. In the coldest part of the winter they throw on a back log of green wood and pull the seats, had benches, didn't have chairs, way back in the middle of the room. It be snow and ice all over the ground. I got wood many a day. Yes, I plowed many a day. I done all kinds of field work, cook and wash and iron. Mid-wife is my talent. I been big and strong and work was the least of my worries.

"I can barely recollect seeing soldiers. They must have just got home from the war. The shiny buttons is about all I can recollect.

"I recollect the Ku Klux. They rode at night, some dressed in dark and some white clothes. They come through our house one time. I got under the cover. I was scared nearly to death.

"Near Cotton Plant there was a log cabin (Methodist?) church—Negro church two and one-half miles northeast direction. They had a Negro preacher. When they went to church they whooped and hollowed along the road. White people lived close to the road. The Ku Klux planned to break it up. They went down there and went in during their preaching, broke up and scattered their seats. One was killed. He may have acted 'smarty' or saucy or he may have been the leader."

Interviewer: Miss Irene Robertson
Person interviewed: Mattie Fannen, Forrest City, Arkansas
Age: 87

MATTIE FANNEN

"My mother was named Silla Davis. She had four children. Her owners was Jep Davis and Tempy Davis. She died and he married her niece, Sally Davis. He had fifteen children by his first wife and five more by his second wife. Wasn't that a plenty children doe? Mama was a field hand. She ploughed in slavery right along. My father was named Bob Lee (Lea?). I never knowed much about him. His folks moved and took him off. Mother was sold but not on a stand. She belong to Bill Davis. He was Jep's brother. They said Bill Davis drunk up mother and all her children. He sold Aunt Serina to a man in Elberton, Georgia and all he had left then was grandma. He couldn't sell her. She was too old and Aunt Kizziah and Aunt Martha lived with her. Mother was born in Georgia. When a child was sold it nearly grieved the mothers and brothers and sisters to death. It was bad as deaths in the families. Jep Davis had forty or fifty niggers. He had six boys. They all had to go to war. They was in the Confederate army. Billy Davis was his daddy's young overseer. He had been raised up with some of the nigger boys then come over them. They wouldn't mind his orders. He tried to whoop them. They'd fight him back, choke him, throw him on the ground. Then the old man would whoop them. We all wanted 'em all to come home but Billy. Billy Davis got killed at war and never come home. His sisters was afraid some of the nigger boys raised up with him on the place would kill him and wanted Jep to make him stay at the house. Jep Davis was a good master and he was bad enough.

"I seen mama whooped. They tied some of them to trees and some they just whooped across their backs. It was 'cordin' to what they had done. Some of them would run off to the woods and stay a week or a month. The other niggers would feed them at night to keep them from starving.

"Jep Davis made a will after his first wife died and give out all his young niggers to his first set of children. His young wife cried till he destroyed it. She said, 'You kept the old ones here and me and my children won't have nothing.' I was willed to Miss Lizzie. They was fixing the wagon for me to go in. I wanted to go to Jefferson on the train. I told them so. I wanted to ride on the train. I never did get off. His young wife started crying. Miss Lizzie lived with her brother. They didn't want this young woman to have their father and he did. They kept a fuss up with her and all left. Then he divided the land.

"I nursed for his second wife, Miss Sally. I was five years or little older when I started nursing for his first wife. I nursed for a long time. I don't like children yet on that account. I got so many whoopings on their blame. I'd drap 'em, leave 'em, pinch 'em, quit walking 'em and rocking 'em. I got tired of 'em all the time.

"Me and Zack (white) was raised up together. He was one of the old set of children. The baby in that set. I'd set on the log across a branch and wait till Zack would break open a biscuit and sop it in ham gravy and bring it to me after he eat his breakfast. One morning the sun was so bright; he run down there crying, said his mama was dead. He never brought me no biscuit. He had just got up. I was five years old. I said I was glad. Emily was the cook and she come down there and kicked me off the log and made my nose bleed. I cried and run home. My mother picked me up in her arms, took me in her lap and asked me about it. I told her I was glad 'cause she kept that little cowhide and whooped me with it. They took me to the grave. She wanted to be buried in a pretty grave at the side of the house off a piece. She was buried there first. There was a big crowd. I kept running up towards the grave and they would pull me back by my dress tail. She was buried in a metal coffin. Susan was the oldest girl. She fainted. They took her to a carriage standing close. The whole family was buried there. Took back from places they lived to be buried in that graveyard. That was close to Nuna, Georgia.

"When the old man Jep Davis married again, Miss Sally must have me sleep in her room on a pallet so I could tend to the baby. The older girls would pick me and I would tell them what they talked about after they went to bed.

"When the War come on, the boys and Jep Davis dug a hole in the henhouse, put the guns in a box and buried them. They was there when the War ended. They had some jewelry. I don't know where they kept it. They sent all of the niggers fifteen miles on the river away from the Yankees. Not a one of us ever run off. Not a one ever went to the War or the Yankees. Jep Davis had been to get his mail on his horse. A Yankee come up at the gate walking and took it. He asked for the bridle and saddle but the Yankee laughed in his face. We never seen our horse no more. 'Babe' we called her. She was a pretty horse and so gentle we could ride her bare back.

"Jep Davis was religious. They had preaching at his church, the Baptist church at Nuna, for white folks in the morning and a white preacher preach for the niggers at the same church in the evening. He'd go to prayer meeting on Wednesday night and Thursday night he would come to the boys' house and read the Bible to his own niggers. We would sing and pray. He never cared how much we would sing and pray but he never better ketch 'em dancing. He'd whoop every one of 'em.

"I learned same of the ABC's in playing ball with the white children. We never had a book. I never went to school in my life. The boys not married but up grown lived in a house to their own selves. They got cooked fer up at Jep Davises house till they got a house built for them and give them a wife. Maybe they would see a woman on another plantation and claim her. Then the master had to talk that over.

Freedom

"Jep Davis had been to town. He got a notice to free his niggers. He had the farm bell rung. We all went out up to his house. He said, 'You are free. Go. If you can't get along come back and do like you been.' They left. Went hog wild. I was the last one to go. He said, 'Mattie, come back if you find you can't make it.' I had a hard time for a fact. I had a sister married in Atlanta. I went with them in

1866. I married to better my living. We quit. I met a man come to Arkansas and sent back for me when he got the money. I was in Atlanta thirty years. I was married in Arkansas in 1895. Been here ever since 'ceptin' visits back in Georgia. My husband was a good farmer and a good shoemaker. He left me six good rent houses and this house here when he died." (She has an income of forty dollars per month—rent on houses.) "He was a hard worker.

"I'd go to see my white folks after freedom. I loved 'em all.

"Jep Davis died out of the church. Him and Jack (Robertson, Robson, Robinson?) was deacons together in the Baptist church and their farms j'ined. Jack had two boys, John and Ed. Ed was killed by Hinton Right over his sister Mollie. Then she married Hinton Right. The quarrel started at La Grange but they had a duel during preaching on the church yard at the Baptist church at Nuna, Georgia. Jack was mean. He had a lot of Negroes and a big farm. He had two boys and four girls. Jennie died. Florence and Lula, old maids; John and Ed and Mollie.

"Jack caused Jep Davis to be put out of the church 'cause he said after freedom he didn't believe in slavery. He always thought they ought to be free but owned some to be like all the other folks and to have a living easy. He was afraid to own that, fear somebody kill him before freedom. When Jack was sick, Jep went to see him. He wouldn't let Jep come in to see him and he died.

"I worked in the field, washed and ironed. I never cooked but a little. In Atlanta when my first baby could stand in a cracker box I started cooking for a woman. She was upstairs. Had a small baby a few days old. I didn't have time to do the work and nurse and get my baby to sleep. It cried and fretted till I got dinner done. I took it and got it to sleep. She sent word for me to leave my baby at home, she wasn't going to have a nigger baby crying in her kitchen and messing it up. She was a Yankee woman. I left and I never cooked out no more.

"I never had no dealings with the Ku Klux. I was in Atlanta then. I heard my mother say they killed and beat up a lot of colored people in the country where she was. Seem like they was mad 'cause they was free.

"Times was hard after freedom. Times is hard now for some folks. Times running away with the white and black races both. They stop thinking. The thing what they call education done ruined this country. The folks quit work and living on education. I learned to work. My husband was a good shoemaker. We laid up all we could. I got seven houses renting around here. I gets about forty or forty-five dollars a month rent. It do very well, I reckon."

Interviewer: Samuel S. Taylor
Person Interviewed: Robert Farmer
1612 Battery Street, Little Rock, Arkansas
Age: 84

ROBERT FARMER

[HW: Tale of a "Nigger Ruler"]

"I was born in North Carolina. I can't tell when. Our names are in the Bible, and it was burnt up. My old master died and my young master was to go to the war, the Civil War, in the next draft. I remember that they said, 'If them others had shot right, I wouldn't have had to go.'

"He talked like they were standing up on a table or something shooting at the Yankees. Of course it wasn't that way. But he said that they didn't shoot right and that he would have to do it for them. They all came back, and none of them had shot right. One sick (he died after he got home); the other two come back all right.

"When my old master died, the son that drawed me stayed home for a little while. When he left he said about me, 'Don't let anybody whip him while I am gone. If they do, I'll bury them when I come back.' He was a good man and a good master.

Brutal Beating

"There were some that weren't so good. One of his brothers was a real bad man. They called him a nigger ruler. He used to go from place to place and handle niggers. He carried his cowhide with him when he went. My master said, 'A man is a damn fool to have a valuable slave and butcher him up.' He said, 'If they need a whipping, whip them, but don't beat them so they can't work.' He never whipped his slaves. No man ever hit me a lick but my father. No man. I ain't got no scar on me nowhere.

"My young master was named Wiley Grave Sharpe. He drawed me when my old master, Teed Sharpe, Sr., died. He's been dead a long time. Teed Sharpe, Jr., Gibb Sharpe, and Sam Sharpe were brothers to Wiley Grave Sharpe. Teed Sharpe, Jr. was the brutal one. He was the nigger ruler that did the beating up and the killing of Negroes.

"He beat my brother Peter once till Peter dropped dead. Wiley Graves who drawed me said, 'My brother shouldn't have done that.' But my brother didn't belong to Wiley and he couldn't do nothing about it. That was Teed, Jr.'s name. He got big money and was called a nigger ruler. Teed had said he was going to make Peter do as much work as my sister did. She was a young girl—but grown and stout and strong. In the olden time, you could see women stout and strong like that. They don't grow that way now. Peter couldn't keep up with her. He wasn't old enough nor strong enough then. He would be later, but he hadn't reached his growth and my sister had. Every time that Peter would fall behind my sister, Teed would take him out and buckle him down to a log with a leather strap and stand 'way back and then he would lay that long cowhide down, up and down his back. He would split it open with every stroke and the blood would run down. The last time he turned Peter loose, Peter went to my sister and asked her for a rag. She thought he just wanted to wipe the blood out of his face and eyes, but when she gave it to him, he fell down dead across the potato ridges.

Family

"Mary Farmer was my mother. William Farmer was my father. I never knowed any of my father's 'lations except one sister. She would come to see us sometimes.

"My father's master was Isaac Farmer. My mother didn't 'long to him. She 'longed to the Sharpes. Just what her master's name was I don't recollect. She lived five miles from my father. He went to see her every Thursday night. That was his regular night to go. He would go Saturday night; if he went any other time and the pateroles could catch him, they would whip him just the same as though he belonged to them. But they never did whip my father because they never could catch him. He was one of those who ran.

"My father and mother had ten children. I don't know whether any of them is living now or not besides myself.

How Freedom Came

"Freedom was a singsong every which way when I knowed anything. My father's master, Isaac Farmer, had a big farm and a whole world of land. He told the slaves all of them were free. He told his brother's slaves, 'After you have made this crop, bring your wives and children here because I am able to take care of them.' He had a smokehouse full of meat and other things. He told my father that after this crop is gathered, to fetch his wife and children to him (Isaac Farmer), because Sharpe might not be able to feed and shelter and take care of them all. So my father brought us to Isaac Farmer's farm.

"I never did anything but devilment the whole second year of freedom. I was large enough to take water in the field but I didn't have to do that. There were so many of them there that one could do what he pleased. The next year I worked because they had thinned out. The first year come during the surrender. They cared for Sharpe's crop. The next year they took Isaac Farmer's invitation and stayed with him. The third year many of them went other places, but my father and my mother and brothers and sisters stayed with Isaac Farmer for awhile.

"As time went on, I farmed with success myself.

"I stayed in North Carolina a long time. I had a wife and children in North Carolina. Later on, I went to Louisiana and stayed there one year and made one crop. Then I came here with my wife and children. I don't know how long I been here. We came up here when the high water was. That was the biggest high water they had. I worked on the levee and farmed. The first year we came here, we farmed. I lived out in the country then.

Occupation

"While I was able to work, I stayed on the farm. I had forty acres. But after my children left me and my wife died, I thought it would be better to sell out and pay my debts. Pay your honest debts and everything will be lovely. Now I manages to pay my rent by taking care of this yard and I get help from the government. I can't read and I can't write.

"I went down yonder to get help from the county. At last they taken me on and I got groceries three times. After that I couldn't get nothin' no more. They said my papers were made out incorrectly. I asked the worker to make it out correctly because I couldn't read and write. She said she wasn't supposed to do that but she would do it. She made it out for me. A short time later, the postman brought me a letter. I handed it to a lady to read for me, and she said, 'This is your old age check.' You don't know how much help that thing's been to me.

Ku Klux

"The Ku Klux never bothered me and they never bothered any of my people.

Opinions

"The young people pass by me and I don't know nothing about 'em. I know they are quite indifferent from what I was. When I come old enough to want a wife, I knowed what sort of wife I wanted. God blessed me and I happened to run up on the kind of woman I wanted. I made an engagement with her, and I didn't have a dollar. I was engaged to marry for three years before I married. I knowed it wouldn't do for me to marry her the way she was raised and I didn't have nothing. It looked curious for me to want that woman. I wanted her, and I had sense. I had sense enough to know how I must carry myself to get her. Now it looks like a young man wants all the women and ain't satisfied with nary one.

"My youngest son had a fine wife and was satisfied. He took up with what I call a whiskey head. He's been swapping horses ever since. That is the baby boy of mine. You know good and well a man couldn't get along that way.

"These young men will keep this one over here for a few days, and then that one over there for a few days. It shows like he wants them all.

Voting

"I have voted. I don't now. Since I lost out, I ain't voted.

Slave Houses

"You might say slave houses was nothing. Log houses, made out of logs and chinked up with sticks and mud in the cracks. Chimneys made with sticks and mud. Two rooms in our house. No windows, just cracks. All furniture was homemade. Take a two by four and bore a hole in it and put a cross piece in it and you had a bed.

"They made stools for chairs and made tables too. Food was kept in the smokehouse. For rations, they would give so much meat, so much molasses, and so much meal. No sugar and no coffee. They used to make tea out of sage, and out of sassafras, and that was the coffee.

Marriages

"I been married twice. The first time was out in North Carolina. The last time was in this city. I didn't stay with that last woman but four days. It took me just that long to find out who and who. She didn't want me; she wanted my money, and she thought I had more of it than I did. She got all I had though. I had just fifty dollars and she got that. I am going to get me a good woman, though, as soon as I can get divorced.

Memories of Work on Plantation

"My mother used to milk and I used to rope the calves and hold them so that they couldn't get to the cow. I had to keep the horses in the canebrake so they could eat. That was to keep the soldiers from getting a fine black horse the master had.

Soldiers

"But they got him just the same. The Yankees used to come in blue uniforms and come right on in without asking anything. They would take your horse and ask nothing. They would go into the smokehouse and take out shoulders, hams, and side meat, and they would take all the wine and brandy that was there.

Dances After Freedom

"Two sisters stayed in North Carolina in a two-room house in Wilson County. There was a big drove of us and we all went to town in the evening to get whiskey. There was one man who had a wife with us, but all the rest were single. We cut the pigeon wing, waltzed, and quadrilled. We danced all night until we burned up all the wood. Then we went down into the swamp and brought back each one as long a log as he could carry. We chopped this up and piled it in the room. Then we went on 'cross the swamp to another plantation and danced there.

"When we got through dancing, I looked at my feet and the bottom of them was plumb naked. I had just bought new boots, and had danced the bottoms clean out of them.

"I belong to the Primitive Baptist Church. I stay with Dr. Cope and clean up the back yard for my rent."

Interviewer: Mary D. Hudgins
Person Interviewed: Mrs. Lou Fergusson
Aged: 91
Home: With daughter Mrs. Peach Sinclair, Wade Street.
[Jan 29 1938]

MRS. LOU FERGUSSON

Zig-zaging across better than a mile of increasingly less thickly settled territory went the interviewer. The terrain was rolling—to put it mildly. During most of the walk her feet met the soft resistance of winter-packed earth. Sidewalks were the exception rather than the rule.

Wade Street, she had been told was "somewhere over in the Boulevard". Holding to a general direction she kept her course. "The Boulevard", known on the tax books of Hot Springs as Boulevard Addition, sprawls over a wide area. Houses vary in size and construction with startling frequency. Few of them are pretentious. Many appear well planned, are in excellent state of repair and front on yards, scrupulously neat, sometimes patterned with flower beds. Occasionally a building leans with age, roof caving and windows and doors yawning voids—long since abandoned by owners to wind and weather.

Up one hill, down another went the interviewer. Given a proper steer here and there by colored men and women—even children along the way, she finally found hereself in front of "that green house" belonging to Peach Sinclair.

Two colored women, middle aged, sat basking in the mild January sunlight on a back porch. "I beg your pardon," said the interviewer, approaching the step, "is this the home of Peach Sinclair, and will I find Mrs. Lou Fergusson here?"

"It sure is," the voice was cheerful. "My mother is in the house. Come around to the front," (the interviewer couldn't have reached the back steps, even if she had wanted to—the back yard was fenced from the front) "she's in the parlor."

Mrs. Lou turned out to be an incredibly black, unbelievably plump-cheeked, wide smiling "motherly" person. She seemed an Aunt Jemimah grown suddenly old, and even more mellow. "Mamma, this young lady's come to see you. She wants to talk to you and ask you some questions, about when—about before the war." (The situation is always delicate when an ex-slave is asked for details. Somehow both interviewer and interviewee avoid the ugly word whenever possible. The skillful interviewer can generally manage to pass it by completely, as well as any variant of the word negro. The informant is usually less squeamish. "Black folks," "colored folks", "black people", "Master's people", "us" are all encountered frequently.)

Five minutes of pleasant chatter preceeded the formal interview. Both Mrs. Sinclair and her guest (unintroduced) sat in on the conference and made comments frequently. "Law, child, we bought this place from your father. He was a mighty fine man." Mrs. Sinclair was delighted to find her guest to be "Jack Hudgins daughter." And later in the chat, "You done lost everything? Even your home—that's going? Too bad. But then I guess at that you're better off than we are. I've been trying for nearly a year to get my mother on the old age pension. They say she has passed. That was way along last March. Here it is January and she hasn't got a penny. No, I know you can't help. Yes, I see what you're doing. But if ever you does get on the pensions work—I'm going to 'hant'[A] you." (a wide grin) [A]

"Hant" was an intentional barbarism.

The old woman rocked and smiled. "Yes, ma'am. I'm her oldest, alive. She had 17 and 15 of them lived to grow up. But I'm about as old as she is, looks like. She never did have glasses—and today she can thread the finest needle. She can make as pretty a quilt as you'd hope to see. Makes fine stitches too. Seems like they made them stronger in her day." A nod of delighted approval from Mrs. Fergusson.

"I was born in Hempstead County, right here in this state. The town we were nearest was Columbus. I lived around there all of my life until I come here to be with my daughter. That was 15 years ago. Yes, I was born on a farm. From what I know, I'm over ninety. I was around 20 when the war ceaseted.

The man what owned us was named Ed Johnson. Yes, ma'am he had lots of folks. Was he good to us? Well, he was and he wasn't. He was good himself, wouldn't never have whipped us—but he had a mean wife. She'd dog him, and dog him until he'd tie us down and whip us for the least little thing. Then they put overseers over us. They was most generally mean. They'd run us out way fore day—even in the sleet—run us out to the field.

Was the life hard—well it was and it wasn't. No, ma'am, I didn't get much learning. Some folks wouldn't let their black folks learn at all. Then there was some which would let their children teach the colored children what they learned at school. We never learned very much.

You see, Master didn't live on the place. He lived bout as far as from here to town" (fully two miles) "The overseer looked after us mostly. No, ma'am I don't remember much about the war. You see, they was afraid that the fighting was going to get down there so they run us off to Texas. We settled down and made a crop there. How'd we get the land? Master rented it.

We made a crop down there and later we come back. No, ma'am we didn't stay with Mr. Johnson more than a month after there was peace. We come on in to Washington. No, ma'am, I never heard tell that Washington had been the Capitol of Arkansas for a while during the War. No, I never did hear that. Guess it was when we was in Texas. Then we folks didn't hear so much anyway.

We stayed in Washington most a year. Was I with my Mother? No, ma'am I was married—married before the war was thru. Married—does you know how we folks married in them days? Well the man asked your mother. Then you both asked your master. He built you a house. You moved in and there you was. You was married. I did some washing and cooking when I was in Washington. Then we moved onto a farm. I sort of liked Washington, but I was born on a farm and I sort of liked farm life.

We didn't move around very much—just two or three places. We raised cotton, corn, vegetables, peas, watermelons and lots of those sort of things. No ma'am, didn't nobody think of raising watermelons to ship way off like they does in Hempstead county now. Cotton was our cash crop. We rented thirds and fourths. Didn't move but three times. One place I stayed 15 years.

I been a widow 40 years. Yes, ma'am. I farmed myself, and my children helped me. Me and the owners got along well. Made good crops, me and the children. I managed to take good care of them. Made out to raise 15 out of the 17 to be grown. There's only 5 of them alive now.

Hard on a woman to run a farm by herself. Well now, I don't know. I made out. I raised my children and raised them healthy. I got along well with the farm owner. You might know when I was let to stay on one place for 15 years. You know I must have treated the land right and worked it fair.

Yes ma'am I remembers lots. Seems like women folks remembers better than men. I've got a good daughter. I'm still strong and can get about good. Guess the Lord has been good to me."

United States. Work Projects Administration

Interviewer: Miss Irene Robertson
Person interviewed: Jennie Ferrell, West Memphis, Arkansas
Age: 65

JENNIE FERRELL

"I was born in Yellowbush County, Mississippi close to Grenada. Grandmother come from North Carolina. They wouldn't sell grandpa. He was owned by Laston. They never met again. She brought two boys with her. She was a Pernell. Her master brought her away and would have brought her husband but they wouldn't sell. She said durin' her forty years in slavery she never got a whoopin'. She was a field hand. After she come to Mississippi they was so good to her they called her free. She was a midwife. She doctored the rich white and colored. She rode horseback, she said, far and near. In Grenada after freedom she walked. They called her free her master was so good to her. I don't know how she learned to be a midwife. Her master was Henry Pernell. He owned a small place twelve miles from Grenada and another place in the Mississippi bottoms. My folks become renters after freedom. I don't know if they rented from him but I guess they did.

"The Ku Klux never bothered them that I ever heard them mention."

United States. Work Projects Administration

Interviewer: Pernella Anderson
Person interviewed: Frank Fikes, El Dorado, Arkansas
Age: About 88

FRANK FIKES

"My name is Frank Fikes. I live between El Dorado and Strong and I am 79 years old if I make no mistake. I know my mama told me years ago that I was born in watermelon time. She said she ate the first watermelon that got ripe on the place that year and it made her sick. She thought she had the colic. Said she went and ate a piece of calamus root for the pain and after eating the root for the pain behold I was born. So if I live and nothing happens to me in watermelon time I will be eighty this year. I was a boy at surrender about the age of fourteen or fifteen.

"My work was very easy when I was a little slave. Something got wrong with my foot when I first started to walking and I was crippled. I could not get around like the other children, so my work was to nurse all of the time. Sometimes, as fast as I got one baby to sleep I would have to nurse another one to sleep. We belonged to Mars Colonel Williams and he had I guess a hundred families on his place and nearly every family had a baby, so I had a big job after all. The rest of the children carried water, pine, drove up cows and held the calves off and made fires at old mar's house.

"I had to keep a heap fire so the boys wouldn't have to

beat fire out of rocks and iron. Old miss did the cooking while all of the slaves worked. The slaves stood around the long back porch and ate. They ate out of wooden bowls and wooden spoons. They ate greens and peas and bread. And old miss fed all of us children in a large trough. She fed us on what we called the licker from the greens and peas with bread mashed in it. We children did not use spoons. We picked the bread out with our fingers and got down on our all fours and sipped the licker with our mouth. We all had a very easy time we thought because we did not know any better then.

"I never went to church until after surrender. Neither did we go to school but the white children taught me to read and count.

"I recollect as well today as if it had been yesterday the soldiers passing our house going to Vicksburg to fight. The reason I recollect it so well they all was dressed in blue suits with pretty gold buttons down the front. They passed a whole day and we watched them all day.

"Old miss and mars was not mean to us at all until after surrender and we were freed. We did not have a hard time until after we were freed. They got mad at us because we was free and they let us go without a crumb of anything and without a penny and nothing but what we had on our backs. We wandered around and around for a long time. Then they hired us to work on halves and man, we had a hard time then and I've been having a hard time ever since.

"Before the War we lived in log cabins. There was a row of log cabins a quarter of a mile long. No windows and no floor. We had grass to sit on. Our beds was made of pine poles nailed to the wall and we slept on hay beds. My mama and other slaves pulled grass and let it dry to make the beds with. Our cover was made from our old worn out clothes.

"On Sunday evenings we played. We put on clean clothes once a week. In summer we bathed in the branch. We did not bathe at all in winter. I went in my shirt tail until I was eleven or twelve years old. Back in slavery time boys did not wear britches. They wore shirts and our hair was long. The slaves say if you cut a child's hair before he or she was ten or twelve years old they won't talk plain until they are that old."

United States. Work Projects Administration

Interviewer: Miss Irene Robertson
Person interviewed: J.E. Filer, Marianna, Arkansas
Age: 76

J.E. FILER

"I was born in Washington, Georgia. I come here in 1866. There was three stores in Marianna. My parents name Betsy and Bob Filer. My mother belong to Collins in Georgia. She come to this state with Colonel Woods. She worked in the field in Georgia and here too. Mama said they always had some work on hand. Work never played out. When it was cold and raining they would shuck corn to send to mill. The men would be under a shelter making boards or down at the blacksmith shop sharpening up the tools so they could work.

"Since we come to this state I've seen them make oak boards and pile them up in pens to dry out straight. I don't recollect that in Georgia. I was so little when we come here. I can recollect that but not much else. My brother was older. He might tell all about it."

[TR: Next section crossed out]

Interviewer's Comment

I didn't get to see his brother. I went twice more but he was at work on a farm somewhere.

United States. Work Projects Administration

Interviewer: Samuel S. Taylor
Subject: Ex-slavery
[May 11 1938]

Person Interviewed: Orleans Finger
Negro (Apparently octoroon or quadroon)
Address: 2804 West Fifteenth Street, Little Rock, Arkansas.
Occupation: Formerly field hand and housekeeper
Age: 79

[TR: Personal information moved from bottom of first page.]
[TR: In text of interview, informant's name is given as Orleana.]

ORLEANS FINGER

Birth, Family, and Master

"I was born in Mississippi in Tippa County not far from the edge of Tennessee. I wasn't raised in Arkansas, but all my children was raised here. I really don't know just where in Tippa county I was born. My mother's name was Ann Toler. Toler was my step father. My real father, I don't know. My mother never told me nothin' bout him and I don't know that; I can't tell what I don't know.

"My grandfather on my mother's side was Captain Ellis. That is the one come after me when I was small to carry me back to my folks. I didn't know him, and I said 'I don't want to go 'way with them strange Niggers'. He's dead now. They're all dead long ago. I have got children over fifty years old myself. I am the mother of nine children—three of them living. One of the living ones is Arthur Finger. He lives in St. Louis. I expected to hear from him today, but didn't. Cornelius Finger. (He is a brownskin boy, spare made), lives in Palestine, Arkansas, near Forrest City. Arthur is my baby boy. Elmira was my baby girl. She's the one you met. She's married and has children of her own.

"Captain Ellis' wife was named Minerva. She was my mother's mother. She's been dead years. I got children older than she was when she died. She died in Mississippi. I got a cousin named Molly Spight. She's dead. My mother's sister was named Emmaline; she is dead now too.

"My mother was colored. I don't know nothin' about my father, and my mother never taught me nothin' 'bout him.

"My step father and mother were both field hands. They worked in the field.

"I don't know just when I was born, but I am just sure that it was before the war. I remember hearing people talk about things in the war.

"My mother's master was named Whitely, I think, because she was named Whitley before she married.

"I have been married three times. The first man I married was 'Lijah Gibbs. The second time I married, I married Joe Finger. The third time I married Will Reese. He warn't no husband at all. They're all dead. Folks always called me Finger after my second husband died, because I didn't live with my third husband long.

House

"They had log houses. You would never see no brick chimney nor nothing of that kind. The logs were notched down and kinda kivered flat—no roof like now. They might have rafters on them, but the top was almost flat. Wouldn't be any steep like they is now. In them times they wouldn't have many rooms. Sometimes they would have two. They wouldn't have so many windows. Just old dirt chimneys. They'd take and dig a hole and stick sticks up in it. Then they'd make up the dirt and put water in it and pull grass and mix it in the dirt. They'd build a frame on the sticks and then put the mud on. The chimney couldn't catch fire till the house got old and the mud would fall off. When it got old and the mud got to fallin off, then they would be a fire. I've seen that since I been in Arkansas.

"Sometimes they would get big rocks and put them inside the fireplace to take the place of bricks. You could get rocks in the forest.

Furniture

"Used to have ropes and they would cord the bed stead. The cords would act in place of springs. When you move you would have a heap of trouble because all that would have to be undone and done up again. You have to take the cords out and them put it together again. The cords would be run through the sides of the bed and stuck in with pegs.

"They used to have spinning wheels and looms. They made clothes and they made the cloth for the clothes and they spun the thread they made the cloth our of. They'd card and spin the thread. There's lots of other things I can't remember.

War Memories

"The Yankess used to come in and have the people cook for them. They'd kill chickens and geese and things. The old people used to take their horses out and tie them out in the woods—hiding them out to keep the Yankees from getting them. The Yankees would ride up, take a good horse and leave the old worn-out one.

"There never was any fighting round where I lived. None of my folks was soldiers in the war.

Right After the War

"I don't remember just what my folks did right after the war. They were field hands and I guess they did that. My mother worked in the field that's all I know.

Life Since the War

"I have been in Arkansas a long time. I have been here ever since I left Mississippi. My first marriage was in Mississippi. The second and last ones was in Arkansas—Forrest City. My second husband had been dead since 1921. I don't know that I count Reese. We married in June and separated in September. He's dead now, and I don't hold nothin' against him.

"I am not able to work now. I do a little 'round the house and dig a little in the garden. I haven't worked in the field since way before 1921. I don't get no help at all from the Welfare. My daughter does what she can for me. I always have lived before I ever heard about the old age pension and I suppose God will take care of me yet somehow.

Cured by Prayer

"I'm puny and no'count. Aint able to do much. But I was crippled. I had a hurting in my leg and I couldn't walk without a stick. Finally, one day I went to go out and pick some turnips. I was visiting my son in Palestine. My leg hurt so bad that I talked to the Lord about it. And it seemed to me, he said 'Put down your stick.' I put it down and I aint used it since. I put it down right thar and I aint used it since. God is a momentary God. God knowed what I wanted and he said, 'Put down that sick,' and I aint been crippled since. It done me so much good. Looks like to me when I get to talking about the Lord, aint nobody a stranger to me.

"I know I been converted but that made me stronger. My son is a siner. He knowed about how I was crippled. He said you ought use your stick. He didn't know what to think about it. Young folks don't believe because they aint had no experience with prayer and they don't know what can happen.

"I done told you all I know. I don't want to tell you anything I don't know. If you don't know nothing, it is best to say you don't."

Everything which Orleana Finger states has the earmarks of being true. There are a great many things which she does not state which I believe that she could state if she wished. She evidently has a long list of things which she things should be unmentioned. She has two magic phrases with which she dismisses all subjects which she does not wich to discuss:

"I don't remember that."

"I better quit talking now before I start lying."

Interviewer: Miss Irene Robertson
Person interviewed: Molly Finley, Honey Creek
3-1/2 miles from Mesa, Arkansas
Age: Born 1865

MOLLY FINLEY

"My master was Captain Baker Jones and his pa was John Jones. Miss Mariah was Baker Jones' wife. I believe the old man's wife was dead.

"My parents' name was Henry ("Clay") Harris and Harriett Harris. They had nine children. We lived close to the Post (Arkansas Post). Our nearest trading post was Pine Bluff. And the old man made trips to Memphis and had barrels sent out by ship. We lived around Hanniberry Creek. It was a pretty lake of water. Some folks called it Hanniberry Lake. We fished and waded and washed. We got our water out of two springs further up. I used to tote one bucket on my head and one in each hand. You never see that no more. Mama was a nurse and house woman and field woman if she was needed. I made fires around the pots and 'tended to mama's children.

"We lived on the Jones place years after freedom. I was born after freedom. We finally left. I cried and cried to let's go back. Only place ever seem like home to me yet. We went to the Cummings farm. They worked free labor then. Then we went to the hills. Then we seen hard times.

We knowed we was free niggers pretty soon back in them poor hills.

"I was more educated than some white folks up in them hills. I went to school on the river. My teacher was a white man named Mr. Van Sang.

"Mama belong to the Garretts in Mississippi. She was sold when she was about four years old she tole me. There had been a death and old mistress bought her in. Master Garrett died. Then she give her to her daughter. She was her young mistress then. Old mistress didn't want her to bring her but she said she might well have her as any rest of the children. Mama never set eyes on none of her folks no more. Her father, she said, was light and part Enjun (Indian).

"John Prior owned papa in Kentucky. He sold him, brother and his mother to a nigger trader's gang. Captain Jones bought all three in Tennessee. He come brought them on to Arkansas. He was a field hand. He said they worked from daylight till after dark.

"They took their slaves to close to Houston, Texas to save them. Captain Jones said he didn't want the Yankees to scatter them and make soldiers of them. He brought them back on his place like he expected to do. Mama said they was out there three years. She had a baby three months old and the trip was hard on her and the baby but they stood it. I was her next baby after that. Freedom done been declared. Mama said they went in wagons and camped along the roadside at night.

"Before they left, the Yankees come. Old Master Jones treated them so nice, give them a big dinner, and opened up everything and offered some for them to take along that they didn't bother his stock nor meat. Then he had them (the slaves) set out with stock and supplies to Texas.

"Mama and papa said the Jones treated them pretty well. They wouldn't allow the overseers to beat up his slaves.

"The two Jones men put two barrels of money in a big iron chest. They said it weighed two hundred pounds. Four men took it out there in barrels and eight men lowered it. They took it to the family graveyard down past the orchard. They leveled it up like it was a grave. Yankees didn't get Jones money! Then he sent the slaves to Texas.

"Captain Jones had a home in Tennessee and one in Arkansas. Papa said he cleared out land along the river where there was panther, bears, and wild cats. They worked in huddles and the overseers had guns to shoot varmints. He said their breakfast and dinner was sent to the field, them that had wives had supper with their families once a day, on Sundays three times. The women left the fields to go fix supper and see after their cabins and children. They hauled their water in barrels and put it under the trees. They cooked washpots full of chicken and give them a big picnic dinner after they lay by crops and at Christmas. They had gourd banjos. Mama said they had good times.

"They had preaching one Sunday for white folks and one Sunday for black folks. They used the same preacher there but some colored preachers would come on the place at times and preach under the trees down at the quarters. They said the white preacher would say, 'You may get to the kitchen of heaven if you obey your master, if you don't steal, if you tell no stories, etc.'

"Captain Jones was a good doctor. If a doctor was had you know somebody was right low. They seldom had a doctor. Mama said her coat tail froze and her working. But they wore warm clothes next to their bodies.

"Captain Jones said, 'You all can go back on my place that want to go back and stay. You will have to learn to look after your own selves now but I will advise you and help you best I can. You will have to work hard as us have done b'fore. But I will pay you.' My folks was ready to 'board the wagons back to Jones' farm then. That is the way mama tole me it was at freedom! It was a long time I kept wondering what is freedom? I took to noticing what they said it was in slavery times and I caught on. I found out times had changed just b'fore I got into this world.

"Some things seem all right and some don't. Times seem good now but wait till dis winter. Folks will go cold and hungry again. Some folks good and some worse than in times b'fore."

Interviewer's Comment

Gets a pension check.

Interviewer: Miss Irene Robertson
Person interviewed: Fanny Finney, Brinkley, Arkansas
Age: 74 plus

FANNY FINNEY

"I was born in Marshall County, Mississippi. Born during slavery. I b'long to Master John Rook. He died during the Civil War. Miss Patsy Rook raised me. I put on her shoes, made up her bed, fetched her water and kindling wood.

"My parents named Catherine and Humphrey Rook. They had three children.

"When Master John Rook died they divided us. They give me to Rodie Briggs. John and Lizzie was Master John's other two children. He had three children too same as ma. My young master was a ball player. I'd hear them talk. Ma was a good house girl. They thought we'd all be like 'er. When I was three years old, I was the baby. They took ma and pa off keep the Yankees from stealing then. Miss Patsy took keer me. When ma and pa come home I didn't know them a tall. They say when they come back they went to Louziana, then 'bout close to Monticello in dis state, then last year they run 'em to Texas.

"Pa was jus' a farmer. Gran'ma lived down in the quarters and kept my sisters. I'd start to see 'em. Old gander run me. Sometimes the geese get me down and flog me wid their wings. One day I climbed up and peeped through a crack. I seen a lot of folks chopping cotton. It looked so easy. They was singing.

"Betsy done the milking. I'd sit or stand 'round till the butter come. She ax me which I wanted, milk or butter. I'd tell her. She put a little sugar on my buttered bread. It was so good I thought Sometimes she'd fill my cup up with fresh churned milk.

"I et in the kitchen; the white folks et in the dining-room. I slep' in granny's house, in granny's bed, in the back yard. Granny's name was 'Aunt' Hannah. She was real old and the boss cook on our place. She learnt all the girls on our place how to cook. Kept one or two helping her all the time. It was her part to make them wash their faces every morning soon as they started a fire and keep their hands clean all the time er cooking. Granny wore her white apron around her waist all time. Betty would make them help her milk. They had to wash the cows udder before they ever milked a drop. Miss Patsy learnt her black folks to be clean. Every one of them neat as a pin sure as you born.

"I was so little I couldn't think they got whoopings. I never heard of a woman on the place being whooped. They all had their work to do. Grandma cut out and made pants for all the men on the whole farm.

"Old man Rook raised near 'bout all his niggers. He bought whiskey by the barrel. On cold mornings they come by our shop to get their sacks. I heard them say they all got a drink of whiskey. His hands got to the field whooping and singing. The overseers handed it out to them. The women didn't get none as I knowed of.

"The paddyrollers run 'em in a heap but Master John Rook never let them whoop his colored folks.

"We lived six miles from Holly Springs on the big road to Memphis. Seem like every regiment of Yankee and rebel soldiers stopped at our house. They made a rake-off every time. They cleaned us out of something to eat. They took the watches and silverware. The Yankees rode up on our porch and one time one rode in the hall and in a room. Miss Patsy done run an' hid. I stood about. I had no sense. They done a lot every time they come. I watched see what all they would do. They burnt a lot of houses.

"A little white boy said, 'I tell you something if you give me a watermelon.' The black man give the boy a big watermelon. He had a big patch. The boy said, 'My papa coming take all your money away from you some night.' He fixed and sure 'nough he come dressed like a Ku Klux. He had some money but they didn't find it. One of the Ku Kluxes run off and left his spurs. The colored folks killed some and they run off and leave their horses. They come around and say they could drink three hundred fifteen buckets of water. They throw turpentine balls in the houses to make a light. They took a ball of cotton and dip it in turpentine, light it, throw it in a house to make a light so they could see who in there. A lot of black folks was killed and whooped. Their money was took from them.

"The third year after the War ma and pa come and got me. They made a crop for a third. That was our first year off of Rook's place. I love them Rook's girls so good right now. Wish I could see them or knowd where to write. I had to learn my folks. I played with my sisters all my life but I never had lived with them. When pa come for me they had my basket full of dresses and warm underclothes, clean and ironed. They sent ma some sweet potatoes and two big cakes. One of them was mine. Miss Patsy said, 'Let Fannie come back to see my girls.' I went back and visited. Granny lived in her house and cooked till she died. I had a place with granny at her house. We went back often and we helped them after freedom. They was good white folks as ever breathed. There was good folks and bad folks then and still is.

"Times is hard. I was raised in the field. I made seven crops here—near Brinkley—with my son. I had two girls. One teaches in Brinkley, fourth or fifth grade; one girl works for a family in New York. My son fell off a tall building he was working on and bursted his head. He was in Detroit. Times is hard now. The young folks is going at too fast a gait. They are faster than the old generation. No time to sit and talk. On the go all the time. Hurrying and worrying through time. Hard to make a living."

Interviewer: Zillah Cross Peel
Information given by: "Gate-eye" Fisher
Residence: Washington County, Arkansas

GATE-EYE FISHER

"I was jes' a baby crawlin' 'round on the floor when War come" said "Gate-eye" Fisher, who lives in a log house covered with scraps of old tin, on what is known as the old Bullington farm near Lincoln. His one room log cabin is "down in the bresh" back of the barn and when new renters come on the place, they just take it for granted that "Gate-eye" just belongs. He bothers no one. No floors, no windows just a door, a bed, stove and a table. Yes and a lantern and a chair.

"Yes mam, my mother, Caroline, belonged to the Mister Dave Moore family. His wife, Miss Pleanie, was a Reagan. Yes mam, they was good folks. When the War come, my pa, Harrison Fisher and my ma stayed on the place, Mister Moore had lots of land and stock—and he and his folks went to Texas, nearly everybody did 'round here, and he took some of his fine stock with him but he called my pa and ma in and told them he wanted them to stay on the place and take care of all the things. Pa was boss over all the slaves. I guess mos' all my white folks is dead. Mos' of them all buried down yan way to Ft. Smith. One of Mister Moore's daughters, Miss Mary, married Dr. Davenport and Miss Sinth (Cynthia) went to live with her."

(The Moores came from Kentucky and Tennessee and settled at Cane Hill, Washington County, about 1829. The Reagans came about the same time. The first schools in the county were at Cane Hill).

"Yes mam, I guess all the colored folks that belonged to Mister Moore, but me, is dead. I guess. My mother, Caroline, stayed in the house nearly all the time and took care of Missy's children, and when they come home from school she'd hear them learn their ABC's. That's how come I can read and write. My ma taught me, out of an old Blue Back Speller. Yes mam, I learned to read and can't write much, jes my own name. Yes mam, I kinda believe in signs that's how come I wear this leather strap 'round my wrist it keeps me from havin' rheumatism, neuralgia. Yes mam, it helps. I used to believe in signs a lot and I used to believe in wishes. I used to wish a lot of bad wishes on folks till one day I read a piece from New York and it said the bad wishes that you made would come back to you wosser than you wished, so I don't wish no more. I got scared and don't wish nothin' to no body."

"After the War Ole Mister and Ole Missey called in my ma and pa and asked them if they wanted to still stay on the place or go somewhere. 'Bout ten of us stayed. Then a while after Mister Moore asked my pa if he wanted to go up on the Tilley place—600 acres and farm it for what he could make. We, my pa and my ma and my sister Mandy, stayed there a long time. Then Mister Moore sold off a little here and a little there and we moved up on the mountain with my sister and her husband, Peter Doss, where my ma died. Then I went down to Mister Oscar Moore's place—he was my Missey' boy."

"Yes mam, I did have a wife. I had a mos' worrysome

time. It is a worrysome time when a man comes to takes your wife right away from you. No'm, I don't ever want her to come back."

"Yes'm, I do my own cooking, and I've put up some fruit. I have a little mite of meat, a little mite of taters, a little mite of beans and peas. I get a little pension too."

"These darkies today nearly all get wild. You can't tell What they are going to do tomorrow. They's jes like everybody—some awful good and some awful bad."

And in the tiny one room shack, of logs and tin, no window, a swing door held by a leather strap, "Gate-eye" does his cooking on a small wood stove. A long bench holds a lantern with a shingly clean globe, a lot of canned fruit, dried beans and peas. The bed is a series of old bed springs. But "Gate-eye" just belongs to the neighborhood, and every one feels kindly toward him. He says he is seventy-one years, past.

United States. Work Projects Administration

Interviewer: Miss Irene Robertson
Person Interviewed: Ellen Fitzgerald
Brinkley, Ark.
Age: 74

ELLEN FITZGERALD

"Mama was named Anna Noles. Papa named Milias Noles. She belong to the Whitakers and he belong to Gibbs. Noles bought them both. They was both sold. Mother was born in Athens, papa somewhere in Kentucky. Their owners, the Noles, come to Aberdeen, Mississippi.

"Grandma, papa's mama, was killed with a battling stick. She was a slender woman, very tall and pretty, papa told me. She was at the spring, washing. They cut a tree off and make a smooth stump. They used a big tree stump for battling. They had paddles, wide as this (two hands wide—eight or ten inches) with rounded-off handle, smoothed so slick. They wet and soap the clothes, put em on that block-tree stump and beat em. Rub boards was not heard of in them days. They soaked the clothes, boiled and rinsed a heap. They done good washing. I heard em say the clothes come white as snow from the lye soap they used. They made the soap. They had hard soap and soft soap, made from ashes dripped and meat skins. They used tallow and mutton suet too. I don't know what was said, but I recken she didn't please her mistress—Mrs. Callie Gibbs. She struck her in the small part of her back and broke it. She left her at the spring. Somebody went to get water and seen her there. They took her to the house but she finally died. Grandpa was dead then. I recken they got scared to keep papa round then and sold him.

"I was born first year of the surrender. Moster Noles told them they was free. They didn't give them a thing. They was glad they was free. They didn't want to be in slavery; it was too tied down to suit em. They lived about places, do little work where they found it.

"We dodged the Ku Klux. One night they was huntin' a man and come to the wrong house. They nearly broke mama's arm pullin' her outen our house. They give us some trouble coming round. We was scared of em. We dodged em all the time.

"I was married and had a child eight years old fore I come to Arkansas. I come to Brinkley first. I was writing to friends. They had immigrated, so we immigrated here and been here ever since. When I come here there was two big stores and a little one. A big sawmill—nothing but woods and wild animals. It wasn't no hard times then. We had a plenty to live on.

"My husband was a sawmill hand and a railroad builder. He worked on the section. I nursed, washed, ironed, cooked, cleaned folks houses. We done about right smart. I could do right smart now if white folks hire me.

"The night my husband died somebody stole nearly every chicken I had. He died last week. We found out it was two colored men. I ain't needed no support till now. My husband made us a good living long as he was able to go. We raised a family. He was a tolerably dark sort of man. My girls bout his color."

The two grown girls were "scouring" the floor. Both of them said they were married and lived somewhere else.

United States. Work Projects Administration

Interviewer: Mary D. Hudgins
Person Interviewed: Henry Fitzhugh
Aged: 90
Home: Rooms at 209 Walnut Street

HENRY FITZHUGH

Several "colored" districts are scattered throughout Hot springs. On Whittington, within a block of the First Presbyterian Church and St. Joseph's Infirmary stand the Roanok Baptist and the Haven Methodist (both for colored). Architecturally they compare favorably with similar edifices for whites. Their choirs have become nationally famous. Sunday afternoon concerts are frequent. Mid-week ones are not uncommon. At such times special sections are reserved for whites, and are usually filled. Visitors to the resort enjoy them immensely.

Across the street a one-time convent school has been converted into a negro apartment house. A couple of blocks up Whittington, Walnut veers to the right. It is paved for several blocks. Fronting on concrete sidewalks are houses, well painted and boasting yards which indicate pride in possession. Some are private homes, some rooming houses and some apartments. Porch flower boxes and urns are mostly of concrete studded with crystals.

Finding Henry Fitzhugh wasn't easy. The delivery boy at the corner chain store "knows everybody in the neighborhood" according to a passer-by. He offered the address 209. That number turned out to be an old, but substantial and well cared for two story house. Ringing the bell repeatedly brought no response.

A couple of women in the yard next door announced that to find Fitzhugh one had to "go around back and knock on the last door on the back porch." This procedure too brought no results. Another backyard observer offered the suggestion that Fitzhugh was probably down at the restaurant eating.

School had just been dismissed. Two well dressed negro children walked along together, swinging their books. "Can you tell me where the restaurant is?" asked the interviewer, stopping them. "Do you mean the colored restaurant?" one of the tots asked, not a whit of embarrassment in her manner, no servility, no resentment—just an ordinary question. "It's right over there."

The restaurant proved to be large, well lighted, scrupulously clean. Tables were well spaced and quite a distance from the counter. Sunshine streamed in from two directions. Fitzhugh was sitting just outside talking to the boot-black.

"Yes, ma'am, I's Henry Fitzhugh. Can't work no more since I got hit by an automoble. Before that I had a shoe-shine place myself. But I can't work no more. Yes 'um I gets the pension. I gets $10 a month. It's not much, but I sort of get by. I's got my room up at 209 and I gets my meals down here at the restaurant. Yes ma'am, pensions seem to be coming in pretty regular now.

Been in Hot Springs a long, long time. Come here in

1876. I remembers lots of the old families here. What yo say your name was? Your Mother was a Dengler? Sure, I remembers the Denglers. Mr. Dengler had a soda-water shop. I remembers him.

When I first come, soon as I was able, I cleaned up for Captain Mallard. Cleaned up all along Central in that block he was in.

How'd I come to Hot springs? I was sick. I had rheumatism. Was down with it so bad the doctor had done give me up. He'd stopped giving me medicine. But the lady I was working for, she run a hotel in Poplar Bluff. They put me on a stretcher and they put me in the baggage car and they brought me clean on in to Hot Springs. They bathed me at the free bath house. I started getting better right away. 'Twasn't long before I was well and able to work. I stayed right on here in Hot Springs.

Yes, ma'am I's all Arkansas. I was born near Little Rock. Ain't never been out of the state but twice. Then I didn't stay long.

I worked on a farm that belonged to Mr. J.B. Henderson. He was an uncle to Mr. Jerome Henderson what was in the bank and Mr. Jethro Henderson what was a Judge.

No, the war didn't bother us none. We wasn't afraid. We heard the shots, but it seemed just like a whole lot of fire crackers to us. Guess we just didn't have sense enough to be afraid. Fighting we did [HW: hear was] near Pine Bluff—the Baxter-Ware trouble. We seen the soldiers when they come through Mt. Pleasant, right smart bunch of them. They was Confederates. We didn't see none of the Yankees.

My father was killed during the war. Went off to help and never came back. My mother, she died when I was a baby. She was lying down in her cabin before the fire—lying on the hearth, letting me nurse. The door was open and a gust of wind blew her dress in the fire. She dropped me and she screamed and run out into the yard. Old Miss saw her from the house. She grabbed a quilt and started out. She got to my mother and she wrapped her in the quilt to smother out the fire. But my mother done swallowed fire. She died. That's the story they tell me. I was too little to know.

I guess I was about eleven when I went into the fields. What's that, pretty young? I didn't go because they made me. I went because I wanted to be with the men. Wasn't nobody around to play with. We was the only family on the farm. It was a pretty good sized farm and they had lots of children. There was Miss Sally and Miss Fanny and Miss Ella and Miss Myrtle and Miss Hattie. Then there was four boys.

Stayed on with the folks three years after the surrender. They treated me good and gave me what I wanted. Treated me nice—very nice—my white folks.

Then I went on down to Marshall—way down in Texas. There I worked for the high sheriff. Drove his carriage for him and cleaned up around the yard. I worked for him a whole year then I went back to Arkansas and then went up in Missouri. Wasn't there long before I got sick. I was working for a woman who had a hotel. She was good to me. Mighty good she was.

Yes ma'am. There has been lost chances I has had to do more than I has. But I's sort of satisfied. There's been lots of changes in Hot Springs since I come. I used to know all the white folks and all the colored folks too. Can't do that today. Place has got too big.

Joe Golden? Yes, I does—I knows Joe. He used to have a butcher shop over on Malvern. Quite a man, Joe was. I hasn't seen him in a long time. How is he? Pretty good? That's fine.

"I remembers Mc—McLeod's Happy Hollow." (Hot Spring nearest approach to a Coney Island in the earlier days). "I remembers that they used to have the old stage coach there what the James and Younger brothers held up. Sort of broken down it was, but it was there.

Law, law, them was the times. I'll never forget when Allen Roane brought in the news. Allen drove a sort of a hack. He come on into town and he whipped up his horse and he run all over town telling about the hold-up. Allen lived just next door to where I does now."

Down the street passed a colored woman, her head held high. Passing the porch where the aged negro man and the young white woman sat talking she paused and gave what was suspiciously like a sniff. Fitzhugh grinned. "She's sanctified," he explained.

"Did you ever hear of Tucky-Nubby? He was an Indian. Bob Hurley used to bring him to Hot Springs every year. What medicine shows they used to have here. Ain't seen nothing like it lately, everybody knowed Tucky-Nubby. Lots of those medicine shows—free shows, used to come here. But Bob Hurley and Tucky-Nubby was the most liked.

Yes, ma'am, I'm all alone now. My sister married a

man a long, long time ago. She didn't live but a couple of years. I's had four children. One of them died when it was born. One died when it was three. One lived until it was seven. One son he lived to be grown. He went to the war. Got as far as camp. One day I got a word saying that he was sick. I went but before I could get there he had died. That left me alone.

What's that? Been married once? I been married eleven times. But it was ten times too many. Besides they is all dead, so you might say that I's been married only once.

Yes, ma'am. Thank you ma'am. The quarter will come in powerful handy. When you tries to make out on $10 a month a little extra comes in powerful handy. Thank you ma'am. I enjoyed talking to you, ma'am."

Interviewer: Mrs. Bernice Bowden
Person interviewed: Mary Flagg
1601 Georgia Street, Pine Bluff, Arkansas
Age: 89

MARY FLAGG

"Yes'm, I was here in Civil War days. I was bout twelve years old when Lincoln was elected. I remember when he was elected. I was big enough to weave and knit for the soldiers. I remember when the war started. Yes ma'm—oh I remember so much. Saw all the soldiers and shook hands with em. Why I waited on the table when General Lee stopped there for dinner on his way from Mobile to meet Sherman. That was in Winchester, Mississippi where I was born. I worked in a hotel, yes ma'm. I was raised up in a hotel, called em taverns in those days. I was born right in Winchester, Mississippi. Used to see the soldiers drill every day. If I could remember, I could tell you a heap of things.

"My mistress' name was Mrs. Shaw. She took me away from my mother when I was four years old—taken me for her body servant. She learned me how to do housework and all kinds of sewin'—cuttin' and makin'. I done all the sewin' for her family.

"I never went to no school but Mrs. Shaw tried to teach me and she slapped my jaws many a day bout my book.

"I married when I was fifteen just fore the war ended

and I forgot everything I ever learned—yes ma'm! I been married four times and they're all dead. I never married when any of em was livin' like a heap of colored folks did.

"The Yankees come within fifty miles of where we was livin' and then they burned the bridge and turned back. White folks never told us what the war was for but a old German man used to read the paper at the table—every battle they'd fight and when the Yankees would whip. Oh them was times then. If I could remember I could tell you a heap of things but my mind's gone from me.

"Old master had about a hundred head of hands and old mistress had a cousin had five hundred.

"White folks was good to me. My father was the carriage driver and old mistress used to carry me to church with her every Sunday.

"I never seen no Ku Klux but I lived where they was, in Mississippi. That was a Ku Klux state. Yes ma'm.

"I remember when General Lee come to Winchester you could hear the horses' feet a mile away, it so cold.

"My great grandfather was a full blooded Indian. I've lived among the Indians in Mississippi and bought baskets from em. They lived all around us. Yes ma'm, I'm acquainted with em. Oh, I been through a little bit.

"I started sewin' and weavin' when I was just big enough to reach the treadles. Used to sew for Mrs. Hulburt in Bolivar County, Mississippi. I remember she started to the Mardi Gras on a boat called the Mary Bell. It got burned and she had to turn back. I used to do a heap a sewin'.

"Everythings changed now. People is so treacherous now. Chile, ain't nothin' to this younger generation. Now I'm tellin' you the truth. They ain't studyin' nothin' good. Sin and corruption all you see now.

"Last man I married was Elder Flagg. He was a preacher in the Baptist church and as good a preacher as I ever heard. They don't preach the Gospel now.

"Well, I wish I could remember more to tell you, but it's been a long time. I'll be ninety if I live till the 4th of next May."

United States. Work Projects Administration

Interviewer: Mrs. Zillah Cross Peel
Person interviewed: Doc Flowers
Age: 85?
Home: Lincoln, Arkansas

DOC FLOWERS

Everybody calls him Uncle Doc. His name is Doc Flowers, and he lives in the last house on a street that is just part of a road in the town of Lincoln, Arkansas.

When you stop in front of the house you will find there is no path. One has to watch his step owing to the fact that there is a zigzaggy branch hidden by the tangle of weeds.

If old Aunt Jinney is on the porch she will say, "Sorry, honey, but de path done growed up."

Uncle Doc is six feet two and as strong as a lion. Whether he is 80 or if he is 90, he is young-looking for his age.

"No'm lady, I'se jes' don' know how old I is. Back in dem days didn't keep up with our ages. No record of the born. Yes'm I was a pretty good chunk of a boy when de war started."

Doc belonged to Edward Choate, who lived on Barron Forks, near Dutch Mills in the Southwest corner of Washington County. Barron Forks is made up from Fly Creek and the River Jordan Creek.

About 1849 Edward Choate came from Tennessee to Arkansas, where he had bought Aunt Marie [TR: 'a slave' marked out here] and her three sons, Doc, Abe, and Dave.

"Yes'm, we had a 100 acres or better all along the banks of de river and good valley land where we raised corn, potatoes, wheat, oats, an' 'bacco. Master Choate had three sons, I recollect, Jack, Sam, and Win. He had a lot of slaves. Some of dem was good, some was bad. An' old Mister Choate had a cat-a-nine-tails. He never did have to whup me, some of dem darkies did get whupped. Dar was one who was always dressing up in wimmins clothes and go walking down by de river.

"My mother was Maria. She worked part time in de kitchen and part time in de field. My mother had three boys and I 'member one of my sisters was sold as a slave. We darkies had cabins all along de river bank.

"During de War we all jes' stayed on de place. Mister Choate and Old Missy stayed too. After peace was made my mother and all of we went up to Prairie Grove to live.

"Yes'm, I voted every chance I got. I voted for Harrison for President. No'm, I don't know which Harrison. Yes'm, I vote Republican.

"I can't say much for these young darkies these times.

"I ben 'roun' some. I went to Caldwell, Kansas, two times. Farming is my occupation. Now we jes' live. I get $10 a month from the state. Yes'm, that there Jinney is my wife. Her mother Celia and she belonged to the Ballards of Cincinnati.

"No'm, I jes' can' tell how old I is. I know I was quite a

chunk of a boy when de War started. Me and Mister Win, one of Mister Choate's boys, was 'bout de same age." (Winston Choate died in the spring of 1935 at the age of 94 years, according to a niece.)

The Choate place down on Barron Forks is still owned by one of the Choates, a grandson of the first owner, Edward Choate.

A granddaughter of Mr. Choate lives in Fayetteville and said that there are four or five graves on the old place where Negro slaves who belonged to her grandfather were buried, and the children on the place would never go near these graves. They thought they were haunted.

So when one asks Uncle Doc how old he is he will say, "I know I was jes' a chunk of a boy when de War started so I mus' be 'bout 83 nex' spring."

Aunt Jinney, his wife, sat on the porch and just rocked back and forth while Uncle Doc was talking. She didn't speak while Doc was speaking.

"Law, honey, I had good white folks. None of dem never struck their colored folks. No'm. Me an' my mother Celia belonged to Mister Ballard at Cincinnati. Old Missey's name was Miss Liza, an' she kept my ma in de house wid her to wait on her. Yes'm all de white folks always kept a little darkey in de house to wait on all of dem. Dem was good times 'fo' de War. Yes'm good times—plenty to eat. Good times. I was jes' a baby crawling on de flo' when de War come."

The interviewer didn't ask Uncle Doc when and why he went to Caldwell, Kansas the two times. She knew that Uncle Doc, big and strong, took another Negro's wife away from him and ran off with her to Kansas and there left her. Later he brought her to Arkansas. Jinney was his wife and took Uncle Doc back, but Gate-eye didn't take his wife back. Nor did the interviewer tell Uncle Doc that she had been to see old Gate-eye Fisher and had heard the long ago story of Uncle Doc taking his wife, and what a worrysome time he had. In an old record marked "Miscellaneous" in the Washington County Courthouse at Fayetteville, Arkansas, one can find this Emancipation paper:

"For and in consideration of the love and affection of my wife for my little Negro girl (a slave) named Celia, about two years old, I do by these presents henceforth and forever give to said Celia her liberty and freedom, and through fear of some mistake, mishap or accident, I now hereby firmly bind myself, heirs and representatives forever in accordance with this indenture of emancipation.

"In testimony whereof witness my hand and seal this 26th day of January 1846.
        Signed: Thomas B. Ballard

        Witnesses: Charles Baylor
        Sumet Mussett"

Jinney, wife of Doc Flowers, is the daughter of the said Celia. "Yes'm," said Jinney, "Miss Liza, my old Missy, always had my mother right by her side all the time to wait on her. She were always good to all her colored folks. No'm she'd never let anybody be mean to her colored folks."

Jinney must have learned the art of house keeping from Miss Liza, for her little three-room home that she and Doc rent for $4 a month is spotless. Maybe the "path is growed up with weeds," but one just can't blame that on Jinney.

United States. Work Projects Administration

Interviewer: Miss Irene Robertson
Person interviewed: Frances Fluker, Edmondson, Arkansas
Age: 77
[May 11 1938]

FRANCES FLUKER

"I was born the 25th day of December 1860 in Marshall County, Mississippi. Our owners was Dr. George Wilson and Mistress Mary. They had one son I knowed, Dr. Wilson at Coldwater, Mississippi. My parents was Viney Perry and Dock Bradley.

"I never seen my pa. I heard about him since I been grown. He left when the War was going on and never went back. Mama had ten children and I am all that's living now. Old mistress set my name and age down in her Bible. I sent back and my niece just cut it out and sent it to me so I could get my pension. I pasted it in the front of my Bible. I was never sold. It was freedom when I first recollect.

"Ma was the cook for the white folks. Grandma Perry come from North Carolina I heard 'em say. She was a widow woman. When company come they would send us out to play. They never talked to us children, no ma'am, not 'fore us neither. I come a woman 'fore I knowed what it was. My sisters knowed better than tell me. They didn't tell me nothin'.

"When it wasn't company at ma's they was at work and singing. At night we was all tired and went to bed 'cause we had to be up by daybreak—children and all. They said it caused children's j'ints to be stiff sleeping up in the day. All old folks could tell you that.

"This young set ain't got no strength neither. Ma cooked and washed and raised five children up grown. The slaves didn't get nary thing give 'em in the way of land nor stock. They got what clothes they had and some provisions.

"Ma was ginger cake. They said pa was black. I don't know. Grandma was reddish and lighter still than ma. They said she was part Cherokee Indian. Her hair was smooth and pretty. She combed her hair with the fine comb to bring the oil out on it and make it slick. I recollect her combing her hair. It was long about on her shoulders.

"I heard about the Ku Klux but I never seed none of 'em. Ma said her owners was good to her. Ma never had but one husband.

"I come to Arkansas 1921. Mr. Passler in Coldwater, Mississippi had bought a farm at Onida. We had worked for him at Lula, Mississippi. Me and my husband come here. My husband died the first year. I cooked some in my younger days but field work and washing was my work mostly. I like' field work long as I was able to go.

"My first husband cleared up eighty acres of land. He and myself done it, we had help. We got in debt and lost it. He bought the place. That was in Pinola County close to Sardis. I had four children. One daughter living.

"What I think it was give me rheumatism was I picked cotton, broke it off frozen two weeks on the sleet. I picked two hundred pounds a day. I got numb and fell and they come by and got a doctor. He said it was from overwork. I got over that but I had rheumatism ever since.

"I learned to read. I went to Shiloah School—and church too—several terms. Mr. Will Dunlap was my first teacher. He was a white man. He run the school a good while but I don't know how long. My name is Frances Christiana Fluker. I been farming all my life, nothin' but farmin'. Never thought 'bout gettin' sick 'cause I knowed I couldn't.

"I jus' get $6 and that is all. It cost more to send get the commodities than it do to buy them. We don't get much of them. I needs clothes—union suits. 'Course I wears 'em all summer. If they would give me yarn and needles I could knit my socks. 'Course I can see and ain't doing nothing else. I needs a dress. I ain't got but this one dress."

NOTE: The two old beds were filthy with slick dirt. They had two chairs and a short bench around the stove and a trunk in which she kept the little yellow torn to pieces Bible tied around the back with a string. The large board door was kept wide open for light I suppose. There were no windows to the room.

I heard the reason she gets only $6 was because her daughter lives there and keeps two of her son's children and they try to get the young grandson work and help out and support his children and mother at least.

United States. Work Projects Administration

Interviewer: Mrs. Bernice Bowden
Person interviewed: Ida May Fluker
Route 6, Box 80, Pine Bluff, Arkansas
Age: 83

IDA MAY FLUKER

"I was born in slavery times in Clark County, Alabama. Clover Hill was the county seat.

"Elias Campbell was old master. I know the first time I ever saw any plums, old master brought 'em. I 'member that same as yesterday.

"I 'member the same as if 'twas yesterday when the Yankees come. We chillun would hide behind the door. Had on blue suits with brass buttons. So you see I'm no baby.

"I 'member my mother and the other folks would go up to the big house and help make molasses. Didn't 'low us chillun to go but we'd slip up there anyway.

"Old missis' name Miss Annis. She was good to us.

"I didn't do nothin' but play around in the yard and tote wood. Used to tote water from the Wood Spring. Had a spring called Wood Spring.

"My mother was the cook and my grandma was the spinner. I used to weave after freedom.

"I know the Yankees come in there and got a lot of

fodder. They was drivin' a lot of cows. We chillun would be scared of 'em—mama would be at the big house.

"Mama belonged to the Campbells and papa belonged to Davis Solomon, and I know every Christmas they let him come to see mama, and he'd bring me and my sister a red dress buttoned in the back. I 'member it same as if 'twas yesterday 'cause I was crazy 'bout them red dresses.

"I used to hear the folks talkin' 'bout patrollers. Yes ma'am, I heered that song

> 'Run nigger run
> Paddyrollers will ketch you
> Jes' 'fore day.'

I know you've heered that song.

"I heered papa talk about how he was sold. He say the overseer so mean he run off in the woods and eat blackberries for a week.

"I guess we had plenty to eat. I know mama used to fetch us somethin' to eat from the house. Old missis give it to her. I know I was glad to get it.

"When the people was freed they was so glad they went from house to house and prayed and give thanks to the Lord.

"Our folks stayed right there and worked on the shares.

"I never went to school but about two weeks. My papa was hard workin'. Other folks would let their chillun rest but he wouldn't let his chillun rest. He sure did work us hard.

"You know in them days people moved 'round so much they didn't have time to keep up no remembrance 'bout their ages. We didn't have no time to see 'bout no ages—had to work. That's the truth."

United States. Work Projects Administration

Interviewer: Miss Irene Robertson
Person interviewed: Wash Ford, Des Arc, Arkansas
Age: 73 or 75?

WASH FORD

"I was born close to Des Arc and Hickory Plains, seems like about half way. Mama's master was named Powell. Papa's master was Frank Ford. My parents was Fannie and Henry Ford. I was the oldest child. There was 6 boys, 4 girls of us.

"They didn't get anything after freedom. They kept on farming. They started working on shares. That was all they could do. If they expected anything I never heard it.

"I heard my mother say when I was small Papa was bouncing me up and down. He was lying on the floor playing like wid me. She looked up the road or 'cross the field one, and said, 'Yonder come some soldiers. What they coming here for?' Papa put me down and run. He hid. They didn't find him. It was soldiers from De Valls Bluff I judge. They made the colored men go wait on them and fight too, if they run up on one. That is what I heard.

"My father voted. He voted a Republican ticket. I do cause he did I reckon. I still vote. If the colored man could vote in the Primary it wouldn't be no better. They know better who to put in office, to run the offices right. I think it is right for a woman to vote.

"I been farming all my life. I was a section hand much

as six months in all my life. I work at the veneer mills but they never run no more. I am having a hard time. I have high blood pressure. I can't pick cotton. I can't even get a mess of turnip greens. The Social Welfare helps me a little and I am janitor up town in two offices. They hand me a little pocket change. It amount to maybe $2 a month. I had that job four years. If I could work I would be on the farm. I could make a living there. I always did. I had plenty on the farm.

"Young folks don't take on no manners. The young folks take care of themselves. It is the old ones seeing a hard time now."

Interviewer: Miss Irene Robertson
Person interviewed: Wash Ford, Des Arc, Ark.
Age: 75?

WASH FORD

"One thing I remembers hearin' my folks talk bout. They had a leader hoeing cotton. His name was John. He was a fast hand. He hoe one row a piece and reach over and hoe the other. He'd get way ahead of the other hands. If they didn't keep up they get a whoopin. So he rest till they ketch up. Once he hoed up to a tree—big shade tree out in the field. He stuck his hoe in the root of the tree and a moccasin bit him bout that time. It bit him right on the toe. They took him up to the house but he died.

"I was born close to Des Arc and Hickory Plains. My parents was Henry and Fannie Ford. Her master was named Powell and his master was named Frank Ford. I was the oldest 'mong six boys and four girls. My folks didn't git nuthing. I don't think they expected freedom much. They heard they goiner be free and knowed they was fightin'. They didn't know what freedom be like. When they was set free at DeValls Bluff they signed up. They went back and went on farmin' lack nothin' ever happened. That what I heard em say when I was small boy.

"I voted—Republican ticket, I believe. If I vote that

what I vote. I reckon the women ought to vote. I still vote that is if I sees fit to vote.

"My father run from the soldiers. He didn't go to the war as I ever knowd of.

"I been farmin' all my life till I got so nocount I ain't able to do nothin' no more. I worked on the section bout six months. I worked some off an on at the veneer mill till it shut down. I does a little janitor work now and the Welfare help me a little.

"The present conditions good if a fellow able to pick cotton but if they run through with it times be hard in the heart of the winter cause they cain't git no credit. Times is hard for old folks."

Interviewer: Samuel S. Taylor
Person interviewed: Judia Fortenberry
712 Arch Street, Little Rock, Arkansas
Age: 75
Occupation: Field hand
[May 21 1938]

JUDIA FORTENBERRY

[HW: Slaves Allowed to Visit]

"I was born three miles west of Hamburg in Ashley County, Arkansas, in the year 1859, in the month of October. I don't know just what day of the month it was.

"My mother was named Indiana Simms and my father was named Burrell Simms. My father's mother was named Ony Simms, and my mother's mother was named Maria Young. I don't know what the names of their parents was.

"My mother's master was named Robert Tucker. My father's master was named Hartwell Simms. Their plantations were pretty close together, but I don't know how my father and my mother got together. I guess they just happened to meet up with each other. The slaves from the two plantations were allowed to visit one another. After their marriage, the two continued to belong to different masters. Every Sunday, they would visit one another. My father used to come to visit his wife every Sunday and through the week at night.

"My mother had ten children.

Houses

"I was born in a log house with one room. It was built with a stick and dirt chimney. It had plank floors. They didn't have nothin' much in the way of furniture—homemade beds, stools, tables. We had common pans and tin plates and tin cans to use for dishes. The cabin had one window and one door.

Patrollers

"I have heard my mother and father tell many a story of the pateroles. But I can't remember them. My father said they used to go into the slave cabins and take folks out and whip them. They'd go at night and get 'em out and whip 'em.

How Freedom Came

"I was so little that I don't know much about how freedom came. I just know he took us all and went somewheres and made him a crop. Went to another man. Didn't stay on the place where he was a slave. He never got anything when he was freed. I never heard of any of the slaves getting anything.

Schooling

"I went to free school after the War. I just went along during the vacation when they weren't doing any farming. That is all the education I got. I can't tell how many seasons I went—four or five, I reckon. I never did go any whole season. I never had much chance to go to school. People didn't send their children to school much in those days. I went to school in Monticello, but most of my schooling was in country schools.

Occupation

"When I first went to work, I picked cotton. That is at a place out near Hamburg. I picked cotton about ten or fifteen years. Then I went to town—Monticello. I washed and ironed. About forty-five years ago, I came to Little Rock, and have been here every since. Washing and ironing has been my support. I have sometimes cooked.

Opinions

"I don't know what I think about the young people. Seems to me they coming to nothing. Lot of them do wrong just because they got a chance to do it. I'm a christian. I belong to the A.M.E.'s. You know how they do.

Song

1

I belong to the band
That good old Christian band
Thank God I belong to the band.

Chorus

Steal away home to Jesus
I ain't got long to stay here.

2

There'll I'll meet my mother,
My good old christian mother,
Mother, how do you do;
Thank God I belong to the band.

I can't remember the music. But that's on old song we used to sing 'way back yonder. I can't remember any more of the verses. You got enough anyhow."

Interviewer: Mrs. Bernice Bowden
Person interviewed: Emma Foster
1200 N. Magnolia, Pine Bluff, Arkansas
Age: 80

EMMA FOSTER

"Yes'm, I was born in time of slavery—seven years before surrender. No'm, I wasn't born in Arkansas. Born in Claiborne Parish, Louisiana.

"I remember hearin' the big guns shoot. I was small and I didn't know what it was only by what they told me.

"My parents belonged to the Harts. My mother run off and left me, a year-old baby.

"I remember better when I was young than I do now.

"After I got big enough—you know, a little old nasty somethin' runnin' around in the yard—after I got big enough, they took me in the house to rock the cradle, and I stayed there till I was twenty-three. I would a stayed longer but they was so cruel to me.

"I didn't know nothin'. I run off and stayed with a colored preacher and his family not far away. You know I was crazy. One day the preacher said some of his members was objectin' to me stayin' there and he was goin' to tell my white folks where I was. And sure enough, he did, and one morning I was out in the field and I saw the son-in-law comin'. So I went back and worked for him and his wife.

"Me? All I did do was farmin' when I was young.

"Oh, I been in Arkansas 'bout fifty years. My oldest boy was fourteen when I come here and he is sixty-four now.

"No, honey, I can't cook now. I'd burn it up. I used to cook. It's a poor dog that won't wag its own tail.

"All I know is I had a hard time, I been married three times. My last husband was a preacher and he was so mean I left him. I told him if all preachers was like him, hell was full of 'em.

"I went to Chicago and lived with my son a while but I didn't like it, so I come back here and I been here right in the yard with Mrs. O'Neal eight years washin' and ironin'—anything come to hand.

"Now if there's goin' to be a death in my family, I can see that 'fore it happens. I was out in the potato patch one day and it started to rain and I come in and somethin' just bore down on me and I started to cry. I didn't know why. I thought, 'Oh, Lord, is somethin' goin' to happen to my son?' But instead it was my grandson. He got killed that evenin'."

Name of interviewer: Mrs. Bernice Bowden
Subject: Birthmarks
Story:—Information

This information given by: Emma Foster (C)
Place of residence: 1200 N. Magnolia Street, Pine Bluff, Arkansas
Occupation: Laundress
Age: 80

EMMA FOSTER

[TR: Personal information moved from bottom of first page.]

"I know I marked one of my babies with beer. It was 'cause I wanted some beer and couldn't get it. And when it was born it had a place on the back of its neck looked like beer and she just foamed at the mouth. And when she was about a week old I got some beer and give it to her with a teaspoon and she quit foamin'.

"And another time there was a boy on the place had a finger that the doctor had done took the bone out. He and I used to love to rassle (wrestle) and one day he said, 'Oh, Emma, you hurt my finger.' And like a fool, you know I took his hand and just rubbed that finger. And do you know, when my baby was born it had six fingers on each hand."

United States. Work Projects Administration

Interviewer: Mrs. Bernice Bowden
Person interviewed: Ira Foster
2000 W. Eureka Street, Pine Bluff, Arkansas
Age: 76

IRA FOSTER

"I was born in slavery because when the people come back from the War I was a pretty good sized yellin' boy when freedom come.

"I heerd 'em tellin' 'bout my young master comin' back from the War.

"Yes ma'am, I was sure born in Arkansas; I won't tell no lie 'bout that.

"My mother's old master was named Foster and after she married she belonged to Hezekiah Bursey.

"She was born in Alabama and she said she was pretty badly treated.

"She was the cook and then she was the weaver and the spinner.

"I never have been to school. Never did learn nothin'. My father put me to work soon as I was big enough.

"I always done farm work all my life till 'bout twenty years ago as near as I can come at it. I went to saw millin' and I didn't do nothin' but manufacture lumber. I worked for the Camden Lumber Company eighteen years and never caused 'em a minute's trouble.

"If I just had enough to live on I wouldn't do a thing but just sit around 'cause I think I done worked my share. Why, some of the white folks say, 'Foster, you ought to have a pension of thirty or forty dollars a month.' And I say, 'Why?' And they say, 'Cause you look just like a darky that has worked hard in this world.'

"I suffers with the rheumatism in my right leg clear up and down. Seems like sometimes I can't hardly get around."

FOLKLORE SUBJECTS
Name of interviewer: Mrs. Bernice Bowden
Subject: Songs of Pre-War Days
Story:—Information

This information given by: Ira Foster
Place of residence: 2000 W. Eureka, Pine Bluff, Arkansas
Occupation: None
Age: 76

[TR: Personal information moved from bottom of first page.]

IRA FOSTER

"'You may call me Raggedy Pat
'Cause I wear this raggedy hat,
And you may think I'm a workin'
But I ain't.'

I used to hear my uncle sing that. That's all the words I can remember."

United States. Work Projects Administration

Interviewer: Samuel S. Taylor
Person interviewed: Leonard Franklin
Temporary: 301 Ridgeway, Little Rock, Arkansas
Permanent: Warren, Arkansas
Age: 70

LEONARD FRANKLIN

[HW: *Mother Whipped Overseer*]

"I don't know exactly the year I was born. But my father told me I was born since the Civil War. I am seventy years old. They always tell me when my birthday come 'round it will be in January—the eighteenth of January.

"My father's name was Abe Franklin and my mother's name was Lucy Franklin. I know my father's mother but I didn't ever know his father. His mother's name was Maria Franklin. My mother's father was Harris Pennington. I never did see her mother and never did see her.

"I was born in Warren, Arkansas. My mother and father were born in Warren. That is on the outer edge of Warren. My mother's slavery farm was on what they called Big Creek. It is named Franklin Creek. Two or three miles of it ran through Franklin's Farm.

"My father's master was Al Franklin. And my mother's master's name was Hill Pennington. One of Hill Pennington's sons was named Fountain Pennington. He lives about five miles from Warren now on the south highway.

"My mother had about three masters before she got free. She was a terrible working woman. Her boss went off deer hunting once for a few weeks. While he was gone, the overseer tried to whip her. She knocked him down and tore his face up so that the doctor had to 'tend to him. When Pennington came back, he noticed his face all patched up and asked him what was the matter with it. The overseer told him that he went down in the field to whip the hands and that he just thought he would hit Lucy a few licks to show the slaves that he was impartial, but she jumped on me and like to tore me up. Old Pennington said to him, 'Well, if that is the best you could do with her, damned if you won't just have to take it.'

"Then they sold her to another man named Jim Bernard. Bernard did a lot of big talk to her one morning. He said, 'Look out there and mind you do what you told around her and step lively. If you don't, you'll get that bull whip.' She said to him, 'Yes, and we'll both be gittin' it.' He had heard about her; so he sold her to another man named Cleary. He was good to her; so she wasn't sold no more after that.

"There wasn't many men could class up with her when it come to working. She could do more work than any two men. There wasn't no use for no one man to try to do nothin' with her. No overseer never downed her.

"They didn't kill niggers then—not in slavery times. Not 'round where my folks were. A nigger was money. Slaves were property. They'd paid money to git 'im and money to keep 'im and they couldn't 'ford to kill 'em up. When they couldn't manage them they sold them and got their money out of them.

"The white people started to Texas with the colored folks near the end of the war and got as far as El Dorado. Word come to 'em that freedom had come and they turned back.

"A paterole come in one night before freedom and asked for a drink of water. He said he was thirsty. He had a rubber thing on and drank two or three buckets of water. His rubber bag swelled up and made his head or the thing that looked like his head under the hood grow taller. Instead of gettin' 'fraid, mother threw a shovelful of hot ashes on him and I'll tell you he lit out from there and never did come back no more.

"Right after the war my folks went to work on the farm. They hired out by the month. [HW: My father] didn't never say how much he got. When they had a settlement at the end of the year, the boss said his wages didn't amount to nothing because his living took it up. Said he had ate it all up. After that, he took my mother's advice and took up part of his wages in a cow and so on, and then he'd always have something to show for his work at the end of the year when it come settling up time. It was ten years before he got a start. It was hard to get ahead then because the niggers had just got free and didn't have nothin' and didn't know nothin'. My father had two brothers that just stayed on with the white folks. They stayed on till they got too old to work, then they had to go. Couldn't do no good then. My father was always treated well by his master.

"I got my schooling at Warren. I went to the tenth grade. Could have gone farther but didn't want to. I was looking at something I thought was better than education. When I got of age, I come up here and just run about.

I was what you might say pretty fine. I was looking so high I couldn't find nothing to suit me. I went 'round to a number of places and none of them suited me. So I went on back home and been there ever since.

"I married once in my life. My wife is still living. My wife is a good woman. No, if I got rid of this one, wouldn't do to take another one. I am the father of ten living children. I made a living by doing anything that come up—housework, gardening, anything.

"I don't get no government help. I don't want none yet. God has seen me this far. I think He'll see me to the end. He is good to me; He's given me such a good time I couldn't help but serve Him. Only been sick once in seventy years.

"I belong to the Baptist church. God is my boss now. He has brought me this far and He's able to carry me across"

Interviewer: Mrs. Bernice Bowden
Person interviewed: Eliza Frazier
2003 Saracen Street, Pine Bluff, Arkansas
Age: 88?

ELIZA FRAZIER

"I don't know when I was born or 'zackly how old I is, but I was born in South Carolina and come here before the War.

"I belonged to Wiley Mosley and he brought me and my mother and my sister here to Arkansas. I don't 'member it at all 'cause I was a baby, but I know what Wiley Mosley and my mother told me.

"Settled in Redland Township. That's what they called it. He bought a plantation there. There was three brothers come to this country and they didn't live very far from each other.

"I 'member hearin' 'em talk 'bout the War and one time I heered the guns a poppin'. They said they was just passin' through. I was just a small girl but I 'member it. I seed the Yankees too. I 'member they'd come up in the yard on hosses and jump down and go in the smokehouse and take the meat and go to the dairy house and get the milk.

"Old master was gone to the War. I 'member when he was gwine and I 'member when he come back. Old missis said he was up in Missouri. Got shot right through the foot once. I know he come home and stayed 'til he was well, then he went back. I don't know how long he stayed but he went back—I know that. And he come back after the War—I 'member that.

"I 'member one time when I upset the cradle. Miss Jane wouldn't 'low me to take the baby up but I rocked the cradle. And one time I reckon I rocked it too hard and it turned over. Miss Jane heard it time it hit the floor and she come runnin'. I was under the house by that time but she called me out and whipped me and told me to get back in the house. I know I didn't turn it over no more.

"The Yankees never said nothin' to me—talked to my mother though, and old mis'.

"They said they was fightin' to free the niggers. There was a boy on the place and while old master was gone to war, he'd just go and come and get the news. He didn't do that when old master was home. I know he brought the news when peace declared. Patrollers got him one night.

"I 'member when peace declared ever'body went around shoutin' and hollerin', 'The niggers is free, the niggers is free!'

"Our folks stayed there on the place right smart while after freedom. I 'member I was gwine out to the field and Woodson, he was the baby I upset, he wanted to go along and wanted me to tote him and I know old master said, 'Put him down and let him walk.'

"They told me I was twenty when I was married—the white folks told me. I know my mother asked how old I was and they said I was 'bout twenty. I 'member it well enough.

"I never went to school but I knowed my ABC's and could read some in the first reader. I ain't forgot about it. I thinks about it sometimes.

"The biggest work I has done is farm work.

"I've had nine chillun and raised all of 'em but one."

NOTE:

Eliza lives with her son who is well educated and a retired city mail carrier and he is now sending three children to the A.M.& N. College here.

United States. Work Projects Administration

Interviewer: Miss Irene Robertson
Person interviewed: Mary Frazier, near Biscoe, Arkansas
Age: 60

MARY FRAZIER

"My parents was Neily and Amos Hamilton. They lived in Marshall County, about forty-eight miles from Memphis. They belong to people by that same name.

"I heard them all say how they come to be way out in Mississippi. The Thompsons owned Grandma Diana and her husband in South Carolina. Master Jefferies went there from Mississippi and bought grandma. They let all twelve of her children go in the sale some way but they didn't sell grandpa. He grieved so till the same man come back a long time afterward and bought him. Jefferies was good to them. I was born in Mississippi. Grandma cooked all the time. Mama and papa both worked in the field. I heard grandma say every one of her children was born in South Carolina. Mr. Jefferies, one of the younger set, lived in Clarendon, Arkansas. Since I come to this country I seen him. I lived over there pretty close by.

"I got no 'pinion worth telling about our young folks. They want to have a big time when they are young. All young folks is swift on foot that way. Times is funny. Funniest times ever been in my life. Is times right now? Ain't no credit no more. That one thing making times so hard. Money is the whole thing now'days."

United States. Work Projects Administration

El Dorado District
FOLKLORE SUBJECTS
Name of Interviewer: Pernella Anderson
Subject: TALES OF SLAVERY DAYS
Story:—Information
[Feb 6 1937]

This information given by: Tyler Frazier
Place of Residence: Ouachita County
Occupation: Domestic
Age: 75

[TR: Personal information moved from bottom of first page.]

TYLER FRAZIER

Ah wus a young nigger bout nine or ten years ole when de slaves wus freed. Ah got freed in Texas. We went tuh Texas on a steamboat an dey wuz a lot uv people on de steamboat. We sho 'joyed dat trip. We went wid our mistress an moster. Dey wuz de Lides, Mistuh John Lide's parents. De Lides run one uv de bigges' stores in Camden now, if yo knows dem dey is de same Lides. One uv de boys wuz named Blackie Lide, one John Lide, one named Hugh Lide. Dem wuz granchillun. Hannah Lide, Minnie Watts now, dey wuz de granchillun. Now let me see, one Miss wuz named Emma Lide. Dem sho wuz good fokes. Ole miss died when we wuz on ouh way tuh dis country. An ole moster been daid since way back yondah. But when we got tuh dis country we settled bout seven or eight miles fum Camden in Ouachita County. Ole moster wuz named Peter Lide. We jes went tuh school nough tuh learn our A.B.C.'s cause we had tuh work in de fiel. We carried our meat tuh de fiel an cooked hot ash cake fuh dinnuh. We kep' spare ribs and backbone all de year roun'. We pickled de backbone an dem spareribs. We worked evah day. Wednesday night wuz wash night. Dat's when de women would do de washin. We'd go tuh de fiel way fo day.

Back in dem days we had er log church. Ah went in mah shirt-tail till ah wuz six. Mis Lide made mah fust pair uv britches. Ah membuhs one time ah went to Miss Lide's garden an stole watuh mellons. Ah put em in a sack an when ah want tuh come outn de garden ah got ovah de fence an got hung an moster caught me. Ah'm tellin de truth. Ah aint had no desire tuh steal since.

Moster Peter Lide's favorite song wus dis: "Hit's er long way tuh heaven." Ah kin mos heah him singin hit now. He wuz a Christian man. He wuz white and owned slaves but he wuz a good Christian. We didn' know bout no money. When we got sick dat's when we got biscuit. We didn' know bout Thanksgiving day and Christmas. We heard de white fokes tawkin bout hit but we didn' know whut hit meant.

When anybody would die dey made de coffin. Didn' have no funeral, no singin, no nothin' jes put dem in de groun. Dat wus all. Nebber stop work. We nevah plowed er hoss. We used oxen teams. We made good crops den. We raised all our sumpin tuh eat.

When ah wus a lil' bitsy boy Mrs. Lide use tuh tell us stories at night. She give us our fireside trainin. She tole us when anybody wuz a tawkin not tuh but in. Ah'm seventy five yers ole now an ah aint nevah fuhgot dat. We ole fokes aint got long tuh stay heah now. We lives in de days dats past. All we knows tuh tawk bout is what we use tuh do. When mah time is up ah is ready tuh go cause ah is done mah bes' fuh mah God, mah country and mah race.

United States. Work Projects Administration

Interviewer: Beulah Sherwood Hagg
Person interviewed: Aunt Mittie Freeman
Aged: 86
Home: 320 Elm St., North Little Rock. In home of granddaughter.
[Aug 27 1937]

MITTIE FREEMAN

"Howdy, honey. Come on in and set down. It's awful hot, ain't it? What you come to see me for? You says old uncle Boss tell you I'se old slave lady? That's right, that's right. Us old war folks never fergits the others. Anything you wants to know, honey, jest go on and ax me. I got the bestest remembrance.

Orange county, Mississippi was where I was borned at but I been right here in Arkansas before sech thing as war gonna be. In slavery, it was, when my white folks done come to Camden. You know where that is?—Camden on the Ouachita? That's the place where we come. Yes Ma'am, it was long before the war when the doctor—I means Dr. Williams what owned my pappy and all us younguns—say he going to Arkansas. Theys rode in the fine carriages. Us slaves rode in ox wagons. Lord only knows how long it tuck a-coming. Every night we camped. I was jest a little tike then but I has a remembrance of everything. The biggest younguns had to walk till theys so tired theys couldn't hardly drag they feets; them what had been a-riding had to get out the ox wagon and walk a far piece; so it like this we go on.

Dr. Williams always wanted to keep his slaves together. He was sure good man. He didn't work his slaves hard like some. My pappy was a kind of a manager for Doctor. Doctor tended his business and pappy runned the plantation where we lived at. Our good master died before freedom. He willed us slaves to his chilrun. You know—passeled (parcelled) us out, some to this child, some to that. I went to his daughter, Miss Emma. Laws-a-Mercy, how I wishes I could see her face onct more afore I dies. I heerd she married rich. Unh-unh! I'd shore love to see her onct more.

After old master died, poor old pappy got sent to another plantation of the fam'ly. It had a overseer. He was a northerner man and the meanest devil ever put foot on a plantation. My father was a gentleman; yes ma'am, he was jest that. He had been brung up that-a-way. Old master teached us to never answer back to no white folks. But one day that overseer had my pappy whipped for sompin he never done, and pappy hit him.

So after that, he sent pappy down to New Orleans to be sold. He said he would liked to kill pappy, but he didn't dare 'cause he didn't owned him. Pappy was old. Every auction sale, all the young niggers be sold; everybody pass old pappy by. After a long time—oh, maybe five years—one day they ax pappy—"Are you got some white folks back in Arkansas?" He telled them the Williams white folks in Camden on the Ouachita. Theys white. After while theys send pappy home. Miss, I tells you, nobody never seen sech a home coming. Old Miss and the young white folks gathered round and hugged my old black pappy when he come home; they cry on his shoulder, so glad to git him back. That's what them Williams folks thought of their slaves. Yes ma'am.

Old Miss was name Miss 'liza. She skeered to stay by herself after old master died. I was took to be her companion. Every day she wanted me to bresh her long hair and bathe her feet in cool water; she said I was gentle and didn't never hurt her. One day I was a standing by the window and I seen smoke—blue smoke a rising over beyond a woods. I heerd cannons a-booming and axed her what was it. She say: "Run, Mittie, and hide yourself. It's the Yanks. Theys coming at last, Oh lordy!" I was all incited (excited) and told her I didn't want to hide, I wanted to see 'em. "No" she say, right firm. "Ain't I always told you Yankees has horns on their heads? They'll get you. Go on now, do like I tells you." So I runs out the room and went down by the big gate. A high wall was there and a tree put its branches right over the top. I clim up and hid under the leaves. They was coming, all a marching. The captain opened our big gate and marched them in. A soldier seen me and said "Come on down here; I want to see you." I told him I would, if he would take off his hat and show me his horns.

The day freedom came, I was fishing with pappy. My remembrance is sure good. All a-suddent cannons commence a-booming, it seem like everywhere. You know what that was, Miss? It was the fall of Richmond. Cannons was to roar every place when Richmond fell. Pappy jumps up, throws his pole and everything, and grabs my hand, and starts flying towards the house. "It's victory," he keep on saying. "It's freedom. Now we'es gwine be free." I didn't know what it all meant.

It seem like it tuck a long time fer freedom to come.

Everything jest kept on like it was. We heard that lots of slaves was getting land and some mules to set up fer theirselves; I never knowed any what got land or mules nor nothing.

We all stayed right on the place till the Yankees came through. They was looking for slaves what was staying on. Now we was free and had to git off the plantation. They packed us in their big amulance ... you say it wasn't a amulance,—what was it? Well, then, their big covered army wagons, and tuck us to Little Rock. Did you ever know where the old penitentiary was? Well, right there is where the Yanks had a great big barracks. All chilluns and growd womens was put there in tents. Did you know that the fust real free school in Little Rock was opened by the govment for colored chullens? Yes ma'am, and I went to it, right from the day we got there.

They took pappy and put him to work in the big commissary; it was on the corner of Second and Main Street. He got $12.00 a month and all the grub we could eat. Unh, Unh! Didn't we live good? I sure got a good remembrance, honey. Can't you tell? Yes, Ma'am. They was plenty of other refugees living in them barracks, and the govment taking keer of all of 'em.

I was a purty big sized girl by then and had to go to work to help pappy. A man name Captain Hodge, a northerner, got a plantation down the river. He wanted to raise cotton but didn't know how and had to get colored folks to help him. A lot of us niggers from the barracks was sent to pick. We got $1.25 a hundred pounds. What did I do with my money? Is you asking me that? Bless your soul, honey, I never seen that money hardly long enough to git it home. In them days chilluns worked for their folks. I toted mine home to pappy and he got us what we had to have. That's the way it was. We picked cotton all fall and winter, and went to school after picking was over.

When I got nearly growd, we moved on this very ground you is a setting on. Pappy had a five year lease,—do you know what that was, I don't—but anyhow, they told him he could have all the ground he could clear and work for five years and it wouldn't cost him nothing. He built a log house and put in a orchard. Next year he had a big garden and sold vegables. Lord, miss, them white ladies wouldn't buy from nobody but pappy. They'd wait till he got there with his fresh beans and roasting ears. When he got more land broke out, he raised cotton and corn and made it right good. His name was Harry Williams. He was a stern man, and honest. He was named for his old master. When my brothers got growed they learned shoemakers trade and had right good business in Little Rock. But when pappy died, them boys give up that good business and tuck a farm—the old Lawson place—so to make a home for mammy and the little chilluns.

I married Freeman. Onliest husban ever I had. He died last summer. He was a slave too. We used to talk over them days before we met. The K.K.K. never bothered us. They was gathered together to bother niggers and whites what made trouble. If you tended to your own business, they's let you alone.

No ma'am, I never voted. My husband did. Yes ma'am, I can remember when they was colored men voted into office. Justice of Peace, county clerks, and, er—er—that fellow that comes running fast when somebody gets killed. What you call him? Coroner? Sure, that's him. I know that, 'cause I seen them a-setting in their offices.

We raised our fam'ly on a plantation. That's the bestest place for colored chilluns. Yes ma'am. My five boys stayed with me till they was grown. They heerd about the Railroad shops and was bound theys going there to work. Ben—that was my man—and me couldn't make it by ourselfs, so we come on back to this little place where we come soon after the war. He was taken with a tumor on his brains last summer and died in two weeks. He didn't know nothing all that time. My onliest boy what stayed here died jest two weeks after his pa. All them others went to Iowa after the big railroad strike here. They was out of work for many years; they didn't like no kind of work but railroad, after they been in the shops.

How I a-living now? You wants to know, honest? Say honey, is you a relief worker—one of them welfare folkses? Lor' God, how I needs help! Honey, last summer when my husband and son die they wasn't nothin' to put on 'em to bury in. I told the Welfare could I get something clean and whole to bury my dead; honey chile, it's the gospel truth, it was two weeks after they was buried when they brought me the close (clothes). Theys told me then I would get $10.00 a month, but in all this time now, I only had $5.00 one time. I lives with my daughter here in this house, but her man been outen work so long he couldn't keep up the payments and theys 'bout to loose it. Lordy, where'll we go? I made big garden in the spring of the year, and sold a heap. Hot summer burnt everything up, now. Yessum, that $5.00 the Reliefers give me—I bought my garden stuff with it.

I got the rheumatiz a-making the garden. It look like I'm done. I knowed a old potion. It made of pokeberry juice and whiskey. Good whiskey. Not old cheap corn likker. Yessum, you takes fine whiskey—'bout half bottle, and fills up with strained pokeberry juice. Tablespoon three times a day. Look-a-here, miss. Look at these old arms go up and down now. I kin do a washing along with the youngish womens.

Iffen you wants to know what I thinks of the young folks I tells you. Look at that grandchile a-setting there. She fourteen and know more right now than I knowed in my whole life. Yes ma'am! She can sew on a machine and make a dress in one day. She read in a book how to make sumthin to eat and go hatch it up. Theys fast, too. Ain't got no time for olds like me. Can't find no time to do nothin' for me. People now makes more money than in old days, but the way they makes it ain't honest. No'am, honey, it jest plain ain't. Old honest way was to bend the back and bear down on the hoe.

Did you ask somethin' 'bout old time songs? Sure did have purty music them days. It's so long, honey, I jest can't 'member the names, 'excusing one. It was "Hark, from the Tombs a Doleful Sound." It was a burying song; wagons a-walking slow like; all that stuff. It was the most onliest song they knowed. They was other music, though. Could they play the fiddle in them days, unh, unh! Lordy, iffen I could take you back and show you that handsome white lady what put me on the floor and learned me to dance the contillion!

I'm a-thinking we're a-living in the last days, honey, what does you think? Yes, Mam! We sure is living in the seventh seal. The days of tribulations is on us right now. Nothing make like it used to. I sure would be proud iffen I knowed I had a living for the balance of my days. I got a clean and a clear heart—a clean and clear heart. Be so to your neighbors and God will make it up to you. He sure will, honey."

Interviewer: Miss Irene Robertson
Person interviewed: Mattie Fritz, Clarendon, Arkansas
Age: 79

MATTIE FRITZ

"I was born at Duncan, Arkansas. Mother died when I was a baby. Old slavery black 'Mammy' raised me. I called her 'Mammy'. My father was born in the State of Mississippi. He got loose there at 'mancipation. His master Jack Oates got killed in battle. They brung him home and buried him in the garden. Down close to Duncan on the place. I played in the yard wid Mr. Jack Oates, Jr. when we was little fellars. Father's master in Tennessee was Bill Tyler. My uncle went back to Tennessee to them. His name was Tyler Oates. Mr. Jack Gates, Sr. used to pat me and call me his little nigger. We thought the world and all of our white folks. We sure did. Some of 'em 'round 'bout Helena they say now. Mr. Jack, Jr., he had two boys and he was a widower.

"My own dear mother was Jane. My father called hisself Bill Tyler. My stepmother was Liddy. The woman what raised me was 'Mammy' all I ever knowed. But her name was Luckadoo.

"Mr. Tyler got killed. Pa had to stay on take care of his mistress. He got sold. Then she died. Then mother died. Jack Oates went to my father and brung him to Mississippi, then to Arkansas.

"Master Jack Tyler hid out. The Yankees come at

night and caught him there and shot him. His wife lived about two more years. She grieved about him. They took everything and searched the house. My pa was hid under the house. They rumbled down in the cellar and pretty nigh seen him once. He was a little bit er black fellar scroughed back in the dark. All what saved him he wore a black sorter coat. They couldn't see him so good. Way he said they would took him to wait on them and be in the fights too. Them Yankees took Massa Jack Tyler off and sont him back in a while. She had him buried in the garden. She didn't know it was him.

"'Mammy' was a slavery woman. She was sold first time from a neighbor man to a neighbor man. He was an old man. She ploughed and rolled logs. Then she was sold to Master Luckadoo close to Holly Grove. They named her Eloise, and she was a farm woman. She was so good to me. She was a worker and never took time to tell me about old times. She said Luckadoo never whooped her. A storm come and blowed a limb down killed her granddaughter and broke my leg. The same storm killed their mule. She raised a orphan boy too. She died from the change of life but she was old, gray headed. Since I'm older I think she had a tumor. 'Cause she was old when she took me on.

"I gets ten dollars from the Welfare. I ain't goiner say nothin' for 'em nor nothin' agin 'em. They's betwix' and between no 'count and good.

"Times too fast. I can't keep up wid them. 'Betwix' and between the fat and the lean.' Some do very well I reckon."

Slave Narratives

www.ingramcontent.com/pod-product-compliance
Lightning Source LLC
Chambersburg PA
CBHW071644160426
43195CB00012B/1352